Rethinking Peace and Conflict Studies

Series Editor: **Oliver P. Richmond**, Professor, School of International Relations, University of St. Andrews, UK

Editorial Board: **Roland Bleiker**, University of Queensland, Australia; **Henry F. Carey**, Georgia State University, USA; **Costas Constantinou**, University of Keele, UK; **A.J.R. Groom**, University of Kent, UK; **Vivienne Jabri**, King's College London, UK; **Edward Newman**, University of Birmingham, UK; **Sorpong Peou**, Sophia University, Japan; **Caroline Kennedy-Pipe**, University of Sheffield, UK; **Professor Michael Pugh**, University of Bradford, UK; **Chandra Sriram**, University of East London, UK; **Ian Taylor**, University of St. Andrews, UK; **Alison Watson**, University of St. Andrews, UK; **R.B.J. Walker**, University of Victoria, Canada; **Andrew Williams**, University of St. Andrews, UK

Titles include:

Sofia Sebastián Aparicio
POST-WAR STATEBUILDING AND CONSTITUTIONAL REFORM IN DIVIDED SOCIETIES
Beyond Dayton in Bosnia

Roland Bleiker
AESTHETICS AND WORLD POLITICS

Thushara Dibley
PARTNERSHIPS, POWER AND PEACEBUILDING
NGOs as Agents of Peace in Aceh and Timor-Leste

Claire Duncanson
FORCES FOR GOOD?
Military Masculinities and Peacebuilding in Afghanistan and Iraq

Kirsten Fisher
TRANSITIONAL JUSTICE FOR CHILD SOLDIERS
Accountability and Social Reconstruction in Post-Conflict Contexts

Julian Graef
PRACTICING POST-LIBERAL PEACEBUILDING
Legal Empowerment and Emergent Hybridity in Liberia

Daria Isachenko
THE MAKING OF INFORMAL STATES
Statebuilding in Northern Cyprus and Transdniestria

Stefanie Kappler
LOCAL AGENCY AND PEACEBUILDING
EU and International Engagement in Bosnia-Herzegovina, Cyprus and South Africa

Roger Mac Ginty
INTERNATIONAL PEACEBUILDING AND LOCAL RESISTANCE
Hybrid Forms of Peace

Sara McDowell and Maire Braniff
COMMEMORATION AS CONFLICT
Space, Memory and Identity in Peace Processes

SM Farid Mirbagheri
WAR AND PEACE IN ISLAM
A Critique of Islamic/ist Political Discourses

Audra L. Mitchell
LOST IN TRANSFORMATION
Violent Peace and Peaceful Conflict in Northern Ireland

Frank Möller
VISUAL PEACE
Images, Spectatorship and the Politics of Violence

Chavanne L. Peercy
LOCAL LEADERSHIP IN DEMOCRATIC TRANSITION

Michael Pugh
LIBERAL INTERNATIONALISM
The Interwar Movement for Peace in Britain

Oliver P. Richmond and Audra Mitchell (*editors*)
HYBRID FORMS OF PEACE
From Everyday Agency to Post-Liberalism

Amaia Sánchez-Cacicedo
BUILDING STATES, BUILDING PEACE
Global and Regional Involvement in Sri Lanka and Myanmar

Emil Souleimanov
UNDERSTANDING ETHNOPOLITICAL CONFLICT
Karabakh, South Ossetia and Abkhazia Wars Reconsidered

Lynn M. Tesser
ETHNIC CLEANSING AND THE EUROPEAN UNION
An Interdisciplinary Approach to Security, Memory, and Ethnography

Mandy Turner and Omar Shweiki (*editors*)
DECOLONISING PALESTINIAN POLITICAL ECONOMY
De-development and Beyond

Rethinking Peace and Conflict Studies
Series Standing Order ISBN 978–1–403–99575–9 (hardback) &
978–1–403–99576–6 (paperback)
(*outside North America only*)

You can receive future titles in this series as they are published by placing a standing order. Please contact your bookseller or, in case of difficulty, write to us at the address below with your name and address, the title of the series and one of the ISBNs quoted above.

Customer Services Department, Macmillan Distribution Ltd, Houndmills, Basingstoke, Hampshire RG21 6XS, England

Practicing Post-Liberal Peacebuilding
Legal Empowerment and Emergent Hybridity in Liberia

Julian Graef
Independent Scholar, USA

© Julian Graef 2015

All rights reserved. No reproduction, copy or transmission of this publication may be made without written permission.

No portion of this publication may be reproduced, copied or transmitted save with written permission or in accordance with the provisions of the Copyright, Designs and Patents Act 1988, or under the terms of any licence permitting limited copying issued by the Copyright Licensing Agency, Saffron House, 6–10 Kirby Street, London EC1N 8TS.

Any person who does any unauthorized act in relation to this publication may be liable to criminal prosecution and civil claims for damages.

The author has asserted his right to be identified as the author of this work in accordance with the Copyright, Designs and Patents Act 1988.

First published 2015 by
PALGRAVE MACMILLAN

Palgrave Macmillan in the UK is an imprint of Macmillan Publishers Limited, registered in England, company number 785998, of Houndmills, Basingstoke, Hampshire RG21 6XS.

Palgrave Macmillan in the US is a division of St Martin's Press LLC, 175 Fifth Avenue, New York, NY 10010.

Palgrave Macmillan is the global academic imprint of the above companies and has companies and representatives throughout the world.

Palgrave® and Macmillan® are registered trademarks in the United States, the United Kingdom, Europe and other countries.

ISBN 978–1–137–49103–9

This book is printed on paper suitable for recycling and made from fully managed and sustained forest sources. Logging, pulping and manufacturing processes are expected to conform to the environmental regulations of the country of origin.

A catalogue record for this book is available from the British Library.

A catalog record for this book is available from the Library of Congress.

For my mother, Mary Gale Garth (1950–2010)

...but not without the help of my father, Stephen Graef, and his partner, Martha Davenport

Contents

List of Figures	viii
Acknowledgments	ix
Acronyms and Abbreviations	x
Introduction	1

Part I A Practice-Based Theory of Peacebuilding

1	A Genealogy of Hybridity in Peace and Conflict Studies	19
2	A Post-Liberal Ontology of Peacebuilding Practice	33
3	The Politics of Post-Liberal Peacebuilding Practice	47
4	Mapping Peacebuilding Practice: A Post-Liberal Methodology	61

Part II Mapping Peacebuilding Practice in Liberia

5	Practicing Justice in Liberia: A Brief History	75
6	Translating Statutory Justice into Legal Empowerment	87
7	Translating Legal Empowerment into Liberian Communities	105
8	Translating Legal Empowerment into a Randomized Controlled Trial	119
9	Translating Legal Empowerment into Political Impact	134
	Conclusion	150

Notes	165
Bibliography	189
Index	200

Figures

6.1	A map of the Community Justice Adviser program (The Carter Center; program document)	97
8.1	The Lighting Round survey design	129
8.2	The Lighting Round process	130
9.1	Weak links in the chain of client–CJA interaction	139
9.2	The Lightning Round schedule (CSAE Survey Team; Lightning Round Proposal)	143

Acknowledgments

This book would not have been possible without the support of a number of incredible people and outstanding organizations. First, I would like to thank Bilal Siddiqi and Justin Sandefur. Had they not been willing to bring me on as a research assistant, I would never have had the academically and personally transformational experience of being part of their extraordinary project. I am very grateful for their patience with my learning curve and their willingness to help me fill in the blanks.

Equally, The Carter Center (TCC) extended every courtesy to me while in Liberia. My informal conversations with Pewee Flomoku, Peter Chapman, Chelsea Payne, Counselor Lemuel Reeves and Rob Pittman were essential in gaining a deep sense of TCC's work there. For their guidance, I am very thankful. Tom Crick, TCC's associate director of Conflict Resolution Programing in Atlanta, and Jeff Austin, TCC's former Southeast Regional program coordinator, provided valuable insights into the background and political context of the Community Justice Advisor (CJA) program. Counselor Jallah Barbu, the chairman of the Liberian Legal Working Group, kindly granted permission to cite his research on Liberia's legal history. I would like to thank the Justice and Peace Commission and each of the CJAs for accommodating my research and helping me to understand the nature of their work. Their contributions were essential.

Finally, this would not have been possible without Professor Oliver P. Richmond and Professor Ian Taylor. Their assistance was instrumental in bringing my ideas to fruition. Additionally, their patience and support through a difficult period of life enabled this to be possible. I would also like to thank Dr Victoria Loughlan, Dr Jaremey McMullin, Professor Stephen Hopgood and Professor David Chandler for their encouraging feedback along the way. The Centre for Peace and Conflict Studies at the University of St. Andrews along with the Russell Trust provided valuable support for conducting the field work which shaped this project. Also, the International Relations Department and the University of St. Andrews have been unwavering in their support for my work despite the setbacks.

Acronyms and Abbreviations

ACS	American Colonial Society
ANT	Actor Network Theory
CJA	Community Justice Adviser
CSAE	Centre for the Study of African Economies
CSO	Civil Society Organizations
DFID	Department for International Development
ICG	International Crisis Group
IDLO	International Development Law Organization
IR	International Relations
J-PAL	Abdul Latif Jamil Poverty Action Lab
JPC	Justice and Peace Commission
L4J	Looking For Justice (USIP Report)
LR	Lightning Round
LWG	Legal Working Group
MoIA	Ministry of Internal Affairs
MoJ	Ministry of Justice
NGO	Non-Governmental Organization
NTC	National Traditional Council
OSF	Open Society Foundation
PBF	Peacebuilding Fund (United Nations)
PCS	Peace and Conflict Studies
PDA	Personal Digital Assistant
PSO	Public Support Office
QAS	Quick Assessment Survey
RCT	Randomized Controlled Trials
TCC	The Carter Center
UNMIL	United Nations Mission in Liberia
USAID	United States Agency for International Development
USIP	United States Institute for Peace

Introduction

The liberal monopoly on peace is gradually giving way to a post-liberal world where the meaning of peace is increasingly contested and the future of peacebuilding appears uncertain. At this precarious juncture of post-liberal emergence, different expressions of power and new visions of emancipation are gradually being folded into peacebuilding practices.This process is changing how peacebuilding interventions are organized and transforming the kind of peace they are designed to bring about. The unstable continuity between the liberal peace and emerging post-liberal world requires a better understanding of how complex processes of change emerge in peacebuilding practices. But change is a difficult phenomenon to capture. In Peace and Conflict Studies (PCS), processes of change are often explored through the concept of hybridity.[1] The notion of hybridity has been used by a number of disciplines to investigate how different entities – organisms, machines, systems and cultures – interact and transform in relation to one another. When applied to post-conflict settings in which myriad international peacebuilding projects are being implemented across an array of local sites, hybrid processes appear particularly dynamic. Attempting to describe the complexity of hybridity in peacebuilding contexts, Mac Ginty presents hybridity as 'a constantly moving piece of variable geometry [that] operates on many levels, through multiple mediums, and impacts multiple (if not all) aspects of life'.[2]

In order to make some sense of this overwhelming complexity, PCS has appropriated the concept of hybridity, defining it as a process driven by the multidimensional interactions between liberal international peacebuilding interventions on the one hand, and local institutions, actors and values on the other. The complex political tension between these international and local entities generates hybrid processes and produces hybrid forms of peace that reflect both international and local input. Presently, peace is largely accepted as a hybrid phenomenon: peace, as it emerges, is not a 'liberal' peace or a 'local' peace, but it is a hybrid peace. However, the status of hybridity remains unsettled in the PCS literature and debate persists.[3] As Mac Ginty points out, the liberal–local distinction is always 'an abstraction and [is therefore] unable to capture the full extent and dynamism of a complex social process. Yet it does allow us to visualise the main axes along which hybridization may be projected or resisted in contexts experiencing liberal peace interventions'.[4] Here Mac Ginty points out the paradox of liberal–local hybridity: while it may explain the overarching tension at play across different international statebuilding interventions, liberal–local hybridity may also conceal how hybrid processes emerge in ways that unsettle and transform the liberal–local boundary and the relationship between power and emancipatory agency that it circumscribes.

The paradox of hybridity

The paradox of liberal–local hybridity conceals *a post-liberal surplus*: expressions of emancipatory agency and demonstrations of power that exceed their liberal–local explanation. Anchored to its liberal–local explanation, hybridity is therefore likely to reproduce the distinction between power and emancipatory agency rather than reveal how the limits of power and emancipation are continually contested and redefined. In PCS, liberal–local hybridity creates and maintains a relationship of alterity. On the one hand, 'the liberal peace' represents how international power circulates; it stands for the top-down imposition of liberal international norms and institutional structures. On the other hand, 'the local' has come to represent a repository of emancipatory post-liberal capacity rooted in local traditions. By creating these distinctions and boundaries, universal claims can be challenged, alternative emancipatory politics become possible and new epistemologies of peace can be advanced. One example of this approach is Mac Ginty's work on local peace indicators.[5] Using the concept of hybridity, Mac Ginty and Richmond have been able to create some post-liberal political space in which they could advance a locally relevant and legitimate alternative to the liberal international epistemology of peace.[6] However, liberal–local hybridity tends to reinforce the difference between these groupings rather than highlight the controversies unfolding within them and cutting across them.

There are two equally important and interrelated dimensions of hybridity: difference and transformation. Yet the PCS literature has tended to emphasize the politics of difference over the politics of transformation. Paradoxically, the transformative politics of hybridity have become trapped between the liberal–local distinctions developed to explain them, and the relationship between power and emancipation has already been determined. The paradox of liberal–liberal hybridity reveals two complementary but distinct approaches to understanding complex processes of post-liberal change in critical PCS: explanatory hybridity and emergent hybridity. Explanatory hybridity is an epistemological and theoretical project. The definition of 'explanation' used throughout the following pages follows Latour's understanding.[7] For Latour, the politics of explanation describe a process through which complex and heterogeneous phenomena become captured by the theoretical name or shape developed to signify and distinguish them. An emergent approach adopts a slightly different orientation toward hybridity. It is an ontological and methodological project; it treats hybridity as an unstable ontological process of transformation. Emergent hybridity is not a secondary outcome generated by the politics of difference; rather, it is the primary ontological inertia that continually destabilizes the explanatory relationship between liberal and local, power and resistance, governmentality and emancipation. Therefore, emergent hybridity is the active ontological process through which the politics of difference are continually transformed. When treated as an emergent phenomenon, hybridity becomes ontologically primary; it is a process, an action, a movement; it is the condition of dynamic transformation that continually upsets and reshapes the theoretical distinctions invented to explain it. Through the process of emergent hybridity, the assumed relationship between internationality and power becomes uncertain and the axiomatic association between localness and emancipatory agency becomes contingent on the transformative politics of emerging hybrid processes.

The post-liberal turn

The recent post-liberal turn in critical PCS has identified the problematic paradox of explanatory hybridity and has laid the groundwork for moving beyond the differential politics between the liberal peace and the local. Chandler's post-liberal approach, for example, attempts to move beyond the liberal peace by redefining how international power circulates in post-conflict conditions.[8] His notion of post-liberal statebuilding incorporates a Foucaultian reading of governmentality. Through the governmental logic of post-liberal statebuilding, local autonomy is produced as a potential risk which must be managed through technologies of governance and deep-penetrating bio-political interventions. For Chandler, post-liberal statebuilding therefore represents a move away from the emancipatory vision for local autonomy embedded in liberal peacebuilding. Crucially, Chandler's post-liberal turn emphasizes methodology over universal theories of power, a move which enables critical research to engage with the contingent politics of policy practices. For him, a practice-based approach explores post-liberal statebuilding 'in its own terms' rather than through an a priori theory of power, such as the liberal peace.[9]

Contrary to Chandler's assertion, Richmond's notion of post-liberalism represents an expansion of emancipation. In order to explore these emancipatory politics, he re-appropriates the epistemological concept of 'the local' and redefines it in spatial terms. In Richmond and Mitchell's reading of post-liberalism, 'the local' is a site of everyday politics.[10] The everyday politics unfolding in peacebuilding sites enable researchers to engage with emerging post-liberal hybrid processes without deferring to the liberal–local dichotomy. From here Richmond points to a post-liberal process of *peace formation* rooted in 'transversal, transnational networks [that merge] both the liberal and the local, the global north and south'.[11] For Richmond, processes of peace formation 'lead to a modification of current global statebuilding agendas and a refocusing on needs at the civil level, rather than mainly on rights'.[12] However, Richmond concludes that the site and the everyday remain ' "fuzzy" concepts, requiring more research in order to open up more critical understandings of peace'.[13] This work hopes to contribute to this post-liberal project.

Both Chandler and Richmond's post-liberal approaches problematize the entrenched liberal–local explanation of hybridity and create valuable methodological space for engaging with hybridity as an emergent ontological phenomenon.[14] Yet, taken together, they also reproduce the relationship between power and internationality as well as the association between emancipatory agency and localness. For Chandler, power is organized through *international* policy practices designed to cultivate neo-liberal subjectivity in post-conflict societies. For Richmond, emancipation is determined by the degree to which peacebuilding reflects *local* customs and is based on local everyday practices and norms. While these are clearly the prevailing dynamics at play in and across peacebuilding sites, the goal over the following pages and chapters is to disrupt the axiomatic relationship holding internationality and power together and to challenge the association between emancipatory agency and localness. The objective is to create some post-liberal space for critical researchers to explore the transformative politics of emergent hybridity in which the limits of power and emancipation are actively contested and reshaped through peacebuilding practices.

Emergent hybridity

In order to expose the transformative aspects of hybridity, the politics of difference must be replaced by an emergent ontology of uncertain and imminent becoming.[15] Instead of deferring to the politics of difference in order to explain complex hybrid processes, an emergent approach exposes the politics of difference to the transformative effects of time. In other words, emergent hybridity is defined by a temporal political tension rather than by the politics of difference and alterity. The temporal politics of emerging hybridity were embraced by Homi Bhabha. He argued that hybridity was characterized by an unstable liminal 'time-lag' in which the politics of difference become unstable and transformative change becomes possible.[16] Whereas Bhabha was interested in the transformation of identity and culture, the approach adopted here explores the emergent politics of transformative hybridity as a material phenomenon. Emergent materialist ontologies grew as a reaction against the cultural and linguistic turns in social and political theory. Material ontologists wanted to reclaim the possibility for change and political subjectivity from the deterministic clutches of language and culture and neo-liberal power.[17] Therefore, they offer very modest claims about the nature of the social world: it consists of the movement of bodies and things through space and time. They make no claim as to the forces, social structures or norms that drive this movement; they do not depend on an ontologically prior politics of difference. This move changes the implicit causal relationship between liberal–local alterity and hybridity. Contrary to efficient causality, the temporal pressures of hybridity are driven by an unstable emergent causality.[18] Emergent hybridity reverses the explanatory direction of liberal–local hybridity: rather than being produced by the politics of difference, emergent hybridity destabilizes alterity and creates an unstable temporal disjuncture in which the politics of difference give way to the politics of *becoming* different.

A practice-based approach

The unstable emergent relationship between being different and becoming different can be exposed using a practice-based approach. Practice is not an effect but the cause, not the outcome but the source. In this view, practice is ontologically stable. Speaking to the ontological primacy of practices, Schatzki defines practices as the situated, embodied everyday doings and sayings that constitute human coexistence, or in Mattern's words, practice is simply 'doing human being'.[19] While practices rest on an emergent and therefore unstable ontology, practices unfold in relatively predictable patterns. In other words, to say that practices are emergent and therefore uncertain is not to say that they are chaotic and disorganized. On the contrary, the organized nature of practice is essential to its ontological integrity.

For Schatzki, there are two dimensions to practice: organization and activity.[20] To reiterate, this is not an attempt to sneak extra-material power or abstract social structures in through the backdoor. Practices are not structured by abstract, extra-material forces, but they are materially organized through various everyday projects, tasks, jobs, contracts or programs that enable the continuity of everyday human existence from one day to the next. In terms of peacebuilding, these projects organize the movement of bodies and things through and between varieties of sites. This movement is organized at many different levels. Peacebuilding projects are organized by rules, methodologies and guidelines; they are limited by ethical standards, codes of conduct and professional norms; projects are constrained by schedules, budgets and capacity. Organized peacebuilding projects establish a hierarchy of tasks and prescribe them a sequence and priority that specifies how and when an activity is supposed to be executed in order to reach a certain goal or objective. Peacebuilding projects are designed for a reason, for some purpose, to do something, to bring something about or to address some perceived problem. In this way, organized practices are inherently political. Although peacebuilding projects are organized, the continuity between organization and practice remains precarious. This continuity depends on the performance of peacebuilding practitioners.

The emergent tension at play in organized practices stretches between how a project is designed and how it is performed.[21] This temporal political strain is expressed as peacebuilding practitioners struggle to realize the objectives specified by their project in sites where those objectives may take on a different meaning and may be contested. While practices are organized and their performance is choreographed, the way it is performed is ultimately indeterminate and uncertain. The unstable relationship between design and performance must be continually and actively managed through and within the constant re-organization and re-stabilization of practices. This precarious condition is defined here as a 'post-liberal political situation'. A post-liberal political situation is a temporal disjuncture between being and becoming, between the liberal peace and the emerging post-liberal world in which new ways of organizing peace and different ways of performing peacebuilding become possible.

The politics of translation

The unstable continuity between the design and the performance of a peacebuilding project must be continually managed through an ongoing process of translation. The concept of translation is invoked by the Actor Network Theory (ANT) to expose the discontinuities that emerge as actors must continually find ways to convert their project into a political reality.[22] The unstable performative nature of a translation also overlaps with Schatzki's notion of practice as an indeterminate situated performance.[23] Translations are not produced, but they are performed; they emerge at the performative front edge of practice as practitioners attempt to realize the goals embedded in their project within and across sites where those goals may be contested. Translations reflect the creativity of practitioners. They depend on a number of subjective agential capacities such as background knowledge, practical understanding, experience, common sense, skill and expertise. The emergent relationship between organized peacebuilding projects and their translation into a performance is described by Freeman as a 'constrained innovation'.[24] A translation marks a subtle change in how things are done, a narrow betrayal of orthodoxy, an improvised deviation from the script. Stretched through the temporal tensions of emergence, a translation exposes performative discontinuities. It is important to clarify that translations must not be confused with emancipatory progress; but translations can expose a debate or controversy about what progress and emancipation amount to. A translation reveals how practitioners must continually appropriate a project, embody and enact its specified practices. Translations reflect how practitioners take responsibility carrying its objectives forward into sites where those objectives may have a different meaning, where a particular practice may have a different significance and may therefore be contested. However, in keeping with the materialist ontology of practices, translation is not the rational individual cast against the backdrop of structured peacebuilding projects. Rather, translations are enabled by and organized through practices.

The post-liberal politics of translation consist of four essential and interrelated components that feed into each other. First, a translation involves *problematization*. This aspect deals with how practitioners establish what is at stake in a given practice; how they identify a particular problem or issue; how they work to unsettle the existing political situation and create a condition in which a new or different way of organizing the existing pattern of practices becomes necessary. Second, a translation entails *appropriation*. When practitioners appropriate a practice, they ascribe their own meaning to a given project and impose their own political situation on its practices. Through appropriation, practitioners co-opt a project, changing how its practices are organized and altering how it is performed. Third, a translation consists of a *performance*. As suggested above, a performance expresses how practitioners embody and enact an appropriated practice. A performance is the material manifestation of a translation and reveals any discontinuities. Lastly, a translation often involves a *re-problematization*. Translations and the changes they reflect may change the political situation which, in turn, may create new problems and expose different challenges, requiring new and different ways of organizing practice. In this sense, translations reveal an ongoing and emergent political process of re-translation, of reorganizing and developing new and different ways to manage the unstable continuity of practices. These four aspects of a translation provide the structure for the empirical sections of this book. Each of the four empirical chapters focus on a single translation which is then broken down and analyzed based on the four dimensions of a translation mentioned above. Stretched out over time, the process of translation exposes a series of performative discontinuities that add up to a post-liberal process of emergent hybridity.

A methodological orientation

The unstable post-liberal politics of translation are difficult to capture through the explanatory lens of liberal–local hybridity. As mentioned above, in critical PCS literature, the liberal peace represents an exercise of international power designed to cultivate liberal subjectivity in post-conflict environments – the art of governance.[25] Meanwhile, 'the local' represents a reservoir of counter-liberal emancipatory subjectivity that emerges as resistance to international peacebuilding power – the art of not being governed.[26] However, tracing the performative discontinuities of peacebuilding practices requires a different research orientation. Rather than adopting a liberal–local reading of hybridity in which the attributes of power and the characteristics of emancipation have already been circumscribed, a practice-based approach requires moving away from critical theory and toward a critical methodology of peacebuilding practice. A critical methodological orientation does not foreclose on the characteristics of power and emancipation but instead maps how limits of power and the meaning of emancipation are continually contested, transgressed and transformed – mapping the art of translation.

In this way, a methodological orientation changes how critical research is practiced. Rather than developing epistemological distinctions and concepts to explain the relationship between liberal international power and emancipatory local agency, a methodological orientation involves developing strategies for exposing how emerging hybrid processes continually transform how power circulates and what emancipation signifies. The methodological strategy developed here incorporates insights form Latour's mapping strategy: sociology of associations.[27] Latour's methodological call to 'keep the social world flat' is a strategy that prevents researchers from re-introducing an extra-material social structure or imposing a priori definitions in order to explain a performance. Yet, his aim is not to ignore unjust systems of domination. Rather, by keeping the social world flat, Latour argues that researchers can gain a better understanding of the constant work required to organize and maintain powerful systems of domination. Relatedly, Latour's mapping strategy calls on researchers to 'follow the actors'. Following peacebuilding practitioners shifts the attention of critical researchers to how practitioners make sense of their own political situation, how they impose their own meaning onto a given project and how their performance may unsettle the circulation of power and expose new emancipatory possibilities. By following peacebuilding practitioners across a flat social landscape, researchers can expose how the logic of international power becomes rewritten and how the meaning of emancipation becomes displaced. Using this ANT-based methodological strategy, this book charts the performative discontinuities that arose in the course of designing, implementing and evaluating a peacebuilding intervention in Liberia and, in the process, maps a process of post-liberal hybridity.

The community justice adviser program

The contingent process that unfolded in the course of launching the Community Justice Adviser (CJA) program illustrates the complicated relationship between power and emancipation in post-conflict Liberia. Liberia is widely understood to have a dual justice system. On the one hand, there is the formal legal system of the Liberian state, and on the other hand there is the customary justice system practiced in rural

Liberian communities. However, when grounded in practice, Liberia's dual justice system is better understood as an ongoing debate about what justice means in Liberia, how it should be practiced and who is authorized to practice it. The CJA program involves training a team of paralegals in the basics of statutory law, conflict resolution and mediation techniques and then dispatching them on motorbikes to assigned rural Liberian communities. It was designed to raise the level of statutory legal awareness in specified communities and to provide free legal services in rural Liberian communities where customary justice is favored. In this way, the CJA program offers an alternative to both the statutory and customary justice practices – legal empowerment – and creates political space for new justice practitioners. The project is organized and coordinated by The Carter Center (TCC), an international NGO specializing in human rights in post-conflict and developing countries. The daily operations of the CJA program are managed by TCC's local implementing partner: the Catholic Justice and Peace Commission (JPC). The CJA program also incorporated two new and increasingly popular peacebuilding practices. First, the CJA's practices were based on an experimental legal empowerment model. Second, in order to determine its impact, this new legal empowerment model was designed within a randomized controlled trial (RCT).

Following the existing lines for critical argumentation, both legal empowerment and RCTs can be practiced in ways that extend and maintain the state monopoly on the practice of justice while supplanting customary justice practices. Legal empowerment may represent a deep bio-political intervention designed to subtly cultivate a sense of legal subjectivity, thereby gradually undermining customary justice practices and the restorative norms they transmit. Meanwhile, RCTs involve the instrumental process of randomization and quantification in which potentially significant disputes and justice take a backseat to the methodological requirements of the evaluation. The data they produce can also be reincorporated into future peacebuilding interventions, making them even more effective in extending statutory law and destabilizing customary justice practices.

For these reasons, it is important to avoid producing a false progress narrative.[28] International peacebuilding projects often invoke the language of local emancipation in order to legitimize projects which only extend statutory practices into local sites just as local political entrepreneurs will appropriate the language of local resistance to extend customary practices that are experienced as unjust by local populations.[29] Equating translations to emancipatory agency and progress must be avoided. Yet at the same time, reproducing the distinction between liberal international power and emancipatory local agency is equally problematic. Instead, translations, as they are understood here, reveal controversies about how power should circulate and expose debates about what emancipation amounts to in the emerging post-liberal world. Seen in this light, both legal empowerment practices and RCT-based methodology are challenging some of the major assumptions that guide liberal peacebuilding interventions.

Legal empowerment

Legal empowerment emerged as a reaction against the liberal approach to legal aid in development and peacebuilding practices. While a legal empowerment intervention is designed to raise a community's level of statutory legal knowledge, its goal is not to simply displace customary justice practices and impose statutory law. Instead, legal empowerment grew for a critique within the legal aid establishment that was increasingly wary of conventional top-down approach to establishing a liberal rule of law in post-conflict and development contexts.[30] In this sense, legal employment adopts the view of legal pluralism. Legal pluralism is concerned with how orthodox rules of law intervention can be appropriated in ways that extend power asymmetries and unjust systems of domination.[31] Rather than prioritizing the institutional structure of statutory law, this approach challenges the ideology of legal centrism and creates political space for a non-essentialized approach to justice that emphasizes function of form.[32] The legal pluralists actively challenge what the law is, how it should be practiced and who can practice it. The CJA program reflects the principles of legal pluralism and organizes them into a legal empowerment intervention. While the CJA program provides legal education and awareness in customary communities, their legal empowerment practices prioritize their clients' justice needs over statutory law. The CJA's task is to provide their clients with the relevant legal information and then assist them in navigating either formal or customary legal systems while advocating on their behalf. In addition to statutory or customary systems, the CJA program provides a third justice option: CJA-led mediation. In this way, the CJA program introduces new justice practitioners and different ways of practicing justice to Liberia's dual legal landscape. However, in order to determine if the CJA program was an effective peacebuilding strategy, it was designed as part of an RCT.

Randomized Controlled Trial

Over the past few years, RCTs have been incorporated into peacebuilding and development practices where they have become the 'gold standard' for establishing a relationship between intervention (cause) and impact (effect).[33] RCTs were originally developed to determine the effectiveness of pharmaceutical interventions. According to the basic methodological structure of an RCT, patients were divided into two groups: treatment and control. The treatment group would be given a drug; the control group would receive a placebo. After a period of time, the two groups could be compared and any difference could be causally attributed to the drug. In the case of the CJA program, legal empowerment is the drug, and in order to measure its effectiveness, two development economists, Bilal Siddiqi and Justin Sandefur,[34] then from Oxford's Centre for the Study of African Economies (CSAE), were enrolled into the process of designing the CJA program. According to the RCT-based design, 176 communities were surveyed in order to establish a baseline reading. Then these 176 communities were separated into 88 'treatment' communities that the CJA would regularly visit and 88 'control' communities where the CJA would not go. After a two-and-a-half year period, the treatment and control communities could be compared and the 'impact' of the CJA's legal empowerment practices could be determined. Like legal empowerment, RCTs are not ideologically committed to undermining customary justice practices and legitimizing the state's claim to a monopoly on justice. Instead, the political economy of data is tilted in favor of politically disruptive findings. There is nothing politically valuable about confirming that common-sense and widely practiced interventions have impacts. But there is something politically valuable about finding that an unconventional intervention generates impacts that more orthodox approaches cannot; likewise, discovering that a common-sense intervention has zero impact is also a politically significant finding. These findings are politically disruptive because they challenge existing approaches to justice and create new political space for different practices and practitioners.

As mentioned above, legal empowerment and RCTs must not be confused with emancipatory progress. Yet at the same time, reducing them to technologies of liberal international power conceals the important post-liberal politics actively transforming the liberal 'peace' into the post-liberal world. Examined through the emergent lens of practice, legal empowerment and RCT-based methodologies reflect a debate about what peacebuilding is becoming. A practice-based approach exposes how these practices are organized into projects, how practitioners ascribe a specific meaning or political purpose to a project and how practitioners struggle to translate that political purpose into sites where it may be contested. On a practice-based account, peacebuilding is not a linear process. On the contrary, it is often replete with controversy and debate. A translation therefore exposes a debate about what peace should be, how peacebuilding and development should be practiced and who is authorized to practice it. It reflects a debate about what 'liberalism' is becoming. In Liberia, the controversies and debates are expressed through translations that reveal a series of performative discontinuities, adding up to a post-liberal process of emergent hybridity. These discontinuities, in turn, expose the fragility of power, the debates and controversies that preclude it from solidifying, and the active and ongoing work of maintaining its precarious connections. In Liberia, the combination of legal empowerment and RCTs functioned to displace the statutory legal monopoly on justice and created a political situation in which customary justice practices and values became essential to the peacebuilding and development repertoire there.

Chapter outline

The following chapters are arranged in two parts. Part I is the theoretical section where the practice-based approach used to map the CJA program is further developed. Part II turns to the designing, implementation and evaluation of the CJA program. Chapter 1 presents a genealogy of hybridity in the PCS literature. It engages with how the hybrid paradigm emerged to displace the liberal peace. It then discusses how hybridity became trapped between the very liberal–local distinction that it disrupts. Finally, it examines how the budding post-liberal in turn lays the foundation for transitioning from liberal–local hybridity to emergent hybrid processes. Chapter 2 advances the 'post-liberal political situation' as the ontological basis for exploring the emergent hybridity at play in the CJA program. It outlines the ontological materiality of practice, undercutting the primacy of difference and alterity at the heart of explanatory hybridity. It then establishes the temporal tensions at play in peacebuilding practices as the ontological basis of emergent hybrid processes.

Chapter 3 focuses on the politics of practice. The chapter reviews a number of practice-based theories, including Foucault's governmentality,[35] Bourdieu's habitus,[36] Adler and Pouliot's community of practice,[37] Schatzki's practical understanding[38] and, finally, Latour and Callon's notion of translation.[39] In the process, it attempts to sketch out the contours of post-liberal notion of political subjectivity – the practitioner. Post-liberal practitioners are not individual actors working within powerful structures. Rather, the fragile material connections that may appear as stable and enduring must be actively maintained by practitioners through the unstable performance of translation. Chapter 4 turns to methodology. It proposes balancing the critical theory's political commitments to exposing power and advancing emancipation with a critical methodology that targets how the relationship between power and emancipation transforms. To this end, it proposes a Latourian mapping strategy designed to mark the points of translation, chart the performative discontinuities that unfold and map unstable processes of emergent post-liberal hybridity.

Part II turns to Liberia and the CJA program. Chapter 5 briefly reviews the history of the dual justice system. However, rather than reinforcing the accepted duality of justice in Liberia, the history presented in this chapter emphasizes how justice is practiced in ways which unsettle the difference between formal and customary law. It highlights how the statutory, liberal meaning of justice envisioned for Liberia's future is being challenged and how a post-liberal political situation is emerging in which customary justice practices are becoming indispensable to peace in Liberia. Chapter 6 introduces the CJA program and maps the process through which TCC *problematized* the liberal monopoly on justice maintained by the Liberian legal establishment; how they re-*appropriated* the liberal meaning of justice to create a post-liberal political situation in which legal empowerment became a political possibility; and how they *performed* (designed and organized) legal empowerment through an intervention called the CJA program. Chapter 7 reviews how the CJA program was translated into an indirect legal empowerment practice by TCC's local implementing partner – the JPC. It maps how the JPC *problematized* an active approach to legal empowerment and how JPC re-*appropriated* legal empowerment in a way that emphasized the restorative customary justice practiced in Liberian communities. The result was an indirect legal empowerment *performance* in which CJAs would attempt to create a political situation in communities in which clients would feel empowered to approach them for help.

Chapter 8 goes on to map how these legal empowerment practices were translated into an RCT. It discusses how the CJA's indirect legal empowerment practices were generating no impact at the intended community level. It maps how the CSAE survey team *problematized* the community-level survey structure and how they *appropriated* legal empowerment, translating its practices into quantifiably measurable indicators economic and social indicators. It then traces how they *performed* a redesign of the community-level RCT in order to capture the impact the CJAs were making at the individual level. This individual-level RCT was called the Lightning Round. Chapter 9 reviews the design and performance of the Lightning Round. The Lightning Round was an entirely new individual-level RCT and therefore required new cases. In order to generate these new cases, the CSAE survey team had to *problematize* the CJA's indirect legal empowerment practice and *re-appropriate* them, translating them into a more active legal empowerment *performance*. After three months, the active legal empowerment approach found some statistically significant improvements in material well-being but did not alter the underlying attitudes and behaviors that influence how Liberians make their justice decisions. The book then concludes with a review and analysis of the post-liberal process of hybridity that emerged in the course of designing, implementing and evaluating the CJA program.

The terms and limits of peace in the emerging post-liberal world are being renegotiated. While liberal–local hybridity captures the overarching and general dynamics at play across many different peacebuilding interventions, it produces a problematic paradox in which the relationship between power and emancipation has already been established. The paradox of liberal–local hybridity is therefore likely to reproduce the existing relationship between power and emancipation rather than exposing how they are contested and reorganized through emerging peacebuilding practices. Contrary to the politics of difference that define liberal–local hybridity, the emergent politics of peacebuilding practices manifest as an unstable relationship between the way peacebuilding interventions are designed and how they are performed. This emergent tension is managed through a process of translation. Translating a peacebuilding project into a performance may incorporate the art of governance or may reflect the art of not being governed; however, in either case they are both expressions of *the art of translation*. The art of translation describes how practitioners continually appropriate and reorganize the way power circulates, how they impose different emancipatory meaning and political significance on the peacebuilding practices they inhabit and how these practices emerge as a new or different performance. The peacebuilding performances unfold as a post-liberal process of emergent hybridity in which the continuity of power is uncertain and the meaning of emancipation in the post-liberal world is always at stake.

Part I
A Practice-Based Theory of Peacebuilding

1
A Genealogy of Hybridity in Peace and Conflict Studies

This chapter traces the emergence of hybridity in the PCS literature. Using a genealogical approach, it maps how the concept of hybridity was translated into PCS and how it was continually re-appropriated by different scholars in order to explain the complex and dynamic processes at play in peacebuilding environments. In the process, the chapter reviews how the transformative properties of hybridity gradually became trapped by the liberal–local distinctions that framed the debate in PCS. However, it also reveals how the recent post-liberal turn in PCS provides opportunities to move the concept of hybridity beyond the liberal–local binary. A post-liberal understanding of hybridity engages with the emerging hybrid processes that are actively displacing and transforming what peace amounts to in the post-liberal world.

This genealogy explores the debate about what hybridity *is*. In the process, this genealogy unpacks what hybridity means in PCS, uncovers the epistemological boundaries developed to understand the relationship between power and emancipation and then exposes how the meaning of hybridity has been retranslated to cope with the complex process reshaping what the post-liberal world is becoming. Foucault describes a genealogy as 'a form of history which can account for the constitution of knowledges, discourses, domains of object etc., without having to make reference to a subject which is...transcendental in relation to the field of events'.[1] Such an approach exposes regimes of truth to the contingent, emergent politics underlying their perceived stability. Using this approach, this chapter grounds the production of knowledge about hybridity within the PCS debate in order to explore how the concept of hybridity became captured by the very liberal–local distinction which post-liberal hybrid processes unsettle and redefine. This genealogy traces the meaning of hybridity through a series of translations. These translations highlight how the international–local distinction at the heart of hybridity is both preserved and subtly redefined by PCS scholars as they struggle to develop better ways to represent the unstable relationship between exercises of power and emancipatory agency in peacebuilding interventions. Through this process, the genealogy exposes the paradox of hybridity: by their very nature, emergent hybrid processes transcend and transform the theoretical and epistemological shapes designed to explain them. Consequently, explanatory hybridity can function to reproduce and reify the liberal–local binary, potentially obscuring the very *emerging hybrid processes* actively shaping what peace and peacebuilding amount to in the post-liberal world.

This argument is presented in three sections. The first part engages with how the liberal peace was debated between problem-solving and critical approaches amid the so-called liberal peace 'crisis' in the early to mid-2000s.[2] The second section reviews how the complex interactions between international peacebuilding and local agency were explained through the concept of hybridity. This section also highlights how explanatory hybridity has reinforced the very distinctions that hybrid processes contest and upset. The final section points to some of the work being undertaken to address the potentially essentializing and reductive effects of explanatory hybridity within the nascent post-liberal paradigm.[3]

From the liberal peace to the local

Prior to the ascendance of the hybrid paradigm, it was 'the liberal peace' that defined theoretical engagement with peacebuilding. The liberal peace emerged in the waning days of the Cold War – specifically from UNTAG, a 1989 peacekeeping mission in Namibia[4] which was gradually codified into international peacebuilding and development policy through a number of precedent-setting policy documents.[5] The rationale shaping this new peacebuilding paradigm flowed from the understanding that a certain kind of state – a market-based democracy organized under the rule of law – mitigates the kinds of tensions that lead to violent conflict.[6] Yet, the drawn-out peacebuilding operations in Bosnia, the transitional administrations in Kosovo and East Timor and the invasions of Afghanistan and Iraq in the early 2000s pointed to a 'crisis of liberal peacebuilding'.[7] The debate between problem solving and critical approaches in PCS emerged in the context of this crisis. According to Newman, problem-solving approaches 'accept the assumptions that underpin existing policy and focus upon optimum effectiveness and performance', while a critical approach 'questions – and if necessary challenges – prevailing discourses or ways of thinking, and the interests they serve'.[8] This distinction was taken up in a number of academic publications in the late 2000s as academics grappled with understanding the reasons behind the apparent liberal peace crisis.

In this context, problem-solving scholars proposed greater international control over peacebuilding interventions. Chopra's notion of 'peace maintenance' reflects such an approach. He argued that the UN must act as 'an outside guarantor of a kind of internal self-determination'[9] which should establish 'a direct relationship with the local people who will eventually, participate in the reconstitution of authority and *inherit the newly established institutions*'.[10] Meanwhile, Kranser's problem-solving approach proposed international trusteeships and shared sovereignty. Under this vision, 'international actors would assume control over local functions for an indefinite period of time'.[11] Arguing along similar lines, Paris called for institutionalization before liberalization which 'begins with the premise that democratization and marketization are inherently tumultuous transformations that have the potential to undermine a fragile peace'.[12] Based on this rationale, Paris concludes that international peacebuilders must 'construct the foundations of effective political institutions before the introduction of electoral democracy and market-oriented adjustment policies'.[13] The implicit 'problem' these examples are attempting to 'solve' is the problem of local politics. Consequently, local post-conflict societies must be transformed into liberal *civil* societies. To this point, Adibe concluded that 'UN authority must seriously embark on social engineering on a scale large enough and deep enough to ensure [the state's] acceptance by successive generations of a population'.[14]

However, there was another response to the liberal peace crisis of the early 2000s. Contrary to the problem-solvers, critical scholars proposed that greater international control was not the solution but the problem. Duffield, for example, observed that the 'liberal peace is a political project in its own right [the aim of which] is to transform the dysfunctional and war-affected societies that it encounters on its borders into cooperative, representative, and especially, stable entities'.[15] Chandler argued that internationally administered democratization in Bosnia had 'undermined autonomy and self-government on the assumption that external assistance is necessary for building an alternative that will more effectively bridge segmented political divisions'.[16] Along with democracy, economic liberalization was also an essential feature of a liberal peace.¹⁷ Pugh's critique of the political economy of peacebuilding maintains that economic liberalization policies are destabilizing and instead argued that local economies should be supported.¹⁸ Meanwhile, Richmond's critique of the liberal peace targeted the deeply embedded Eurocentric cultural assumptions which legitimize such international interventions. According to his line of critique, the liberal peace is 'sometimes colonial and racist in that it implies the transference of enlightened knowledge to those who lack the capacity and the morality to attain such knowledge themselves'.¹⁹ Summarizing the theme of critical scholarship in PCS, Tadjbakhsh notes that it coalesced around the idea that the liberal peace 'fails to recognize the agency and capacity of local and indigenous institutions and often appears to be impositionary rather than a liberation'.²⁰

Richmond's critical approach seeks to create some conceptual space for an alternative emancipatory approach to peacebuilding based on local epistemologies of peace.²¹ PCS's critical turn to 'the local' introduced an alternative to 'the liberal peace', one which could be grounded and legitimized through bottom-up, local processes, through a politics which reflected local culture, knowledge and practice as opposed to the top-down internationally led method favored by problem-solving approaches. To this end, Richmond draws on postcolonial scholars such as Spivak, Bhabha and Scott²² to explore expressions of hidden resistance and postcolonial agency: the subtle, often hidden, ways that local politics manifest in the face of domination. As Richmond observes, 'local agencies, whether resisting aspects of statebuilding or co-opting it, have begun to find ways of claiming ownership of a politics that responds to [local] needs and identity issues, appropriating liberal peacebuilding, ignoring it or modifying it'.²³ Arguing along similar lines, Mac Ginty notes that the relationship between local agency and liberal peacebuilding is not necessarily adversarial but also complimentary. His research explores the 'ways in which internationally supported peace-making interventions can be improved by their inclusion of traditional and indigenous approaches to peace-making'.²⁴ Through this critical line of scholarship, 'the local' gradually emerged as the counterpoint to the problem-solving approach and their advocacy of the liberal peace. The critical literature began to cluster around two overlapping and interrelated claims: international peacebuilding represented an exercise in coercive neo-liberal power which limits space for local autonomy; meanwhile, local agency represented an emancipatory expression of resistance against international power, reflecting plurality, local autonomy and local subjectivity.

However, in the midst of the liberal peace crisis, the local was viewed more as a cause of conflict than an alternative foundation for peace.[25] In this context, problem-solving scholars responded with skepticism toward 'the local' and a defense of the liberal peace. Newman, for example, argued that liberal peace critics tend to overestimate the capacity of the liberal peace to actually transform entire societies. He suggests that some critics of the liberal peace tend to view it as 'dominated by a single coherent hegemonic agenda', reducing the agency of liberal peacebuilders to that of instruments of 'a global conspiracy'.[26] Therefore, he concludes that 'the critical approach to peacebuilding suffers from the analytical weakness of meta-theorizing'.[27] Meanwhile, Paris argued that the local is 'no panacea', pointing out that 'if the post-conflict society could organize its own governance arrangements without international assistance, there would have been no need or demand for peacebuilding in the first place'.[28] Paris maintains that 'there appears to be no viable, preferable alternative to some form of liberal peacebuilding'.[29] Hence, he concludes that local customs and practices should be incorporated 'within' a liberal framework.[30]

For Paris and Sisk 'retreating from the post-war statebuilding project would be tantamount to abandoning tens of millions of people to lawlessness, predation, disease and fear'.[31] Based on this reasoning, they turned to the task of managing the problems that arise from building a liberal state: the 'dilemmas analysis approach'.[32] This approach aims to acknowledge the contradictions, incoherency and messiness of statebuilding in order to then manage these dilemmas in a way which results in more effective liberal peacebuilding. Following this rationale, Belloni maintains that relying too much on 'the local' generates a problematic self-determining 'dilemma of civil society' in which people organize not only around democratic and liberal values, but also around values that can be seen as 'uncivil'.[33] He concludes that the risk of a locally rooted and locally situated civil society is too great: 'the best avenue to favor the emergence and development of a domestic civil society [...] is to strengthen the state.'[34] Similarly, Donias cautions that local 'activist civil society organizations may not necessarily be pro-peace, but might just as easily engage in the type of factionalized, zero-sum politics that stand in the way of sustainable peacebuilding'.[35]

Despite calls from the problem solvers to be cautious of 'the local', the need for local ownership, local participation and local empowerment was increasingly understood as essential to the success of international peacebuilding endeavors.[36] However, as the local emerged alongside the liberal peace, it was filtered through the academic debate between problem solving and critical scholars. While, problem solvers clustered around the idea that better international peacebuilding techniques were necessary to mitigate the destabilizing impact of local politics, critical scholars concluded that liberal peacebuilding was itself the problem. They argued that for peacebuilding to be locally legitimate and sustainable, international interventions must addresses local context, emphasize local needs and embrace local customs. As a result, the lines of the theoretical debate between problem solving and critical scholarship were projected onto the complex ontological hybrid processes actually unfolding in international peacebuilding environments, producing a liberal–local binary.

Explaining hybridity: Between the liberal peace and the local

With the increasing relevance of local participation to international peacebuilding processes, the academic and policy debates shifted away from the liberal peace and began to emphasize the interactions between international and local entities. However, post-conflict environments are highly dynamic, and the interactions between international and local entities are complex and contingent. In order to make sense of such overwhelming ontological complexity, critical scholars introduced the concept of hybridity to the PCS literature. Hybridity represented a continuation of the postcolonial turn in critical PCS and its accompanying emphasis on how local resistance and agency manifest in the context of international power.[37] However, hybridity also introduced a particular way of understanding the relationship between liberal and local entities – one which involves two essential components that stretch out along a temporal continuum: difference and transformation. According to Bhabha's influential postcolonial approach, hybridity is a temporal phenomenon in which difference becomes unstable; it is a *moment* in a colonial encounter when the continuity of difference can be disrupted and transformed.[38] Understood temporally, hybridity begins with the notions of difference, alterity and otherness; but it simultaneously involves the contested transformation of that difference and the emergence of new entities and different forms of difference.

Yet, as hybridity was incorporated into the peacebuilding debate, the concept's causal, differential characteristics were emphasized over its temporal transformative properties. By applying the concept of hybridity to explain the agonistic tensions between liberal and local entities, the critical PCS literature was able to cut through the overwhelming ontological complexity at play in and across a shifting array of contexts and shed new light on the relationship between the exercise of international power and expressions of emancipatory local agency. However, the explanatory power of hybridity also tended to emphasize the contested interactions *between* international power and emancipatory local agency rather than the transformation *of* what international power and local agency amounted to. It takes international power and emancipatory local agency for granted. While liberal–local hybridity provided a valuable framework for explaining the overarching tensions and general dynamics at play between and across peacebuilding contexts, it was less useful in exposing how the meaning of power and emancipation were themselves being transformed. The critical literature grappled with the contradictory tension embedded in the concept of hybridity; it sought to strike a balance between the explanatory utility of international–local hybridity, on the one hand, and the transformative process of hybridity which continually exceed these explanations, on the other.

Critical scholars such as Brown et al., for example, caution that hybrid orders have 'no clear-cut boundaries' between the liberal and local and instead describe 'processes of assimilation, articulation, adoption, and transformation at the interface of the global/exogenous and the local/indigenous'.[39] Nevertheless, they maintain that the liberal–local distinction is 'helpful' insofar as it indicates 'specific local indigenous characteristics that distinguish them from introduced institutions that belong to the realm of the state and civil society'.[40] Mac Ginty's understanding of hybridity reflects the same tension. He defines hybridity as 'processes that are a composite of exogenous and indigenous forces'.[41] Yet he also cautions that it is 'crucial that hybridity is not understood as the grafting together of two separate entities to make a new third entity'.[42] Nevertheless, Mac Ginty seeks to salvage a reading of hybridity which does not overly problematize its liberal–local constituent parts arguing against 'interrogating concepts so rigorously that we find that our language is rendered useless [and] concepts such as endogenous and exogenous, indigenous and international risk losing their currency'.[43] Therefore, he arrives at the following conclusion: 'recognise the shortcomings of concepts and language and move on.'[44] He favors accepting the liberal and the local as the 'main axes along which hybridization may be projected [in] liberal peace interventions'.[45]

While critical approaches treat hybridity as a consequence of local resistance to the liberal peace, problem-solving scholars introduced the idea of 'hybrid peace governance'.[46] According to Belloni and

Jarstad, hybrid peace governance refers to 'the activity of governing' a hybrid condition in which 'liberal and illiberal norms, institutions, and actors coexist, interact, and even clash'.[47] They envision hybridity as a range of governing conditions extending along a 'continuum' stretching out from liberal Westphalian states toward 'illiberal, often authoritarian, repressive state[s]'.[48] Yet, despite the so-called illiberal nature of these local norms and forms, they find that such a 'hybrid condition may also contain significant opportunities to make peace processes more stable and provide domestic institutions with the kind of locally rooted legitimacy that liberal peacebuilding has been unable to impart'.[49] For these reasons, Belloni concludes that hybridity offers a post-hegemonic alternative to 'the liberal peace' and therefore requires a move 'beyond the ontological and methodological dominance of Western actors and approaches to engage with bottom-up, local views of politics and society'.[50] The appropriation of hybridity by the problem-solving scholars reflects the increasing recognition that the ultimate success of the statebuilding endeavor depends on reaching out to local actors and incorporating local institutions and practices into the process. This shift signaled a move beyond simply managing the dilemmas of statebuilding. The explanatory utility of hybridity compelled problem-solving research to engage with the local. By the end of 2010, liberal–local hybridity emerged as the central theoretical framework used by both critical and problem-solving scholars.

Although the ascendance of the hybrid paradigm decentred the existing monopoly of the liberal on peace theory, it also manifested in ways which proved problematic. As hybridity was translated into the PCS debate, the concept's agonistic and differential tensions were emphasized over its transformative properties. On the one hand, the critical literature overemphasizes the emancipatory characteristics of local agency along with the counter-emancipatory power of the international peacebuilding apparatus. Although these are important dynamics, this explanation can also conceal unjust exercises of local power as well as expressions of emancipatory agency exercised through international peacebuilding. The problem-solving literature, on the other hand, overemphasizes the emancipatory power of international peacebuilding while portraying local agency as counterproductive to that effort. Yet, this position tends to delegitimize local grievances and alternatives while legitimizing often counterproductive international practices. Through this process, hybridity became trapped between the liberal–local distinctions that were developed to explain it. Consequently, the highly dynamic and transformative relationships between power and emancipation were gradually supplanted by the explanatory distinction between the liberal peace and the local.

This creates and preserves a problematic ambiguity in which the actual ontological tensions at play in emerging hybrid processes are substituted with the theoretical tensions between the liberal peace and the local. As Peterson points out, the liberal–local explanation of hybridity establishes a simplistic binary of otherness between local and external entities which also preserves the homogeneity within each group.[51] For Peterson, the international–local binary at the heart of hybridity raises questions about 'the capacity of hybridity to drive us conceptually forward by moving us away from binaries and the homogenisation of groups.'[52] Therefore, she cautions, 'when utilising hybridity as an analytical frame, there is a balance to be struck in terms of focusing solely on agency on the one hand and more structural analyses of power on the other.'[53]

Recently, a number of PCS scholars have started advocating for a move beyond the liberal peace and the local and challenging the fixed relationship between power and emancipatory agency they preserve. Chipping away at the homogenizing effects of the liberal peace, Zaum, for example, argued that it '[offers] little analytical purchase'.[54] He maintains that the liberal peace unacceptably reduces the complexity of peacebuilding interventions. Adopting a similar position, Heathershaw notes that 'by essentialising the nature of the state or the international intervention or by drawing a binary between internal and external actors, the analyst is blind to how the formal is intertwined with the informal, the international with the local'[55] Therefore, he finds that 'it is high time that critical scholars developed sharper theoretical tools to understand and explain the complex empirical cases that are thrown up by the liberal peace.'[56] Both Heathershaw's and Zaum's critiques suggest that the liberal peace distracts from the more important dynamics at play in actual emerging ontological peacebuilding *practices*.

Meanwhile, critical scholars were also attempting to disentangle emancipatory agency from 'the local'. Mitchell, for example, explores how power circulates within local politics. She finds that local communities use mechanisms of control and power in order to preserve a quality of life. She proposes that 'control need not emanate "from above" or even from relatively powerful actors. Rather, it may occur at a local level and in the medium of conflictual forms of world-building.'[57] Tom, meanwhile, challenged the way in which the power – agency binary at the center of liberal–local hybridity reinforces the axiomatic relationship between local agency and emancipatory inertia. He defines emancipatory hybridity as a process 'which does not only challenge the hegemony of the liberal peace, but also dominant local structures as well as [local] marginalisation and exclusion'.[58] In his reading, local processes which reinforce oppressive customary leaders while withholding benefits to the general population should not be considered emancipatory by virtue of their localness.

These lines of critique signaled a subtle but important turn in the PCS literature: a shift away from explaining hybrid outcomes through the politics of difference in favor of the more transformative dimensions of emerging hybrid processes. As the explanatory limitations of liberal–local hybridity were gradually revealed, critical PCS scholars attempted to move beyond the liberal–local tension at the heart of the hybrid paradigm and instead lay the foundations for a post-liberal paradigm. For example, Chandler's post-liberal turn flowed from a concern with 'the way that the term 'liberal' appears to have become an easy and unproblematic assertion of critical intent'.[59] Meanwhile, Richmond's post-liberal turn attempted not 'to exaggerate a local-international binary [as] such categories inevitably capture only part of the political tensions within peacebuilding'.[60] Contrary to the explanatory epistemological distinction between liberal and local entities, the nascent post-liberal literature instead focuses the material expressions of power and emancipatory agency as they ontologically emerge in peacebuilding contexts.

The emerging post-liberal world: Hybridity after the liberal and the local

As the PCS debate drifted from the explanatory hybrid paradigm into a more transformative and emergent one, critical PCS faced a new post-liberal problem: how to advance the PCS literature beyond the liberal–local distinction and break down the fixed relationship between power and emancipatory agency that it preserves. For Chandler, post-liberalism represents a new mode of international governmentality: post-liberal statebuilding. His approach stems from the assertion that critical scholars misinterpreted the liberal peace 'crisis' as being the result of *too much* liberalism.[61] On the contrary, he proposes that the nature of liberalism itself had changed. Chandler argues that post-conflict interventions do not resemble a 'liberal' peace at all but instead signal the rise of a new governing paradigm in which the emancipatory ambitions of the liberal peace are supplanted by the governmental logic of post-liberal statebuilding. Under this post-liberal governmental logic, local autonomy is constructed as a risk to be managed rather than the objective to be supported. The risk posed by local autonomy requires proactive management through deep-penetrating bio-political and techno-methodological social interventions. The aim of these deep social interventions is to transform the ungoverned social conditions in which local agency is understood as 'risky' into neo-liberal conditions which produce a civil society.[62] The central innovation of Chandler's approach is his introduction of 'international policy-practices' to the post-liberal debate.

Drawing from Foucault's methodological insights, Chandler finds that emphasizing policy-practice allows researchers to bypass problematic theoretical universals such as the liberal peace.[63] He argues that by embracing nonuniversal international policy-practices we can better understand statebuilding as a 'meaningful set of practices; a meaningful way of constructing problems and solutions'.[64] This is an important ontological contribution as it provides a way for international statebuilding interventions to be 'analysed as a policy discourse and set of practices which make sense on their own terms [and] judged by their own criteria' as opposed to the universal theoretical frameworks often imposed by outside academics.[65] However, while Chandler's emphasis on policy-practices lays the foundations for a methodological engagement with post-liberal processes, he emphasizes the international dimensions of post-liberalism. Therefore, Chandler's approach may potentially obscure the subtle ways in which the logic of post-liberal statebuilding changes. It may conceal the unstable process through which international policy-practices are transformed as they confront the local autonomy they are designed to manage. As a result, 'the local' remains abstract and without agency; likewise, expressions of emancipatory agency by internationals may be subsumed under the overarching paradigmatic logic of international statebuilding.[66]

Contrary to Chandler, Richmond argues that post-liberalism is the continuation of an emancipatory process rather than the end of one. According to him, a post-liberal peace represents a process of emancipation *from* the international statebuilding approach described by Chandler. For Richmond, this emancipatory post-liberal energy is nested in 'the everyday'. Richmond's post-liberal turn to the transformative processes of everyday life stemmed from a concern with the way 'the local' was increasingly being deployed uncritically, as shorthand for non-liberal, parochial, indigenous and lacking critical capacities.[67]

To this end, the everyday is an attempt to redefine 'the local'. Rather than treating 'the local' as the dialectical opposite of 'the international', he proposes that the local should be understood materially, as 'the specific socio-geographic space in which peace interventions... unfold'.[68] This is an important contribution which dislodges post-liberalism from the theoretical limits imposed by the international–local binary. Like Chandler's practice-based approach, the everyday creates important ontological space for exploring the proactive expressions of power and emancipation through which the liberal peace is gradually transformed into a post-liberal peace.

Richmond coins the term 'critical agency' in order to marshal these proactive and transformative expressions of emancipatory agency.[69] This critical agency, he argues, moves beyond statebuilding's preoccupation with cultivating local ownership and liberal civil society; it goes 'far deeper', getting at 'local-local' peacebuilding as it unfolds in the everyday.[70] For him, these everyday expressions of local–local and critical agency cannot be essentialized; they exist outside of the liberal–local binary and instead constitute a plural 'transnational and transversal community of political subjectivities'.[71] In order to capture these emancipatory post-liberal processes, Richmond introduces the term *peace formation*.[72] For him, peace formation extends beyond the limits of the international–local boundary and is instead 'networked across the state or the international' and 'has contributors who act with a notion of an emancipatory form of peace in mind.'[73] Therefore, post-liberal peace-formation processes should not be understood as an outcome of liberal–local difference but by a tension between emancipatory 'positive hybridity' and coercive 'negative hybridity'.[74] Yet according to Richmond's reading, the positive emancipatory value of peace formation is measured by the degree to which it reflects local customs, norms and culture. It is defined by a shared stake in promoting a postcolonial civil society that is locally relevant and reflects local needs. While these transversal everyday material practices offer a new way of understanding how emancipatory process shape post-liberal processes, they also preserve a reflexive relationship between emancipatory activity and localness.

While Chandler prioritizes how international power circulates, Richmond's approach prioritizes the local nature of the emancipatory activities unfolding in everyday sites. Taken together, they may have the effect of obscuring the ways in which emancipatory agency is expressed by international actors, and it may conceal how local actors exercise power in ways which may contravene emancipatory processes. As a result the differential tensions and theoretical boundaries created to explain the relationship between power and emancipatory agency may, paradoxically, obscure the very post-liberal processes reshaping what power and emancipation are becoming in the emerging post-liberal world.

Conclusion: Beyond international power and emancipatory local agency

The post-liberal contributions of both Chandler and Richmond push the peacebuilding debate beyond the epistemological limits of the liberal–local binary. Taken together, their post-liberal approaches disrupt the axiomatic distinction between the liberal peace and the local and establish the ontological foundations for exploring the more transformative dimensions of emerging post-liberal processes. Yet, they also preserve the explanatory tension between internationality and power and between emancipation and localness. On the one hand, this distinction is necessary and useful; it explains the central, overarching political tension driving post-liberal processes in peacebuilding and development contexts. Yet, on the other hand, these explanatory distinctions are projected onto the complex and uncertain post-liberal hybrid processes in which the limitations of power and meaning of emancipation are actively being contested and transformed. As a result, these approaches may paradoxically conceal the very transformative post-liberal processes they seek to expose.

This ambiguity is rooted in the undefined relationship between two overlapping and interrelated approaches to exploring the emerging post-liberal world: an *explanatory* approach and an *emergent* one. The explanatory approach is epistemological in nature; it aims to develop concepts and analytical frameworks for making sense of the overwhelming ontological complexity of emerging post-liberal processes. However, the emergent approach is ontological in nature; it is concerned with tracing the messy post-liberal processes emerging in ways that exceed and transcend their explanation. Contrary to an explanatory project, an emergent project maps the post-liberal processes unfolding in ways which continually destabilize that which is international or local about peace. From this emergent perspective, the issue becomes how to engage with uncertain post-liberal processes in a way which does not distribute the attributes of power and properties of emancipatory agency according to an a priori distinction between 'the international' and 'the local'. For this purpose, this book draws from the emergent aspects of both Chandler's *practice*-based approach and Richmond's *peace formation* approach and then combines them with insights from Practice Theory and Actor Network Theory in order to further develop ontological scaffolding for engaging with the emergent hybrid processes shaping what the post-liberal world is becoming.

2
A Post-Liberal Ontology of Peacebuilding Practice

The meaning of emancipation and the limits of power have become trapped between the liberal peace and the local. Liberal–local hybridity maintains and projects an a priori relationship between power and emancipatory agency onto the complex ontological processes though which this relationship is continually contested and transformed. In other words, the liberal–local explanation of hybridity produces a problematic paradox: it conceals the expressions of power and emancipatory agency that are actively reshaping post-liberal world. Rather than exposing the active, ontologically transformative properties of hybridity, liberal–local hybridity preserves hybridity as an outcome, a by-product, a secondary effect of a more fundamental, more significant tension between liberal international power and emancipatory local agency. However, concealed within the paradox of liberal–local hybridity, there is an alternative and previously unidentified *emergent* post-liberal project. By way of comparison, the explanatory orientation is epistemological in nature; its purpose is developing concepts, analytical frameworks and theoretical distinctions in order to make sense of the overwhelmingly complex ontological phenomena. The emergent approach, however, is ontological in nature. It is oriented toward mapping ontological complexity and tracing *the post-liberal surplus*: activities that exceed and reshape the distinctions on which explanatory hybridity depends.

The emergent approach is adopted here. An emergent ontology attempts to disrupt the axiomatic relationship between liberal international power and emancipatory local agency; its goal is to move beyond the differential and agonistic tension that functions as the driving force at the heart of the liberal–local explanation of hybridity. However, in order to move beyond the causal explanatory political tension between internationality and localness, an emergent ontology of hybridity must supply an alternative way of engaging with the circulation of power and expressions of emancipatory agency – one which does not rely on the continuity of a liberal–local political tension. In order to present an alternative approach for exploring the exercise of power and expressions of emancipatory, the emergent post-liberal approach outlined in this chapter is based in peacebuilding *practice*. A practice-based approach does not defer to the a priori agonistic relationship between the liberal peace and the local but is instead based in the material relations in which peacebuilding practices emerge. This chapter presents a practice-based approach to exploring the hybrid processes that give shape to the emerging post-liberal world.

From explanation to emergence

In order to explore the more transformative dimensions of post-liberal hybridity without reproducing another explanatory distinction, an alternative ontological foundation must be developed. An alternative practice-based ontology must disentangle the exercise of power and the expression of emancipatory agency from its explanatory epistemological roots in the liberal peace and the local. An emergent approach instead explores how the limits of power and meaning of emancipation are contested and reshaped in the emerging post-liberal world. Therefore, a post-liberal ontology of practice must remove the exploration of hybrid processes from the explanatory politics of difference; instead it must ontologically situate emerging hybrid processes upon the unstable politics of transformation. To this end, Bruno Latour's critique of the politics of explanation is instructive.

A leading proponent of ANT, Latour argues that the names, shapes, boundaries and distinctions designed to explain complex social phenomena are shaped by the 'politics of explanation'.[1] In describing the politics of explanation, he distinguishes between the 'elements to be explained' (which tend to be confusing, new, different, messy and incoherent, and thus the imperative to explain them) and the 'elements providing an explanation'.[2] Defined as such, an explanation becomes a 'one-to-many ratio' between the elements providing an explanation and the complex, messy 'elements being explained'.[3] This 'one-to-many' explanatory relationship applies where 'the same social factors are used to explain many natural or objective elements.'[4] Latour finds that powerful explanations allow 'one element [to] "replace", "represent" and "stand for" all the others, which are, in effect, made secondary'.[5]

Therefore, he treats explanatory formulations as an exercise of power: the ability of one 'social factor' to 'hold' various contingent, concrete, inchoate, messy social phenomena to as few social factors as possible. In Latour's reading, the differential relationship between international power and local agency represents a powerful explanation. Translated as 'the local', a vast and differentiated pattern of activities and practices emerging across many sites can be *replaced*. Meanwhile, 'the liberal peace' *stands in* for a wide spectrum of projects, institutions and actors, organized by varying mandates and mobilized for different purposes. Through the politics of explanation, these complex, dynamic ontological processes gradually become substituted by the name invented to explain them.

Latour points to a problematic implication that results when ontological complexity becomes theoretically arrested by its explanations: cause becomes confused with effect; the phenomena requiring an explanation are mistaken for the explanation.[6] When complex ontological activity is replaced with the theoretical shape assigned to it, then the activity becomes secondary. In this way, complex webs of interlacing micro-interactions are reduced to an outcome generated by something else, namely, interactions between entities called 'the liberal peace' and 'the local' and the relationship between power and agency that they signify. Problematically, when explanations stand in for activity, the very dynamics which challenge and upset powerful explanations cannot be detected. While the explanatory tension between international power and emancipatory local agency may capture the main tensions and asymmetries at play amid the complex messiness of contested post-liberal processes, it is less useful for exposing the ways in which these very processes displace the flow of international power and redefine the limits of emancipation. In other words, the theoretical boundaries developed to explain what post-liberalism *is* may paradoxically obscure the emergent processes reshaping what the post-liberal world is *becoming*. This produces a problematic paradox which, if left unaddressed, is likely to reproduce the international–local binary rather than redefine it.

In order to circumvent the paradox of liberal–local hybridity, it must be disentangled from the epistemological politics of explanation and instead situated within the unstable ontological politics of emergence. There is a subtle but important difference in the nature of the political tension at play between explanatory and emergent hybridity: the political tensions at play in emerging hybrid processes are temporal – the politics of emergence are shaped by the pressures of time. These temporal political tensions extend beyond the explanatory relationship between international power and emancipatory local agency and instead actively unsettles the limits of power and continually reshapes the meaning of emancipation as the emerging post-liberal world continually takes shape.

Contrary to the political tension of *being different*, emergent hybridity is shaped by the politics of *becoming different*. While the political tensions at play in explanatory and emergent readings of hybridity are closely related, emergent hybridity emphasizes the more transformative dimensions of hybrid processes. The emergent politics of becoming includes, but extends beyond, the differences of being local or being international; yet it goes further by exposing the politics of difference to the ontological stresses of time that cut through and run between all manifestations of difference. These temporal tensions continually disrupt different ways of being, stretching them into different ways of becoming. The temporal relationship between being and becoming is emergent and is therefore uncertain. It continually oscillates between order and disorder, continuity and discontinuity and between stability and instability.

The subtle shift from being different to becoming different has significant implications. The uncertain process of becoming post-liberal demands active and ongoing management. This active ontological reading fundamentally reverses the cause-and-effect relationship at the center of explanatory hybridity. Rather than a secondary outcome, or by-product of differential tensions, the uncertain politics of emergence are active political processes through which the post-liberal world is always taking shape. On this emergent reading, hybridity is a verb not a noun; a source not an outcome. Therefore, the post-liberal world should be understood as an open-ended, emerging ontological process of uncertain becoming in which the limits of power and the meaning of emancipation are always at stake. In order to expose and trace this active post-liberal political process of hybridity, they must be grounded in the peacebuilding practices through which it emerges.

Practice: Between being and becoming

In order to identify and map the complex ontological politics of emergent hybridity, a practice-based approach is very useful. Practices are ontologically primary, not secondary outcomes. The genealogical roots of what can loosely be described a practice approach stem from Heidegger's ontology of immanent becoming (Dasein)[7] and Wittgenstein's[8] work on language and rule-following.[9] They understood practice as a critical point of entry for challenging the enduring philosophical binary between powerful but abstract social structures and the equally abstract rationality of individual actors.[10] The post-foundational potential of 'practice' was used in different ways through Foucault's work on the body as a site of power,[11] De Certeau's exploration of everyday tactics,[12] Butler's notion of performative gender[13] and Latour's ANT.[14] A diverse range of disciplines call on practice theory as well. Sociology explores practice in the works of Bourdieu's habitus,[15] Giddens' structuration[16] and Schatzki's site-based ontology of social practices.[17] Practice is central to science and technology studies (STS), which excavates contingencies embedded in scientific practices and the production of knowledge.[18] Practices are explored in anthropology,[19] in human geography[20] and have recently been incorporated into international relations (IR)[21] in order to redirect the perceived overemphasis on structure, institution and culture in IR theory while also avoiding the myth of the transcendentally rational individual.[22]

Following the general direction of the present argument, practice-based approaches are not a homogenous school of thought. Rather, the multidisciplinary range of practice approaches constitutes an ongoing debate concerning the nature of practice, what a practice approach is and what it should be. To the extent that there is a common theme among practice theorists, it stems from a concern that the complex and uncertain ontological processes that make up the world have become trapped in an endless dialectical cycle between competing structural and individualist ontologies of the social world. Practice theorists are concerned with the meta-theoretical practices that allow scholars to transcend the world's complex emergence, to name it, to map it, to categorize it, to re-present it, to establish its limits and then project these limits into an uncertain future. For practices theorists, the complex ontological processes shaping the emerging world always exceed the attempt to explain it.

Therefore, practice theorists start with fairly simple ontological claim: *practice is doing*. According to Schatzki, practices are the everyday 'doings and sayings' that comprise human coexistence.[23] Speaking to this basic ontological claim, Mattern defines practice as 'doing human being'.[24] A practice-approach therefore treats 'what people do', or *how people go about doing their human being*, as the basic and fundamental unit of analysis. Mattern argues that practice-approaches treat the doings of actors as irreducible; she finds that practices are 'the foundations, or the smallest units of social life'.[25] Yet, the uncertain flow of these everyday practices is far from chaotic; it unfolds in relatively organized and predictable patterns. If practices are not the by-product of individual actors negotiating powerful social structures, then how do practice approaches account for relative continuity of social order? According to Schatzki, the everyday activities of human coexistence are *organized*. For him, the organized nature of practice is essential to its ontological integrity.[26] And therefore, understanding the organized nature of practice is crucial to understanding how the emergent and uncertain continuity between being and becoming is actively managed. In order to explore the organized nature of practice without deferring to the transcendental rationality of individuals or reinforcing explanatory distinctions between international power and local agency, a practice-approach turns to the *material relations* of practices themselves.

The materiality of practice

As mentioned, proponents of practice-based approaches set out to circumvent the entrenched, explanatory relationship between structuralist and individualist ontologies. To this end, practice approaches claim to restore the material dimension to social research. Their aim is to offer a novel point of departure from traditional Cartesian distinctions between subject and object, self and world. To say that practice is material is to say that practice is ontologically nested in bodies and things.[27] While the implications of this definition carry far beyond the purposes of the present inquiry,[28] there are two important ontological aspects of the materiality of practice: practices are carried or transmitted through bodies and artifacts.[29] First, practices are embodied. According to Schatzki, 'the body demands attention in practice theory as the common meeting point of mind and activity and of individual activity and society.'[30] Rouse notes that the body functions 'as both the locus of agency, affective response and cultural expression, and the target of power and normalization'.[31] In other words, practices are exercised through and upon bodies. However, it is important to note the distinction between embodied *practices* and individual *agency*. A materialist ontology holds that practice remains 'ontologically prior' to agency.[32] According to Schatzki, 'human agency must [...] be understood as something contained in practices'.[33] Mattern agrees, pointing out that according to a practice-approach 'agency is a *result* of practice rather than its source'.[34] Therefore, contrary to 'individual' agency, embodiment can be read as the materialized expression of practice, or what Reckwitz terms 'embodied understanding'.[35]

Diane Coole's attempt to reconceptualize agency through 'embodiment' is useful here. She redefines agency in material terms as the 'agentic capacities' located in individual bodies.[36] Coole's notion of embodiment 'does not begin with an idealist model of agents [and] then seek their facsimile in the real world'.[37] Her materialist approach parallels practice approaches insofar as they both resist 'ascrib[ing] any specific political orientation to the body *a priori*' and therefore avoid 'reifying or simply modelling the body on a traditional sense of agency (as a unified, intentional, active source of freedom or dissent)'.[38] For Coole, bodies are only 'contingently, not ontologically identified with rational, individual agents'.[39] The contingent nature of embodied agency suggests that 'the body is never merely a passive transmitter of messages but plays an active role in the generation of perceptual meaning'.[40] She maintains that an emphasis on the materiality of agency clears new ontological space hence 'opening up a field of inquiry and recognition of immanent, contingent emergence'.[41] In this sense, the ontological body is simultaneously the cause and effect of practice; it is at once effected and effecting. The body is both shaped by practice, yet the body is also a locus of 'agentic capacities' which can reshape and reform the practices. In this sense, the body is an active participant in organizing the emergent relationship between being and becoming, continuity and discontinuity, between the liberal and post-liberal worlds. In order to signify the distinction between individual agency and embodiment, the term *practitioner* will be used to capture the contingent performance of a specified practice.

The relationality of practice

In addition to displacing ontological individualism, the material foundations of practice approaches sought to undermine its binary opposite: ontological structuralism. Therefore, practice approaches had to address the organized and patterned social *relations between practitioners* without deferring back to abstract powerful structures. Latour's post-humanist materialism is useful for displacing the human body as the sole site of agency. Along with fellow ANT proponents, Latour argues that 'anything that modifies the state of things, making a difference is an actor'.[42] With this move, Latour decouples agency from its housing in the intentionality of individual minds and expands it to include materials such as technology, documents, tools and maps. On this materialist reading, artifacts are 'more than just objects of knowledge, but are necessary, irreplaceable components of certain social practices'.[43] ANT proposes that objects and artifacts are *'participants* in the course of action waiting to be given a figuration'.[44]

Speaking of the ontological significance of the relational nature of practice, Rouse argues that practices 'cannot be properly characterized or understood apart from their belonging to or participation within a practice sustained over time by the interaction of multiple practitioners and/or performances'.[45] Meanwhile, Reckwitz observes that 'when we talk of "social fields" or "institutions", in the end we find nothing more than nexuses and sequences of social practices'.[46] To this ontological point, Schatzki identifies the relational nature of practice as the 'linchpin' of a practice-approach.[47] For him the material-relationality of practice is 'how determinant entities are laid out and hang together [the ways] in which they relate and are positioned with respect to one another'.[48] However, these arrangements of bodies and artifacts are not fixed but instead have to be actively held in place. Therefore the material relations of practices are not static but are ontologically embedded in and transmitted through the emergent flow of organized practices. As such, practice approaches are primarily interested in the material relations through which the unstable emergent tension between being and becoming are actively organized and managed through practices. In order to explore theses unstable material relations, Schatzki suggests turning to the *sites* in which they emerge.

The site: A material ontology

Practices emerge in sites. Schatzki's site-based ontology of practice maintains that 'the character and transformation of social life are both intrinsically and decisively rooted in the site where it takes place'.[49] It is important to note that Schatzki's distinction between practice and sites is only *analytical* not ontological. Ontologically, practice and the site are not distinct opposing units of analysis; they are not abstract forces that break down along binary lines which can then be juxtaposed like individual and institution or agent and structure. Rather the distinction between practices and the sites in which they unfold collapses into the same dynamic ontological material-relational condition. According to Schatzki, the social site is defined by the practices circulating through it, not the other way around. As such, the site is not simply the location, place or geographical space upon which practices emerge. Rather, practices are brought forth into the site, giving it shape and imbuing it with contingent and sometimes contested social meaning. This leads to a fairly open and dynamic reading of the site. In this sense, sites are simply the material clusters and nexuses of practices emerging in space. Practices and the sites in which they emerge are composed of the same fundamental material elements – the organized movement of bodies and things – and the continually shifting relations between them. Stretched out along the temporal tension of emergence, the site is simultaneously an unstable context and a clearing.

A site as a context

Understood as a context, the site is 'the place' in which materials (bodies and things) interact, it is where everyday life unfolds. In this way, the site functions as the material-relational context in which practices emerge. Context, in this sense, is what Schatzki identifies as the particular 'orders' or 'arrangements' – the materials clustered in a given site, effecting the flow of activity.[50] For Schatzki, in this contextual sense, the site 'surrounds' or 'immerses' practice; sites are where bodies and things are 'suspended' and action is 'determined' and 'prefigured'.[51] In this way, the site–context shapes and channels the forthcoming flow of emerging practices. However, a practice approach eschews any ontological distinction between sites and practice. Practices are not 'suspended' *in* structure, 'immersed' *in* global forces or 'ordered' *in* sites; nor do sites represent an outside structural, normative or extra-material organizing principle or rationality.

In Schatzki's account, the contextual elements of a site are 'not self-standing or self-propagating configurations'.[52] Instead, the 'within-ness' of a site – context separates the site as a 'special sort of context'.[53] A site is where 'entities are intrinsically part of their own context'.[54] In other words, the site within which practice emerges is itself composed of the movement generated by the practices sustaining it. Practices generate their own context; sites are the living context of practices unfolding among a multiplicity of co-emerging practices. *Sites are practices emerging in material relation to other practices in space.* For example, a prison can be either a site of incarceration or a museum, depending on what practices are emerging there at different times. A site therefore is not simply the material context within which practices emerge; a site does not simply constrain emerging practices or order activity. Rather a site is a dynamic and shifting context defined by the practices emerging there.

A site as a clearing

Therefore, sites are more than context; they are also a *clearing* of relative contingence where practices may emerge in new ways and take on different meanings. The site–context reflects the emergent, shifting material relations animated by practitioners. Amid this context, sites are simultaneously replete with 'spaces', 'openings', 'mediums', 'clearings' and 'fields'.[55] The organized movement of practitioners through a site generates unstable pockets, opportunities and moments of imminent possibility in which practices can emerge anew and continually (re)shape and (re)define their context. In these clearings, the routine, scripted, teleoeffective ordering effects embedded in a given practice open up to the contingent possibility of change. It is through this emergent and uncertain process that practices are continually forced to confront the world they seek to organize. In such clearings, a gap opens up in the organized temporal stream of emergent practices. A fundamental component of Schatzki's site ontology is the position that 'all the [order] in the world cannot sew up agency before it occurs. The endless becoming of social life effected in human actions transpires in a social site that qualifies paths in numerous ways of import for action'.[56] Accordingly, practices 'continually evolve because of changing circumstances, accumulating experience [...], and shifts in the orders and practices that the actions engage or are part of'.[57]

Yet, as Schatzki points out, 'lives hang together not just in and through single settings, but also across multiple ones.'[58] While practices emerge locally in the site, the ordering effects they produce may overflow and extend far beyond the local site of their emergence, just as they may flow in from other sites. In other words, the practices emerging in one site are often implicated in practices emerging in other sites. Experience gained from encounters in different sites may serve as a resource in another. To the extent that the site is an 'entity', it is a very porous and dynamic one. Practices pass through and between sites. Practices inhabit and shift within a site, altering existing material-relational patterns, changing the nature of the site as they pass through and between them. This movement can also be assisted and extended with technology and artifacts. Practices can be transcribed onto artifacts, digitally encoded and electronically transmitted between sites allowing the practices emerging in one site to endure beyond the site of its immediate emergence.[59] For Latour, artifacts such as these explain the durability of certain practices where 'social forces' are unable to.[60] In this way, a practice approach can account for the durability of certain 'ways of doing' outside of face-to-face, single-site limited interactions without invoking extra-material social phenomena such as identity, culture, institution or the differential tension between international power and emancipatory agency.

For Latour, the connections between sites are of primary ontological significance. He is centrally concerned with *how* such connections are designed, forged, stabilized, strengthened and entrenched; how these connections break down, are reformed and diversify; and how these connections must be constantly managed and maintained. The relative durability of these connections is a function of how the movement of bodies and things through and between sites is organized. These linkages must be constantly managed, maintained, redeveloped and reconfigured through the organized circulation of practice in and between sites. Sites are therefore the material nexuses, the spatial nodes in which the temporal tension between being and becoming is actively negotiated and the uncertain and emerging relationship between the liberal and post-liberal worlds is actively managed.

A political situation

The near-infinite complexity of international peacebuilding and development interventions renders charting the connections through and between the vast landscape of sites an overwhelming task; hence, the explanatory utility of liberal–local hybridity. However, human geography provides a more dynamic ontological alternative for exploring the material linkages that hold various configurations of sites together while under constant emergent temporal strain. In a series of articles, Woodward, Jones and Marston argue that the material relations running through and between sites should be grounded on a flat spatial ontology.[61] A flat ontology of emergent material relations, they argue, problematizes the legacy of Cartesian binaries embedded in hierarchical epistemologies of power and geographies of scale that are 'anchored by the endpoints of the local and global'.[62] They maintain the hierarchical scaling of power 'assigns[s] the global more causal force, assume[ing] it to be more orderly (if not law-like) and less contingent'.[63] As a result, the local is relegated to the secondary status of a 'case study', a mere laboratory for confirming global power. Instead, they argue that a flat, site-based ontology requires no 'transcendental organizing principle or category beyond the swarms of material articulation and differentiation'.[64] According to Escobar, their flat ontological approach displaces 'the centering essentialism that infuses not only the up–down vertical imaginary but also the radiating (out from here) spatiality of horizontality' enshrined in the core-periphery cartographic binary.[65] A flat ontological formulation therefore eschews the vertical, topological landmarks and concentric horizontal mile-markers of power which allow lived space to be transcended, neatly divided and explained from above. All that remains is the messy and chaotic flat ontological landscape upon which the disassembled and unstable nature of everyday life continually plays out.

However, this raises a critical question: what about power, domination and injustice? Flat ontologies do not ignore unjust asymmetries and powerful systems of domination. Rather, flat ontologies attempt to disrupt the assumed continuity between how power is organized and how power emerges. From a flat, emergent and therefore uncertain ontological position, the continuity of unjust power and domination can be re-interrogated, and the question of how such arrangements are held in place can be reposed. For Latour, power 'is the final result of a process and not a reservoir, a stock, or a capital that will automatically provide an explanation. Power and domination have to be produced, made up, composed'.[66] However, this outcome remains uncertain and must therefore be actively managed. Latour maintains that while the power asymmetries and domination characterizing the social world do exist, 'they are not behind the scenes, above our heads, and before the action, but after the action, below the participants and smack in the foreground. They do not cover, nor encompass, nor gather, nor explain; they circulate, they format, they standardize, they coordinate'.[67] In this way, Latour argues that a flat, emergent landscape forces 'any candidate with a more "global" role to sit beside the "local" site it claims to explain'.[68]

From this flat ontological position, he observes that it is 'possible to [...] foreground the *practical means* to keep ties in place, the ingenuity constantly invested in enrolling other sources of ties, and the cost to be paid for the extension of any interaction'.[69] Fellow ANT proponent John Law holds that what appears to be powerful are instead rather 'precarious' connections that require 'constant maintenance'.[70] Therefore he points out that the assumption of power underpinning the relative continuity of social order instead suggests that 'everything is uncertain and reversible, at least in principle. It is never given in the order of things.'[71] Therefore, the task is to trace the practical means by which the shifting and unstable connections running through and between sites are actively managed in such a way that they appear durable and stable.

In order to better capture the contingency and uncertainty at play in actively managing the continuity of the practical connections between sites, Woodward et al. reconceptualize the site as an emergent *political situation*. The incessant motion of a site, they argue, is 'always a matter of labor, of work'.[72] They describe the site as a ' "state of affairs" open to a perpetual "state of play" ' and therefore suggest that 'we must approach sites as aggregating negotiating and *working* materialities – bodies in motion, affecting and effecting – that sometimes enfold the labors of purposeful subjects'.[73] The purposeful organization of practice suggests that it is organized for some reason, to do something, to address some perceived problem and to bring about some change. Importantly, however, the purpose of organized practices are embedded in and articulated through practices themselves rather than through an abstract structure or extra-material norm. As Woodward et al. remark, when understood as a purposeful political situation, a site becomes 'a dynamically composed aggregate whose "map" is drawn according to its own internal "logics", rather than any generalizing laws'.[74] This 'internal logic' or 'situated reasoning' is concerned with the ongoing management of the unfolding and uncertain political situation. This management consists of the continual, situated negotiation, arbitration and trading-off between how a given practice is designed to emerge and how it emerges in practice. The post-liberal politics of practices can be glimpsed at the emergent disjuncture between being and becoming continually held open in an uncertain political situation.

Conclusion

The political situation provides a dynamic ontology grounded in space and stretched by time. A post-liberal political situation is simultaneously (a) the site, (b) the specific practices circulating and emerging there and (c) the unstable condition generated by what those practices are organized to bring about in the site. Taken together, the practical situation is an imminently unfolding material condition requiring constant management. Contrary to a liberal–local explanation of hybridity, a political situation draws attention to the organized labor of practitioners as they move through and between sites attempting to organize how peacebuilding practices circulate through and between them. Ontologically speaking, a political situation is the imminently emerging condition in which the unstable relationship between being and becoming is actively managed. A political situation provides a dynamic ontological platform – a flat ontological landscape – on which to explore the post-liberal politics of becoming. From here, one need not turn to power, to structure or to 'the liberal peace' in order to give shape to the political tension at play. Instead the politics of practice can be re-interrogated as they are forced to confront the complex world they attempt to explain and organize.

A political situation draws attention to the political purpose of a given set of practices as it is materially circumscribed through specified goals, methods and in the strategies through which the labor of practitioners is organized. Therefore, peacebuilding practices are political; they are organized to do something, to address some perceived problem, to bring about some change, to manage some situation. A political situation provides an emergent ontological basis that allows researchers to account for how practitioners actively manage the emerging relationships between order and disorder, stability and instability, continuity and discontinuity and between the liberal and emerging post-liberal world.

3
The Politics of Post-Liberal Peacebuilding Practice

The previous chapter outlined a post-liberal ontology of practice. This chapter turns to the post-liberal politics of practice. When peacebuilding practices are subjected to emergent pressures and tensions of a post-liberal political situation, the unstable relationship between being and becoming can be explored. In addition to the agonistic political tensions between different ways of being, a political situation subjects different ways of being to the emergent tensions actively reshaping what they are becoming. In post-conflict environments, the unstable temporal bridge connecting being to becoming is continually and actively constructed through the organized management of peacebuilding practices. Practices are organized activities; they are organized for some purpose, to address some perceived problem, to bring about some kind of change. While embedded in the past, peacebuilding practices are oriented toward the future. However, peacebuilding practices and the future they are organized to bring about may be contested. Therefore, the temporal politics at play in actively managing the continuity of this relationship stretches out along an uncertain, unfolding continuum in which the limits of power and meaning of emancipation in the post-liberal world are being actively reshaped.

In such an unstable political situation, the post-liberal politics of practice unfold at the emergent disjuncture between *how practices are organized and how organization is practiced*. The politics of peacebuilding practices can be exposed in the management of the unstable relationship between how practices are designed and how they are performed, between how practices should emerge and how they actually emerge. This unstable emergent political tension must be actively managed by practitioners. When organized peacebuilding practices are stretched out along an emerging continuum, the continuity of that organization becomes unstable. As practitioners grapple with managing the unstable continuity of these performances, they must actively organize and reorganize how practices circulate through an often diverse array of sites so as to maintain the unstable associations between them. This chapter explores how practitioners manage this disjuncture between design and performance, organization and reorganization and liberal and post-liberal worlds.

Therefore, the issue of agency and subjectivity is at the center of this discussion. Hence, this chapter explores the degree to which peacebuilding practices are structurally predetermined and, conversely, the extent to which practitioners can actively reorganize existing organized patterns of practices. However, in keeping with the emergent ontology outlined in the previous chapter, practitioners must not be understood as individuals exerting autonomous agency to transform powerful structures. Instead the capacity to act in a way that appears as agency should be understood as something which is enabled though an unstable continuum of organized practices. In order to walk this fine line, this chapter reviews the politics of practices first as it was envisioned in Foucault's biopolitics, then in Bourdieu's habitus, Adler and Pouliot's 'community of practices', through to Schatzki's notion of practical understanding and, finally, Callon and Latour's notion of the politics of translation. The point of this discussion is not to disprove or overly problematize a particular reading of practice, but to gradually construct post-liberal notion of situated practical agency: *the post-liberal practitioner*. This chapter focuses on how practitioners attempt to *translate* their purposefully organized practices as they move through and between complex and shifting arrangement of sites in which the peace they are attempting to bring about may be contested. The chapter then develops a practice-based reading of translation which involves four interrelated processes: *problematization, appropriation, performance* and *re-problematization*. Through this ongoing and active process, the various points and moments of translation can be traced along an unstable emerging continuum. These points of translation reveal a series of performative discontinuities that add up to a post-liberal process of emergent hybridity.

Organizing peacebuilding practices

Peacebuilding practices are organized. As mentioned in the previous chapter, the organized nature of practice is essential to its ontological integrity. The continuity of everyday life and the stability of social order are nested in the organized continuum of circulating social practices.

Speaking to the organized nature of practices Büger, for example, defines practice as 'collectively shared and routinised forms of behaviour that are materially anchored in bodies and artifacts'.[1] According to Adler and Pouliot, practices 'tend to be patterned, in that they generally exhibit certain regularities over time and space. In a way reminiscent of routine, practices are repeated, or at least reproduce similar behaviour with regular meanings'.[2] The relatively predictable motion of practices therefore provides a smooth and patterned backdrop against which translations can be cast.

However, in keeping with the materiality of practices and the flat ontological landscape across which they move, practices are not organized by powerful structures or abstract systems of meaning. As the above descriptions suggest, human activities are organized *within and through* practices. Nevertheless, practices can be organized in ways which produce powerful effects. According to Schatzki, the relative continuity and stability of organized practices should be understood as the situated prefiguration of forthcoming activities – the shaping or channeling of emerging activities within and through practices that are ontologically grounded in sites.[3] However, practice theory emerged as a reaction against post-structuralism's turn away from the subject along with the possibility for transformative change. Practice theorists wanted to recover some semblance of agency, some manifestation of subjectivity from the deterministic clutches of culture, language and economic order while also avoiding a modernist ideology of individualism. However, walking the fine line between social and individual ontologies raises questions about the limits of agency and the ability of practitioners to bring about transformative change.

Governmentality

Foucault's theories of power and resistance are at the center of the hybrid paradox in critical PCS. His notion of governmentality has been particularly influential in explaining how international power circulates.[4] Likewise, Foucault's politics of resistance has been equally influential in understanding how peacebuilding interventions are resisted by local actors and institutions.[5] However, Foucault's work originally set out to problematize liberal humanism and to decenter the individual subject as the source of rationality and the engine of history.[6] He wanted to investigate how subjectivity is produced through the tactics and strategies of governing.[7] Such governmental practices were directed toward the population and designed to act on the possibilities of action. However, rather than acting directly on bodies or through disciplinary power, governmentality operated discretely by shaping the socioeconomic conditions in which subjectivity is cultivated.[8] Yet, according to the Foucauldian maxim, 'where there is power there is resistance', when governmental strategies designed to conduct human conduct are exposed, counter-conduct emerges.[9]

However, as Pickett cautions, resistance must not be mistaken for the 'antimatter' of power.[10] He finds that Foucault's notion of resistance is always embedded in the field of power it is attempting to transform. Therefore, he remains trapped in a bind where expressions of resistance reproduce 'the very system we are trying to escape because it will be rebellion in the name of ideals drawn from modern power'.[11] For these reasons, Caldwell argues that Foucault's radical decentering of the subject and preclusion of emancipatory agency fails to account for the emergent possibility of change: 'Ultimately, without a synthetic concept of agency you cannot have a credible conception of change. Agency must include not only the capacity to resist or "act otherwise", but also the possibility of "making a difference".'[12] Therefore, he maintains that in order to account for a process of change, a 'practice-oriented concept of agency would have to mediate between classical ideas of intentional action, autonomy and choice and ideals of embodied agency as always changing and always open to reinvention.'[13] Although Foucault's theories of power and resistance are at the center of the hybrid paradox in PCS, he also lays the foundations for moving beyond the power/resistance, structure/agency dichotomy that often frames hybridity and paves the way for exploring the relationship between power and resistance as materially embodied *practices*.[14]

Habitus

Like Foucault, Pierre Bourdieu wanted to understand how everyday life unfolds in relatively stable and predictable patterns. However, he also wanted to reclaim some subjectivity from Foucault's discursive determinism and move beyond the limitations that linguistic rules imposed on the subject's ability to act in ways which exceed those limits. Bourdieu observes extra-linguistic factors at play in social interactions – factors that function to synchronize and harmonize the perceptions of agents in ways which generate continuity of social order.[15] He proposes that this continuity is supplied by the habitus. According to Bourdieu, the habitus is a 'system of durable, transposable dispositions, which integrates past experiences and functions at every moment as a matrix of perception, appreciation, and action, making possible the accomplishment of infinitely differentiated tasks'.[16] The practical matrix of dispositions continually provided by the habitus is a subconscious relational resource of background knowledge and experience that supplies agents with the perceived ability to respond consciously and objectively to a given situation in an organized and intelligible way.[17] Therefore, habitus is more than simply the rules one follows, it is the preconscious synthesis of meaning, social convention, history, norms, inarticulable know-how, intuition, etc. Understood in this way, the habitus is the source of practices.

Yet, while it provides agents with the semiconscious dispositions to respond to situations in relatively predicable ways, the habitus does not determine practices. Instead, the habitus is 'the durably installed generative principle of regulated improvisations'.[18] Understood this way, the habitus is a dynamic organizing system that continually produces regulated improvisations through practices which then reproduce the habitus. However, for Bourdieu, this dynamic reproductive process is situated in a field of practice. The field of practice represents the intersubjective social condition – the overlapping relationships between actors and institutions – within which a habitus is dynamically actualized. Through the ongoing reproductive feedback cycle between habitus, the field and practices, a relationally shared 'common sense' is generated and sustained.[19] However, despite his attempts to develop a theory of practice that exceeded the deterministic limits of social structures, Bourdieu has been critiqued for relying on the generative tensions between the habitus and the field.[20] By emphasizing the structuring effects of the tensions between the field and the habitus, the ontological status of practice remains ambiguous – it is reduced to a secondary outcome that can be *explained* by the tensions between the habitus and the field. Nevertheless, Bourdieu's practice-based approach moved in an important direction. It broke from both structural and post-structural traditions by proposing that both cultural–linguistic structures and the subject are secondary outcomes produced and reproduced through practices. This insight has become increasingly influential as it was incorporated into International Relations.[21]

Communities of practice

As Bourdieu's ideas were gradually incorporated into International Relations, practice theory's proponents in Security Studies shifted emphasis from explaining the continuity of social order to exploring innovation and change.[22] Attempting to recoup some subjectivity from Bourdieu, Bigo cautions that 'habitus is not obedience. It generates resistance, but resistance does not mean opposition, mobilization, or revolution.

Resistance is carried out in each field, in everyday practices, through limited but effective possibilities generated by the inventiveness of the habitus.'[23] In order to explore these expressions of subjective agency in International Relations, Adler and Pouliot turn to Wenger's notion of a community of practice.[24] A community of practice is 'a configuration of a domain of knowledge that constitutes like-mindedness, a community of people that "creates the social fabric of learning" and a shared practice that embodies "the knowledge the community develops, shares and maintains"'.[25] Using the 'community of practice', they are able move away from the structuring effects of the habitus and focus more on the possibility for change:

> Change not stability is the ordinary condition of life. 'Change takes place because most of the time most people in an organization go about what they are supposed to do; that is, they are intelligently attentive to their environments and their jobs'. Stability...is an illusion created by the recursive nature of practices [...] new ways of thinking or doing necessarily emerge from the contingent 'play of practice' in which meanings are never inherently fixed or stable.[26]

For Adler and Pouliot, 'reflexivity and judgment are also at the foundation of practice.'[27] Based on this insight, they argue that practice approaches enable 'a superior formulation of the agency-structure conundrum, where agency and structure jointly constitute and enable practices'.[28] However, as Mattern points out, Adler and Pouliot's community of practice rests on an 'amalgamated' ontology of practice in which practices remain 'suspended' between structure and agency.[29] This claim reveals an instructive, if subtle, debate. Mattern argues that the community of practice depends on maintaining the very theoretical distinction it sets out to problematize and therefore 'disaggregates practices into the very ontological dichotomies that [...] practice exceeds'.[30] Mattern argues that habitus and other amalgamated ontologies of practice reduce 'practitioners [...] to mechanistic carriers and executors of competencies they "inherit" from the habitus; and practical action devolves into a self-reinforcing "locked-in" structure that is impervious to change'.[31] By suspending practices within a 'community', they remain ontologically trapped within the very agent-structure binary they set out to transcend.[32]

While Pouliot maintains that practice is 'ontologically prior' to agency and structure,[33] Mattern's critique of habitus and the community of practice debate is nevertheless instructive insofar as it illustrates the fine line between the explanatory and emergent politics of hybridity.

When practice is treated as a constitutive or amalgamative outcome generated by a tension between communities of practice and practitioners, it loses ontological viability; practice simply becomes that which is being ordered – a secondary phenomenon.[34] This in turn drives interest, emphasis and focus to the extra-material social forces which then must be called upon to 'explain' this ordering. In the process, practices are made dependent on some other explanatory variable.[35] However, Schatzki's site-based ontology of practice avoids a similar amalgamated explanatory bind. As Mattern points out, Schatzki's site-based ontology of practice 'offers a post-Cartesian account of agency' in which 'agency is a result of practice, not its source'.[36] Such an approach maintains the ontological primacy of practices over both the structuring effects of organization and transcendental capacities of rational individual actors.

Practicing organization

While the practice-based approaches outlined above demonstrate a tendency to rely on the structural effects of practice, the opposite tendency is at play in this section: overemphasizing individual rationalism. When the organization of practice is prioritized, the crucial question then becomes 'how are practices organized?'. However, when the practice of organization is emphasized, then practice itself assumes ontological priority, and the crucial question then becomes 'how do practitioners perform organized practices?'. Posed in this way, the question becomes an emergent one: how do practitioners actively manage their post-liberal political situation? These emergent questions change the emphasis of the investigation from explaining social order to tracing the unstable performative continuity of practices through which order must be actively maintained. Schatzki's site-based ontology of practice avoids overemphasizing the agential capacities of individual practitioners by instead exploring how practices emerge as part of the material-relations of the site.

Practical understanding

For Schatzki, practices are organized activities. However, his practice approach grew from a general dissatisfaction with the ways post-structural theories, such as Bourdieu's habitus, Giddens' structuration and Deleuze and Guitari's assemblage, treated practices as the embodied 'substantialization' of 'abstract machines'.[37] Therefore, Schatzki wanted to materially ground practices in the site where they emerge. Contrary to the relatively ambiguous extra-material organizing properties embedded in habitus, the field, communities or assemblages, Schatzki demystifies practices by tracing how practices are materially organized through *projects*. For Schatzki, projects articulate, synthesize and arrange practices into 'a set of hierarchically organized set of doings and sayings'.[38] In this reading, projects are organized by rules: 'explicit formulations, principles, precepts and instructions that enjoin, direct or remonstrate people to perform specific actions'.[39] The performance of these rules is informed and organized by a *practical understanding* of how to enact a given practice. A practical understanding is essential for carrying out or performing a given practice; it is a socially shared understanding of how to go about 'doing' something. For example, in order to perform the role of a legal empowerment practitioner, one must have a practical understanding of the rules, language, protocols and procedures that enable a particular performance to be recognized as legal empowerment.

While the organized nature of practice is a fundamental aspect of a given project, Schatzki's approach emphasizes how organized practices are performed. In his reading, the 'ontological primacy' of one practice always supersedes and cuts across 'the different actions that a person performs at any given moment'.[40] The ontological primacy embedded in a given project is expressed as its goal, purpose and political significance woven into the design of the project; it specifies what is at stake in a project's outcome. This ontological priority represents the meaning practitioners assign to a given project and specifies that which must be 'managed' by practitioners. For example, the ontological priority of a legal empowerment intervention in Liberia may be to supplant customary justice or to challenge statutory legal authority. Whatever the ontological priority is, it must be supported and managed by a number of subordinate and overlapping tasks such as applying for funding, training practitioners and monitoring processes. When practitioners manage their projects, they are attempting to find ways to maintain the continuity of this ontological priority, to manage any breakdowns and discontinuities in the performance through which the political purpose of a project is transmitted. When practitioners manage their political situation, they are managing performative discontinuities.

In this way, projects purposefully orchestrate practices toward a future outcome. Therefore, like habitus, the notion of a practical understanding embraces the idea that the 'persistence and transformation of life, rests centrally on the successful inculcation, of shared embodied know-how'.[41] However, Schatzki cautions that while a practical understanding 'resembles habitus [...] in being a skill or capacity that underlies activity [it] differs in almost never determining what makes sense to people to do, [and] almost never, therefore, governing what people do'.⁴² For Schatzki, *how* practitioners perform their organizing function is never foreclosed. As practitioners navigate between the living sites in which their purposeful practices ensnare them, the organizing effects of peacebuilding practice give way to the fundamental 'indeterminacy of action' embraced by Schatzki's practice approach.⁴³ According to Caldwell, the indeterminacy of action in Schatzki's reading of practice 'avoids any hint of predetermination or theoretical reductionism by insisting that participation within a practice only takes on a determinate form as it happens'.⁴⁴

The tension at play as peacebuilding practices unfold in sites is therefore temporal, not differential. As Schatzki observes, projects 'almost always constitute further actions in the context in which they are performed'.⁴⁵ Peacebuilding practices are future oriented; they are designed for a purpose and are therefore political. Drawing attention to the political purpose embedded within organized practices, Rouse points out that projects always 'point ahead of themselves toward something essentially contestable'.⁴⁶ He argues that organized practices 'must constitute something at issue and at stake in their outcome'.⁴⁷ Rouse defines these political stakes as 'the difference it would make to resolve [an] issue one way rather than another. But that difference is not already settled; working it out is what these practices continue to be "about" '.⁴⁸

Peacebuilding projects, interventions, experiments and programs are a material manifestation of organized practices. They are organized for some purpose, to do something, to address some perceived problem, to maintain or establish an existing arrangement of practice or to bring about some change. Yet, the nature of this change remains unsettled, contested and therefore subject to re-appropriation and open to the possibility of change. Therefore, 'what practitioners do' is of primary ontological significance. The difference between how practices are organized to emerge and how practitioners actually perform this organization reveals how practitioners actively manage the always-emerging disjunction between the liberal and post-liberal world. As ANT proponent John Law comments, 'there is no social order. Rather there are endless attempts of ordering.'⁴⁹ To tease this emerging and unstable process out with greater detail, ANT's performative notion of translation is helpful.

Translation

The politics of peacebuilding practice emerges through the active and unstable process of translation. As Freeman observes, the politics of translation are 'to a large extent normative [and] concerned with what good translation is or should be'.⁵⁰ Using linguistic translation as an example, he pinpoints the essential tension at play in a translation: 'should a translation conform to the structure and vocabulary of the target language, "domesticating" the foreign text, or should it retain a sense of foreignness, enriching the target language with new resources?'⁵¹ The play between 'faithful' and 'free' translations is very much a practical tension which has to be negotiated 'in such a way as to preserve the essential symbolic structure ("topology") of both source and receptor language'.⁵² Translation, Freeman notes, 'is thus a "bounded" or "constrained" innovation'.⁵³ Therefore, the free play that emerges within a translation can perhaps be understood as something like technique.

Good technique slightly aggravates the tension between faithful and free translation; it may be expressed as the subtle bending of rules, a narrow betrayal of orthodoxy, a creative innovation or it may be expressed more dramatically as a new and different direction or a paradigm shift. Translations may involve cutting corners, spending extra time, going over-budget; they may include enrolling new practitioners from other sites with a different practical understanding. This active and indeterminate process of translation may include course corrections, strategy revisions, overhauls and changes of plans. Translations manifest as the subtle and dramatic adjustments, adaptations, compromises and innovations that emerge as practitioners constantly ply their practical understanding toward meeting the ends specified in their project, or altering its specified ends altogether. As Freeman concludes, translation is a vital tool as '[it] takes place on the ground, as practitioners (including researchers and policy makers) talk and write about *new ways of doing things*'.⁵⁴ Stretched through the temporal tensions of organized practice, translations reveal the discontinuity of practice; they uncover the constrained innovations that unfold at the emergent front edge of organized peacebuilding projects. These constrained innovations are expressed as practitioners must continually find ways to actualize the goals circumscribed in a given project as they move across an unstable arrangement of sites where those goals may be constrained by a variety of factors and contested for many different reasons.

Michel Callon's sociology of translation highlights the discontinuity between project design and performance.⁵⁵ Callon followed three marine biologists investigating a decline in the scallop populations in St. Brieuc Bay, France. These biologists were tasked with developing a cultivation strategy for increasing scallop production. However, the cultivation project was plagued by a number of problems where 'the strategy of the three researchers begins to wobble'.⁵⁶ In this unstable situation Callon observed that 'not only does the state of beliefs fluctuate with a controversy but the identity and characteristics of the implicated actors change as well.'[57] These fluctuations reflect a process of translation. For Callon, the process of translation reveals 'the continuity of the displacements and transformations' that emerged as various practitioners attempted to manage their unfolding political situation.[58] Managing this unstable political situation can therefore be understood as the art of translation.

The art of translation

Callon's sociology of translation uncovered four 'moments of translation' in which the three biologists sought to 'impose themselves and their definition of the situation on others'.[59] These moments of translation emerged as an overlapping and continual phased process, like links in a chain. Each link in the chain represents a point at which a practitioner re-appropriates the situation, imposing their own meaning upon it, changing the practice and performing it in new and different ways. Again, practitioners are not individual actors able to transcend their political situation. Instead practitioners act within their political situation; it is the political situation through which a course of action is filtered. Each moment or point of translation that emerges along this chain consists of four interrelated and overlapping processes: *problematization, appropriation, performance* and *re-problematization*. These four intrinsic components expose a series of performative discontinuities.

By identifying the points of translation that emerged in the course of designing and implementing a legal empowerment intervention in Liberia – the CJA program – a post-liberal process of emergent hybridity rises to the fore. Taken together, these points of translation reveal how the meaning of justice at the heart of the CJA's legal empowerment practices was continually problematized, appropriated and performed and then re-problematized as the various practitioners involved continually retranslated the meaning of legal empowerment and reshaped the political situation in which the CJA program was operating. In the process, the CJA program became unstable as the legal empowerment practices the program was designed to transmit were continually transformed for different purposes and performed in different ways.

Problematization

As with Callon's definition, problematization refers to the process by which practitioners attempt to define the terms of a given situation and qualify a certain course of action. In defining the nature of the problem, practitioners can shape the politics of the situation. Problematization involves identifying the obstacles that need to be overcome as well as delegitimizing alternative ways of understanding the problem and different ways of addressing them. Therefore, problematization involves contestation, controversy and tension; it includes the continual production and reproduction of difference and similarity. This may allow a practitioner to shape the purpose, the end or goal around which a possible solution can be articulated and a project can be designed. Problematization circumscribes what needs to change, what needs to be maintained and what needs to be strengthened. Through this process, disjunctions and discontinuities are created as the political purpose of a project becomes reframed. This allows practitioners to determine what is at stake in the outcome of a given project, thereby shaping the way in which a project becomes politically significant and meaningful.

Appropriation

Appropriation is a process which flows directly from problematization. Appropriation is the point between problematization and performance where meaning becomes unstable and new ways of practicing become possible. If problematization allows practitioners to create politically meaningful stakes, then appropriation is the process by which practitioners ascribe their own meaning to a given project, how they impose their own political situation onto its practices. But *how* practitioners engage a problem, *how* they incorporate a purpose, *how* practitioners interpret its stakes and assign meaning to their political situation remains uncertain. It highlights how practitioners become enrolled into a project, embody its purpose and become participants in shaping the way a project emerges. Appropriation is always a matter of re-appropriation. Therefore, appropriation should be understood as the re-inscription of meaning. Practices are rarely faithfully translated but instead reflect a re-appropriation of the meaning embedded in a project, a re-inscription of purpose. Appropriation is how and where a project's meaning becomes unstable and its intended purpose becomes seized. It is how practices become imbued with different significance and meaning. It is how projects are co-opted and reincorporated into a different political situation. It is how meaning becomes embodied and domesticated. However, even subtle re-appropriations of a project's purpose may have significant impacts on how a practice may be performed.

Performance

Performance reflects the materially embodied expression of a translation. A performance necessarily flows from the processes of problematization and appropriation. A performance introduces a number of overlapping political situations and inserts the often conflicting relations between varieties of sites. Performances exhibit meaning and demonstrate ontological priorities. A performance necessarily incorporates the purpose of a given project. A performance exhibits a practitioner's history; it bears their experience; it reflects the influence of their relative dispositions and is constrained by the limits of their practical understanding. However a performance also reflects a practitioner's expertise, their technique, their creative and improvisational capacity to apply their practical understanding in new and innovative ways. Understood this way, performances display discontinuity. They are the material expression of appropriation. Performances indicate that a different meaning has been assigned to a project. Performances reveal a displacement, a disruption and a disjuncture. These performative discontinuities express an active debate about what a project means, what its purpose is, how it should be practiced and what is at stake in its outcome.

Re-*problematization*

These performative discontinuities often lead back to a re-*problematization* and therefore indicate the ongoing and continual cycle of problematizing, appropriating and performing a given project. The cycle of re-problematization emerges as practitioners reflect on the new obstacles, attempt to maintain performative continuity and manage their ever-changing political situation. Practitioners must constantly problematize and adapt their performances to an unstable political situation shared by a host of practitioners. Practitioners must actively manage the performative continuity of their project against the destabilizing effects of the ongoing process of translation and the performative discontinuity it generates. This is a highly dynamic situation which requires constant management. When stretched out over time and space, a pattern of performative discontinuity can be exposed. A series of performative discontinuities uncovers points of translation. Points of translation, in turn, reveal a process of emerging post-liberal hybridity in which the limits of power and emancipation are actively being shaped and the meaning of peace in the post-liberal world is what is at stake. Following Callon's lead, the approach taken here is to identify the displacing moments of translation – the performative discontinuities – that emerged in the course of designing, implementing and sustaining a legal empowerment intervention in rural Liberia.

Conclusion

The post-liberal politics of translation offers an alternative to the power/resistance model of explanatory hybridity outlined at the beginning of the chapter. According to Latour's reading, the liberal–local explanation of hybridity rests on a diffusion-based model of power. For a diffusion model of power, 'everything may be explained by either talking about the initial force or by pointing to the resisting medium.'[60] Rather than invoking a resisting medium to explain the discontinuity of power, Latour suggests exploring power as a process of translation. A translation-based model places power 'in the hands of people; each of these people may act in many different ways [...], modifying it, or deflecting it, or betraying it, or adding to it, or appropriating it'.[61] A translation-based model is one in which practitioners are 'doing something essential for the existence and maintenance' of power.[62] He argues that when an order is given, 'the chances are that the order has been modified and composed by many different people who slowly turned it into something completely different as they sought to achieve *their* own goals'.[63] This translation model breaks the axiomatic explanatory relationship between power and resistance that sits at the heart of the hybrid paradox. A translation-based approach to hybridity would therefore focus on how practitioners problematize, re-appropriate and re-perform power. It would emphasize how practitioners actively manage their uncertain political situation and struggle to maintain the performative continuity of the practices circulating through and between unstable arrangements of sites. The post-liberal politics of hybridity are shaped through this ongoing process of translation and retranslation. Through this emerging hybrid process, the meaning of the liberal peace and the local are actively displaced, the limits of power and emancipation are contested and the meaning of peace in the post-liberal world is always at stake.

4
Mapping Peacebuilding Practice: A Post-Liberal Methodology

Engaging the post-liberal politics of hybridity requires a methodological orientation rather than a theoretical one. As the previous two chapters outlined, the uncertain material ontology of politically contested post-liberal practices is emergent in nature. Practices may be organized but the relationship between organization and performance is unstable. A performance only takes shape as it emerges and may express new meanings and introduce different ways of performing. Therefore, a theoretical approach in which the limits of power and emancipation have already been established is less attuned to exposing the processes through which these limits are exceeded and redefined. Hence, a methodological orientation is needed to explore the emerging post-liberal world, one which is attuned to how the limits of power and meaning of emancipation are continually contested and reshaped. However, critical methodology remains underdeveloped in critical PCS where the epistemological distinction between international power and emancipatory local agency is often maintained. As a result, important expressions of post-liberal power and emancipatory agency slip by undetected.

The post-liberal literature has already recognized this methodological gap. Chandler starts from the position that critical PCS must move away from problematic universals such as the liberal peace and the local, and instead understand statebuilding policy-practices in their own terms.[1] Meanwhile Richmond's post-liberal turn also recognizes the need for greater attention to methodology in critical PCS. His approach to the everyday calls for new 'ethical, ethnographic and active research methodologies' that would enable the creation of an 'ethnoscape of both liberal interventions and local modifications.'[2] To this end, Richmond advocates for a multi-methodological approach that draws pragmatically from ethnography and sociology.[3]

The goal in this chapter is to sketch out the contours of a critical methodological orientation toward peacebuilding practices, one which avoids rendering a priori decisions about how power and emancipatory agency can be expressed in practice. In other words, the political purpose of the methodological orientation advanced over the following pages is to disrupt the assumed relationship between internationality and power and between emancipatory agency and localness that sits at the heart of the explanatory paradox of hybridity. Understood in this way, the goal of this chapter is to develop a post-liberal methodological approach. A post-liberal methodology would focus on the unstable performance of peacebuilding, the ad hoc translations and improvisations that emerge as practitioners traverse the flat, yet dynamic, ontological landscape between the unstable arrangements of sites that practitioners are attempting to manage. In order to capture the emergent politics of translation, the methodological approach outlined here is based on Latour's mapping strategy.

To this end, this chapter is organized into three sections. The first section introduces methodology as a practice, one which is contingently performed by the researcher. It attempts to move beyond a critical theoretical orientation and lay a methodological foundation for mapping post-liberal hybrid process. The second section further develops the need for methodological orientation when exploring emergent hybridity and then outlines a mapping strategy based on Latour's ANT-based approach which calls on researchers to 'follow the actors' as they traverse the complex, flat social world. The last section briefly reviews how this methodological strategy maps the series of translations that unfolded in the course of designing and implementing a legal empowerment project in rural Liberian communities.

Practicing critical methodology

Methodology is a practice; methodology is a purposefully organized arrangement of activities which must be performed and actively managed. Defining methodology as practice has some interesting implications as it always implicates the researcher. The relationship between the practices of the mapper and the practice that the mapper is mapping is precarious and uncertain. It must be constantly managed. A methodological performance aggravates the emergent tension between how a mapping strategy is designed and how it is practiced. There is always a reflexive dimension to methodology.[4] This section briefly reviews the inherently political role of the researcher (me) as a methodological practitioner, as designer and practitioner of a mapping methodology.

Mapping a peacebuilding intervention requires inside access. Therefore I applied for a position as a research assistant on a small survey team led by two researchers (Bilal Siddiqi and Justin Sandefur) from Oxford's Centre for the Study of African Economies (CSAE). They were surveying a new legal empowerment intervention being managed by TCC, called the CJA program. The CJA program involved deploying local Liberian paralegals to remote communities for the purpose of raising community awareness on the rule of law and to assist community members in resolving disputes. Gradually, I was enrolled into the CSAE research team,[5] and I became a practitioner, a quasi-project-insider, folded into the political situation shaped by the CJA program and operated according to the project's internal logic. This ongoing process of enrollment consisted of acquiring practical understanding, picking up 'know-how' and becoming familiar with the practices, the practitioners and the crosscutting political stakes involved in the project's outcome. This enrollment process extended to general discussions, gossip and chatter, all of which provided some practical sense of the political situation into which I was being enrolled. Operating as a project insider often required active problem solving. This involved acting instrumentally and developing more effective intervention strategies. It entailed participation in the internal processes of designing, training, piloting, redesigning, repiloting, changing strategies, redesigning new research frameworks, then retraining and reimplementation. As an insider, my work was directed toward the ends of the research project in which I was being enrolled; my labor was shaped by the political situation generated by implementing a legal empowerment project in Liberia.

However, insider access is a double-edged sword. As Richmond and Mitchell point out, peacebuilding 'norms such as care and social health or well-being may lead to a form of "soft" or even "affective biopolitics"'.[6] These deep social interventions 'may, from a critical perspective, appear as a force for the colonization and domination of the everyday, although it may, paradoxically, be experienced as a form of emancipation'.[7] Richmond cautions that critical research must take into account how power can appropriate hybridity, using it to extend patterns of domination, 'otherwise, any engagement with the everyday will be skewed toward the current predominant "liberal" modes with its attendant contradictions, masquerading as hybridity.'[8] The critical orientation tends to view international interventions in postcolonial civil society as inherently problematic; its political aim therefore is to expose the hidden power relations in these interventions that reproduce unjust systems of domination. However, as an insider, I was folded into a development-based political situation, one in which abstaining from intervention was inherently problematic.[9]

Managing one's insider position then is a difficult political situation. Researchers must take care to balance the potentially corrupting effects of becoming an 'insider' against the equally corrupting effects of remaining a 'critical' outsider, simply reproducing existing theoretical distinctions. As a self-described 'critical' researcher, the insider position was a precarious one. Critical researchers set themselves the task of disrupting reductive binaries that conceal how power and emancipatory action circulate across artificial epistemological frontiers. Yet, from an insider position, the assumed relationship between internationality and power appeared unstable, and the theoretical association between emancipatory agency and the local became problematic. Important post-liberal expressions of emancipatory agency and demonstrations of power were obscured behind their liberal–local explanation. There was more; there was a remainder, a surplus of unaccounted for power and agency emerging in ways that were challenging the limits of power and emancipation. Contrary to explaining the relationship between power and emancipation, liberal–local hybridity was concealing a post-liberal surplus – processes that were challenging liberal limits of power and local limits of emancipation.

In order to expose this post-liberal surplus, it was necessary to move beyond the explanatory theoretical limits of liberal–local hybridity and develop a methodological strategy that exposed how expressions of power and emancipatory agency were challenging the liberal–local limits imposed on them. However, this raises a number of important reflexive questions about the tension between the risk and reward of conducting insider research: Had I been co-opted by the 'the liberal peace'? Had I been captured by the very power I set out to critique? Was my translation a victim of a classic hybridity trap – to confuse colonization with emancipation? Or, alternatively, had I been disciplined by critical theory? As Dwyer and Buckle point out, the 'insider role status frequently allows researchers more rapid and more complete acceptance by their participants. Therefore, participants are typically more open with researchers so that there may be a greater depth to the data gathered'.[10] However, they point out that access may come at a cost:

> the researcher's perceptions might be clouded by his or her personal experience and that, as a member of the group, he or she will have

difficulty separating it from that of the participants. This might result in an interview that is shaped and guided by the core aspects of the researcher's experience and not the participant's. Furthermore, its undue influence might affect the analysis, leading to an emphasis on shared factors between the researcher and the participants and a de-emphasis on factors that are discrepant, or vice versa.[11]

However, they maintain that the insider–outsider distinction 'traditionally existed more strongly in theory than in practice'.[12] Therefore rather than attempting to either conceal this insider–outsider tension or to over-problematize it, Dwyer and Buckle embrace the in-between position. They propose that 'surely the time has come to abandon these constructed dichotomies and embrace and explore the complexity and richness of the space between.'[13]

Nevertheless, managing an insider–outsider political situation is difficult. To this end, Brigg and Bleiker's defense of auto-ethnography provides some useful guidance about the role of an inside researcher: 'Our suggestions [...] are based on the proposition that insights developed through an exploration of the author's position should be evaluated not by some *a priori* standard of reference, but by their ability to generate new and valuable insights for particular knowledge communities.'[14] Following Brigg and Bleiker's auto-ethnographic approach, the crucial question is not whether or not one is co-opted by a priori definitions of 'power'. The critical question is whether the researcher can draw from their conflicted insider–outsider position in a way which exposes the fragility of power, highlights its lack of coherence, its controversies and traces the process through which power becomes unstable and its logic rewritten. Such a critical methodological orientation would therefore encourage researchers to become enrolled into the political situation of a given peacebuilding project, to become familiar with its practical understanding, its purpose, its methods and the practices it is designed to organize. It would create critical space for researchers to 'play' with their insider–outsider position, to aggravate its liminal tensions in order to generate interesting and useful insights into the contested politics of post-liberal becoming.

A methodological orientation

In order to expose the post-liberal dynamics at play in emergent hybridity, a critical theoretical orientation must be substituted for a critical methodological orientation. Smiths's institutional ethnography[15] has been a particularly influential methodological approach in critical PCS[16] since it emphasizes the lived, everyday experience, perceptions and practices of actors. However, comparing the nuanced distinction between ethnography and ethno-methodology reveals the emergent orientation of the latter. Pollner and Emerson argue that ethnography overemphasizes 'shared internalized norms' and 'theoretical "top-down" solutions'.[17] Rather than focusing on the internal order and coherence of a social group or institution, they maintain that for ethno-methodologists, 'society consists of the ceaseless, ever-unfolding transactions through which members engage one another and the objects, topics and concerns that they find relevant'.[18] While ethnographers may not agree with this characterization, it does frame the subtle but consequential difference between theoretical and methodological orientations toward emerging hybrid processes. Ethno-methodology highlights how peacebuilding practices and projects often cut through and across a number of different organizations, institutions, geographies and sites; it focuses on how peacebuilding practices orchestrate the labor and working materialities of practitioners moving through and between these porous 'entities'. Hence the ethno-methodological approach adopted here resists the urge to superimpose a priori theoretical shapes and boundaries upon the complex living social phenomena circulating through and between sites.

Consequently, a methodological orientation requires a different set of practices. It changes the political situation of the researcher and transforms the purpose of their labor. Rather than the researcher focusing on the theoretical task of explaining complex hybrid processes as an outcome of political tensions between different entities, the researcher's labor is instead focused on the methodological task of developing a strategy that accounts for emerging practices. A methodological orientation, therefore, reverses the explanatory relationship and instead directs the researcher toward the methodological work of developing a strategy for exposing how peacebuilding practices emerge in ways which transform how power circulates and what emancipation signifies. Such an orientation foregrounds how practitioners define their own political situation, how they identify the desired change they wish to bring about and how they deploy their world-building capacities accordingly and then map performative discontinuities that emerge in the process.

Mapping peacebuilding practices

This section sketches out a mapping strategy designed to chart the performative discontinuities that emerged in the course of designing and implementing the CJA program in Liberia. Latour's ANT-informed methodological orientation provides the basis for the mapping strategy outlined here. Adapting his approach, this section presents a mapping strategy designed to trace the unstable post-liberal politics of translation that emerge as practitioners navigate through the flat, but dynamic, living ontological terrain of sites as they struggle to manage the performative continuity of their given project. The methodological task is therefore to develop a *methodological strategy* that accounts for (a) how practitioners make sense of their own projects and the purpose and meaning they ascribe to their political situation; and then (b) map how these practitioners set about the messy process of translating that ascribed meaning into sites where that meaning may be contested.

As discussed previously, Latour's critique of the politics of explanation stems from a concern with sociological attempts to explain complex and heterogeneous localized activities by pointing to global structural power.[19] In order to avoid reproducing another iteration of a structure/agency, power/resistance or global/local dialectic, he proposes that researchers must 'try to keep the social domain completely flat'.[20] In addition to being an ontological claim, keeping the social world flat is also a methodological strategy that compels the researcher to resist turning to structure, power or global forces to explain the complex material relations that circulate through sites. However, a flat methodological orientation should not be confused with an attempt to conceal established hierarches of power and spatialities of domination. Instead a flat orientation aims to problematize and expose how powerful and dominating configurations are established and maintained.[21] By maintaining a flat methodological orientation, researchers can 'capture those many connections without bungling them from the start by some *a priori* decision over what is the "true size" of an interaction of some social aggregate'.[22] Latour argues that 'it is only by making flatness the default position of the observer that the activity necessary to generate some difference in size can be detected or registered.'[23] When approached methodologically rather than theoretically, the fragility of these powerful configurations can be exposed and the active and contingent process of translation rises to the foreground.[24]

To this end, Latour proposes a sociology of associations.[25] Contrary to conventional sociology, ANT sets itself the task of mapping the movement of practitioners through and between the sites, to account for their attempts to harmonize the practices circulating through them and strengthen the connections between them. A flat methodological orientation allows researchers to account for the actual work that goes into designing, establishing and stabilizing the material connections between sites which may appear to be durable and powerful. By keeping the social world flat, Latour seeks to map the specific movements between one place and another as they are laid. This orientation, therefore, engages with the ontological labor of rendering new practices into a stable configuration of sites. This work is practiced. It is enacted, executed and carried out in observable, traceable pathways and in circulating patterns of organized practice moving through and between living sites. Mapping, according to Latour, is therefore a matter of cartography.[26]

In order to identify and map these fragile connections, Latour advises that we just follow the actors.[27] For Latour, ANT is 'a very crude method to learn from the actors without imposing on them an *a priori* definition of their world-building capacities'.[28] As he explains, 'actors know what they do and we have to learn from them not only what they do, but how and why they do it. It is us, the social scientist, who lacks knowledge of what they do, and not they who are missing the explanation of why they are unwittingly manipulated by forces exterior to themselves and known to the social scientist's powerful gaze and methods.'[29] Such a methodological orientation calls on researchers to allow actors to 'deploy the full range of controversies in which they are immersed. It is as if we were saying to the actors: "We won't try to discipline you, to make you fit into our categories; we will let you deploy your own worlds, and only later will we ask you to explain how you came about settling them"'.[30] Therefore, ANT embraces 'the rich vocabulary of the actors' practice [and avoids] replacing their sociology, their metaphysics, their ontology with those of the social sciences'.[31] Allowing practitioners to define their own political situations has significant implications. Rather than attempting to explain or understand hybridity in theoretical terms, the methodological task is to account for how actors deploy their own capacities, how they organize their own activities and struggle to bring them forth amidst the complex play of living sites.

Therefore, instead of deploying theoretical distinctions to explain the post-liberal politics of peacebuilding, the methodological imperative is to allow practitioners to explain their own practical situation and to follow them as they actively translate their purposefully organized practices into complex living sites inhabited by multiplicities of purposeful practitioners. As practitioners continually manage this unstable political situation, they must find new and creative ways to perform these translations while actively maintaining the continuity of the project. The methodological goal is to chart these course changes; to mark the points of innovation, the moments of ad hoc improvisation that unfold as practitioners continually attempt to maintain the purposeful heading embedded in their project. The objective is to map the organized but nonlinear movement of practitioners and to reveal the performative discontinuities that emerge in the course of implementing a peacebuilding project.

Mapping a legal empowerment project in Liberia

This section turns from defining the mapping strategy to how this strategy will be implemented; it explores how the methodological strategy outlined above will be practiced – how it will be performed. The present mapping strategy begins with a peacebuilding project – the CJA program – rather than with an organization, institution, community of practice or with individual actors. The CJA program was conceptualized, designed and organized around a legal empowerment model. The model deploys a paralegal to Liberian communities in order to establish, maintain and increase the circulation of legally empowered practices there. While CJAs are tasked with providing free legal assistance, their ultimate goal is to 'empower' Liberians to use to use the law to protect themselves from perceived exploitation and injustice and improve the quality of their lives. Understood this way, the raison d'être of the CJA program is to organize the performance of justice in a legally empowered way. Yet the political situation generated by the CJA program was very complex; it demanded the ongoing management of how legal empowerment interventions should be performed, what legal empowerment means, how to maintain the performative continuity of the CJAs' legal empowerment practices and how to go about translating it into Liberian communities.

Therefore, a number of practitioners and organizations participated in developing, implementing, overseeing and assessing the program. It involved a large number of Liberian communities – complex social sites where customary justice practices predominate and international interventions are viewed with suspicion. The CJA program itself is experimental, and the legal empowerment practices on which it is based are new to the peacebuilding and development repertoire. Therefore, they remain somewhat controversial among more orthodox practitioners both in Liberia and beyond. Given the complexity of this political situation, the performative continuity of legal empowerment became unstable as practitioners struggled to translate their legal empowerment project into legally empowered performances in Liberia. In order to

70 A Practice-Based Theory of Peacebuilding

identify and trace these performative discontinuities, the methodological strategy to map the shifting performance of legal empowerment was continually retranslated in new ways by different practitioners sharing an overlapping but crosscutting political situation.

To this end, the strategy is to follow the legal empowerment practitioners, to chart their movement as they circulate through and between different sites, moving back and forth form offices, to communities, to conference rooms and to class rooms. The goal is to account for the unstable process through which legal empowerment was continually retranslated by a series of different legal empowerment practitioners involved in designing, managing, implementing and evaluating the CJAs' legal empowerment practices. Such a strategy draws attention to how practitioners attempt to impose their own political situation on legal empowerment. It emphasizes how these practitioners *problematize* legal empowerment, re-*appropriate* its meaning, and how they *perform* legal empowerment in new and different ways. This mapping strategy reveals a series of performative discontinuities that highlight the points at which the meaning of the CJAs' legal empowerment practices became unstable, giving rise to a chain of translations. By mapping these translations, the following chapters uncover a post-liberal process of hybridity emerging in Liberia. This post-liberal hybrid process is actively reshaping what justice amounts to in Liberia, how justice can be practiced in Liberia and who is authorized to practice it. The active and contested negotiation over the limits and meaning of justice in Liberia is simultaneously a negotiation over the limits of power and meaning of emancipation in post-liberal Liberia. And the implications of this negotiation carry into sites far beyond Liberia where the purpose of peacebuilding and the meaning of peace in the post-liberal world is also being actively contested and renegotiated.

Conclusion

This chapter articulates a methodological strategy for exploring the performative discontinuities that emerge in post-liberal hybrid processes. The mapping approach outlined above attempts to subject the axiomatic link between international power and emancipatory local agency to the unstable politics of translation that actively contest and reshape limits of power and emancipation through peacebuilding practices. A methodological orientation toward peacebuilding practices leads to a different understanding of hybridity. It compels the researcher to focus on the situated, unstable and transformative politics of emergence rather than invoking powerful global structures or systems of meaning to explain them. A post-liberal mapping strategy does not require the researcher to look to an existing theoretical explanation for what is unfolding; it does not require the researcher to ascribe the terms and limits of political agonism prior to their performance. Instead it compels the researcher to map how practitioners define their own problems, co-opt the projects into which they have been enrolled, impose their own meaning and perform them in new and different ways. Such a mapping strategy allows practitioners to determine what power and emancipation mean as opposed to the researcher. In addition to capturing the agonistic politics of asymmetrical difference represented by the liberal–local hybridity, a methodological orientation also exposes the unstable emergent politics of post-liberal hybridity. A methodological orientation exposes active and uncertain processes that cut across the international–local distinction. It highlights the controversies within these unstable entities and reveals how international power can be exercised in ways that contest how power circulates and how emancipatory local agency can be enacted to contest how local justice practices are performed.

Part II
Mapping Peacebuilding Practice in Liberia

5
Practicing Justice in Liberia: A Brief History

This chapter presents a brief history of justice in Liberia. It traces the unstable and dynamic relationship between the statutory and customary justice practices through the colonial period and into emerging history of Liberia's peacebuilding enterprise. The statutory justice system in Liberia is based on an American model of legal liberalism. It is anchored by a national constitution that divides power between three branches of government, granting the judiciary branch the power to determine which laws, court rulings, executive order and legislative acts are constitutional and which are not. Under the Liberian Constitution, the state is the ultimate arbiter of justice and claims a monopoly over who can practice justice and how justice can be practiced. However, the statutory claim to a monopoly on the legitimate practice of justice is not reflected in practice.

The vast majority of Liberians rely on the customary system for their everyday justice needs. Customary justice is restorative. Contrary to the adversarial relationships between plaintiff and defendant, winner and loser, innocent and guilty that are maintained through the procedural practices of statutory justice, the restorative practices of customary justice practice are based on repairing adversarial relationships. Restorative justice values community cohesion over punishing the guilty or establishing innocence. Customary justice enforces community cohesion through trials by ordeal. In Liberia, trials by ordeal are generally referred to as 'sassywood' and can be socially coercive (e.g. swearing a public oath) or physically coercive (e.g. burning the accused with a hot cutlass or hot oil). These practices are seen as highly problematic by local and international human rights and rule-of-law advocates.

Clearly, the political tension between these two justice systems is a significant feature of Liberian history. On the one hand, the state has continually attempted to extend its authority into the interior, to supplant the competing authority of customary law with statutory law, and secure its claim to a legitimate monopoly on the practices of justice. On the other hand, this attempt has been unsuccessful, revealing both the limits of state power and the relative legitimacy of customary justice practices. In addition to the political tension *between* customary and statutory justice practices, Liberian history also exposes the politics *for and about* justice – how justice in Liberia should be practiced and who is authorized to practice it.

Colonial history

Liberia is the oldest independent republic in the African continent. It was founded in 1847 by an ex-slave community from the United States and funded and supported by the American Colonial Society (ACS). The justice system of the Liberian state is based on an American constitutional model which limited the division of government between executive, legislative and judicial branches along with the protection of certain basic rights of Liberian 'citizens' – a legal status not originally extended to the indigenous population.[1] After forcibly expelling the indigenous people from the coastal area and establishing Monrovia as Liberia's capital, the original policy of the Americo-Liberians was one of non-interference vis-à-vis the indigenous Liberians.[2] However, under external pressure from the British and French colonies and internally challenged by a Mandingo trade monopoly, the Americo-Liberians turned to the Hinterland in order to secure Liberia's borders and Monrovia's position as a destination for export trade.[3]

Through the second half of the 19th century, the government negotiated a number of treaties with the Hinterland kings in order to protect the free passage of commerce across tribal boundaries.[4] During this early colonial period, the Liberian Supreme Court issued two consequential opinions regarding the legal status of the Hinterland inhabitants under the Liberian Constitution and formal law. In 1862, the court ruled that 'native inhabitants are bona fide subjects of the state (Liberia), and the political authority of the same covers them in all relations.'[5] While this ruling implies that indigenous Liberian's would be subjected to the laws and rights of the formal constitution, a Legislative Act passed in 1869 suggested otherwise. With this act, the Legislature established the Interior Ministry (later changed to the Ministry of Internal Affairs) as an office of the executive branch charged with managing 'matters affecting the aborigines of the country'.[6] The 1869 Act contradicted the constitution by vesting an executive office with judicial power over Hinterland subjects, thereby violating the separation of powers. Consequently, Hinterland subjects were not bona fide Liberian citizens under the law. Although the 1869 legislative act violated the principle of the court's 1862 ruling by creating an exception in the constitution for the Hinterland subjects, it was passed and the Interior Ministry was given authority to preside over customary courts in the Hinterland.

By the end of the 19th century, these policies enabled President Coleman's administration to criminalize the intertribal trade tariff system, attempting to bring the Hinterland trade under the control of the state.[7] However, Coleman's administration was short-lived as his interior policy was plagued by resistance and attack from established beneficiaries of the intertribal trading networks.[8] Nevertheless, Coleman's Hinterland policies were extended after President Barclay's election in 1904. Under Barclay, the 1905 Legislative Act, *Providing for the Government of Districts within the Republic, Inhabited by Aborigines*, declared 'Hinterland subjects' as Liberian citizens.[9] However, in a landmark Supreme Court ruling in 1907 (Gray v. Beverly), the court paradoxically upheld the earlier 1869 Legislative Act, thereby reinforcing the jurisdictional segregation of the Hinterland subjects under the Ministry of Internal Affairs (MoIA) rather than the Judiciary.[10] With this ruling, the Supreme Court sanctioned the vestige of judicial power under the executive office of the MoIA. According to the current chairman of the Liberian Legal Working Group (LWG), Counselor Jallah A. Barbu, the court ruling 'allowed the constitution to be negated because of its holding that the [Minster of Internal Affairs] could exercise judicial power over the natives.' Therefore Barbu concludes that the judicial practices of 'the Court more than anything, proves its support of the violation of the constitution in this case. Thus, the first major conflict between the constitution and statutory laws relative to customary law arose'.[11]

By upholding the extra-constitutional legality of the MoIA's judicial authority over the Hinterland, the court de facto sanctioned a dual legal system in Liberia along with two classes of Liberian citizenship that existed under two separate legal jurisdictions. In order to establish the authority of the MoIA in the Hinterland, Barclay founded the Liberian Frontier Force in 1908 and placed it under the authority of the MoIA.[12] The force was deployed to establish 'law and order throughout the republic and for the prevention and detection of crimes on the frontier and in the interior of the country'.[13] However, according to Akingbade, the force gained a reputation for 'wanton cruelty, harassment, indiscipline and rapine' the result of which being that 'the indigenous people perceived the settlers as colonizers and began to speak of them in the same breath as the European colonizers of Africa.'[14] Under Barclay's Hinterland policy, the administrative boundaries between the customary jurisdiction of the Hinterland and the County courts governed by statutory jurisdictions were extended 44 miles inland and formally codified into law.[15]

However, at the same time that the court and the legislature were entrenching the distinction between Hinterland and County jurisdictions, the circulation of cases between them was also formalized. The Liberian king system was transformed into a chieftaincy and the town and clan courts retained relative jurisdictional autonomy. Paramount chiefs stood for local elections as officers of the highest regional customary courts (though only after approval from the Executive). Above the paramount chief, the MoIA appointed a district commissioner to preside over appeals from the paramount chief's customary court by applying statutory law.[16] Counsellor Barbu notes that under this distinct but contiguous dual–legal hierarchy, cases *'travel [...] from the customary legal system to the formal legal system though the customary legal system does not form a part of the formal legal system'*.[17] The movement of cases between the formal and customary systems highlights the fluidity of justice *practices* in Liberia relative to the 'systems' that signify the difference between them.

After crushing a Grebo rebellion in Harper in 1910, the Barclay government moved to 'bring the vast hinterland communities into the administrative organ of the republic' by implementing a system of 'indirect rule'.[18] According to Barbu, '[t]he government's policies, established for administering the hinterland thereafter, were vigorously enforced' by the Frontier Force.[19] Between the 1910s and the Second World War, a number of Supreme Court decisions regarding the status of the Hinterland administration were rendered. Jedah v. Horace (1916), Karmo v. Morris (1919), Posum v. Pardee (1935), Darnenoh v. Republic, (1935) and Karpeh v. Manning (1936) generated yet further ambiguity. The court vacillated between deferring to the authority of customary courts under the unitary executive of the MoIA while later issuing a ruling declaring the very idea of a judiciary authority exercised by any office outside the judiciary as 'utterly inadmissible' finding that 'such a statute must be declared as being not only voidable, but, void *ab initio*'.[20] As Barbu notes, the rulings characterizing this period of the court 'suggest the existence of a gap, some ambiguity or confusion in interpretation as to the jurisdiction of the Judicial branch, or at least, *what judicial power is*'.[21] In other words, when examined through the lens of legal practice, Liberian judicial history is more than the continual expansion of the judicial power over Hinterland communities; it also reveals a debate about the meaning of judicial power in Liberia.

While the interwar period (1918–1939) in Liberia was characterized by an ambiguity in the legal and constitutional status of the Hinterland, the postwar period was one of state consolidation. The election of Americo-Liberian president William Tubman in 1944 secured Liberia's status as a US Cold War semi-protectorate. Resources flowed to Western markets allowing Tubman to make more ambitious political and economic inroads into the Hinterland. Tubman established vast patronage networks thereby creating a centralized relationship of upward dependency wherein Monrovia controlled the downward flow of resources in exchange for legitimacy among the chiefs.[22] A series of new regulations governing the administration of the Hinterland accompanied Tubman's economic incursions.

The Hinterland Regulations of 1949 revised the earlier 1905 Legislative Act and effectively cleared up any ambiguity related to the application of judicial practices under the executive administration of customary areas. As Barbu notes, the Hinterland Regulations 'successfully vested in the Executive a separate legal authority from the statutory legal system that governs the "judicial system" of Liberia'.[23] While they were superseded in 1956 by the Aborigines Law, the Hinterland Regulations remain the more commonly cited precedent by customary authorities and are more practically relevant in the daily exercise of customary justice.[24] Nevertheless, Barbu explains that the 1956 Aborigines Law was notable insofar as it formalized the extra-constitutional authority of the MoIA and solidified the dual-legal status of the Hinterland subjects while codifying their hierarchical relationship under the law.[25]

After his death in 1971, Tubman was replaced by President Tolbert who, in turn, issued a series of executive orders in 1972 related to the administration of the Hinterland. Significantly, the Administrative Procedure Act further secured the dual authority of the MoIA in the Hinterland. Under this provision the MoIA was authorized to 'manage tribal affairs and all matters arising out of tribal relationships, draft rules, regulations and procedures for tribal government and courts including fees allowable in such courts, and, administer the system of tribal courts'.[26]

In addition to Tubman's Hinterland policies, Tolbert also inherited his established patrimonial networks which he used to brutal effect until 1980 when Samuel Doe, a master sergeant from the Krahn tribe, mounted a coup against Tolbert, assassinated him in the executive mansion and had his cabinet publically executed on Barclay Beach in Monrovia. Doe proceeded to enact authoritarian policies, granting preferred access to his ethnic kin, the Krahn, while brutalizing the Hinterland with his Armed Forces of Liberal (AFL) troops.[27] In 1989, after nearly ten years of Doe's control, the National Patriotic Front of Liberia (NPFL), a rebel group trained in Libya and lead by an Americo-Liberian – Charles Taylor, swept through the countryside toward Monrovia initiating the first Liberian Civil War. Despite a brief ceasefire, the Liberian conflict continued until 2003 when the comprehensive peace agreement was signed in Accra. During the conflict, the statutory justice system ceased to function.

Peacebuilding: An emerging history

Liberia's peacebuilding strategy was informed by two different approaches. Despite significant nuances which will be discussed below, these two approaches were in general agreement regarding the causes of the conflict: Liberia was a weak Weberian state with a strong informal society.[28] In other words, the Liberian state was highly centralized, predatory and authoritarian with shallow, patrimony-based legitimacy outside of elite Monrovia circles. Meanwhile, the 'informally' arranged networks based on kin, ethnicity, custom, the gray economy and rooted in Liberian communities enjoyed greater everyday legitimacy. However, despite the general consensus about the political situation that resulted in the conflict, two different peacebuilding strategies emerged, both of which have shaped Liberia's peacebuilding process.

Top-down peacebuilding

In order to understand how Liberia's peacebuilding strategy evolved, a number of prominent Liberian and West African scholars[29] point to the ideas presented in Richard Kaplan's influential work *The Coming Anarchy*.[30] According to Kaplan's rationale, the Liberian conflict was linked to broader post–Cold War trends in the early 1990s that were defined by the pervasiveness of ethic, kin and tribal populations and weak, corrupt states. He argues that these communal connections supersede national identities and the boundaries they demarcate. In the absence of a strong national identity and state monopoly on legitimate violence, Kaplan forecasted increasing destabilization and conflict.[31] Echoing the ethno-cultural dimensions of the conflict, Ellis links the particularly brutal practices characterizing the conflict in Liberia with its spiritual or supernatural practices, its culture of deference to authority and Liberian proclivities for secrecy.³² Ellis traces these practices to Liberia's colonial history, characterized by Americo-Liberian attempts to promulgate and enforce a new moral code.³³ Citing a 1914 ban on customary secret societies, Ellis notes that these attempts resulted in the 'spread of practices of subterfuge as people practice in secret types of behaviour which they are not allowed to practice in public [leading to] extremes of deception and evasion which become part of the political culture'.³⁴

However, turning from Liberian culture to the international political economy, Reno argues that West African conflicts are rooted in the intersection between international commerce and weak or failed states.³⁵ In these conditions, warlords draw their legitimacy from the use of international resources and credit for purposes of maintaining their domestic patronage networks and quelling resistance.³⁶ For Reno these informal patronage networks function to distribute 'resources in a way that is mutually reinforcing to the state's leader and those who are beneficiaries of the client/patronage relationship. The result is a weak and corrupt bureaucratic state'.³⁷ Reno argues that neo-liberal economic policies advocated by the World Bank 'aim to dismantle the existing patronage system'.³⁸ However, these very market liberalization policies also serve to undermine attempts to strengthen the state.³⁹

Richards agrees. Contrary to the tribal or ethnic nature of the violence described by Kaplan and Ellis, Richards alternatively proposes that West African conflict is, 'moored, culturally, in the hybrid Atlantic world of international commerce'.⁴⁰ His work takes place along the Mano River Basin separating the Mano speaking tribes on both sides of the Sierra Leonean–Liberian border. He concludes that West African conflicts are 'a product of this protracted, post-colonial crisis of partrimonialism'.⁴¹ Yet he argues that a stronger state is needed to check the power of informal patrimonial institution. Richards argues that customary institutions were a significant factor in creating the underlying climate of resentment; therefore, he maintains that the chieftaincy must be replaced by a strong state.

In each of these assessments, the cause of the Liberian conflict is ultimately a weak state coupled with the relative strength of informal, traditional or economic associations. However, despite significant nuances, this formulation tends to emphasize how customary institutions and practices contributed to the outbreak of the conflict. The peacebuilding strategy which follows from this assessment naturally emphasizes building a strong state which legitimately enjoys a monopoly of violence and can effectively mitigate the negative effects of informal ethnic, customary or economic connections and cleavages. And indeed, as it pertains to the rule of law and justice sector reform, the vast majority of funding for justice sector reform is channeled into developing the formal, procedural statutory justice system and building national capacity to that end. However, as Liberia was emerging from conflict, the top-down consensus in favor of statebuilding was being challenged.

Bottom-up peacebuilding

The second peacebuilding strategy flows from a different logic. This approach did not view customary systems, institutions and practices as antithetical to Liberian peace but as essential to its sustainability. As such, the bottom-up approach advocated a decentralized peacebuilding approach anchored in the very communities and traditional associations described above as precluding any consolidation of peace. In 2005, Amos Sawyer, president of the interim Liberian transitional government (1990–1994), concluded that the Liberian conflict was a not a problem of an illegitimate and weak state but the opposite. He argued that the 'over-centralization' of government was the problem that the Liberian peacebuilding strategy should address.[42] According to Sawyer, the Liberian peacebuilding project should not attempt to rebuild what Hinterland Liberians experienced as a predatory entity.[43] Instead Sawyer proposed that the Liberian state should be 'reconstituted on the basis of a theory of limited or shared sovereignty and not on a theory of a unitary sovereignty'.[44] He suggested embracing a model of 'poly-centric change', not 'good governance' as set forth by the World Bank but 'self-governance'.[45] This peacebuilding strategy looks to local government as the cornerstone of postwar governance in Liberia:

> Liberians have employed wholesome and ingenious entrepreneurship to cope; many communities have taken recourse in their own social organization to provide education for their children, health services and security protection. This capacity of entrepreneurship and community self-organization constitutes the foundation of self-reliant development and potentially and self-governed order.[46]

In 2006 the International Crisis Group (ICG) published a report confirming Sawyer's assertion of the durability of community life in Liberia. It found that that while the Liberian state and statutory legal system had collapsed during the conflict, the customary system remained intact and functioning.[47] The ICG report suggested that the reform of Liberia's justice system should be a top-priority of the policy framework.[48] Citing the 'predatory' nature of state encroachment into the interior and the resulting suspicion of state institution sown by such policies, the ICG report raised questions about the top-down statebuilding approach then dominating debates between donors and the Liberian government. The report pointed out that the top-down approach is based on the idea that if the statutory system could be reformed and corruption could be rooted out, then ordinary citizens would prefer statutory justice to customary justice. But, the report maintained that policies based on this assumption 'may be short-sighted'.[49]

Instead the ICG report found that the customary system enjoys greater popular legitimacy, noting that 'aspects of customary law that are simply more appealing to many'.[50] Therefore the report suggests that while statutory mechanisms should be reformed and strengthened, a 'parallel/hybrid system that acknowledges various customary systems may be the best interim solution but it will be necessary to ensure that it does not lead to unequal and illegal forms of justice'.[51] As such, the report suggested that the Liberian government and international donors fund 'the internal strengthening of state-sponsored customary law through short-term reforms such as creation of rural community education and paralegal programs, [reforming] the antiquated Rules Regulating the Hinterland, and training of customary officials'.[52] The report concludes that 'justice reform can succeed if the government puts it prominently on the agenda, community-based approaches to justice are taken, and donors deliver money quickly and in sufficient quantities'.[53] However, in 2006 Liberia's peacebuilding strategy was to establish a state monopoly on the legitimate practice of justice, not to strengthen customary institutions.

Peacebuilding in practice

The ICG report reshaped the political situation in which Liberia's peacebuilding strategy was being developed. By asserting that customary justice practices institutions were essential to long-term Liberian peace, its findings ran contrary to the prevailing liberal peacebuilding assumptions. The ICG findings generated some political legitimacy for customary justice practices and compelled those developing Liberia's peacebuilding strategy to engage with the customary justice practitioners and design bottom-up peacebuilding interventions. In the wake of the ICG report, a new political situation emerged, one which demanded an experimental blend of the top-down and bottom-up approaches. Beginning with the publication of the Poverty Reduction Strategy (PRS) in 2008, the Liberian government set out to articulate a 'coherent strategy to harmonize the statutory and customary justice systems'.[54]

Under this 'harmonization' strategy, the Liberian government and United Nations Mission in Liberia outlined a Peacebuilding Priority Plan that addressed large donors' concerns such as corruption, mismanagement of resources, poverty, food insecurity and regional instability. However, it also suggested reaching out to and training local civil society organizations (CSOs) and improving the channels through which local input could be incorporated into the peacebuilding process. On the one hand, the peacebuilding strategy set out to expand the authority of the state especially in rural areas. Yet, on the other hand, it created a framework for training local CSOs, facilitating a national dialogue, drawing from community-based conflict resolution capacities and improving channels for local input into these processes.[55] In this way Liberia's peacebuilding strategy blended the top-down and bottom-up approaches, cohering around the simultaneous expansion of the formal legal institutions of the state along with the strengthening of customary institutions and practices. The rationale guiding this approach was to gradually *harmonize* the customary system under the laws of the formal state constitution.

As it relates to the rule of law, the harmonization strategy called for practitioners to 'accelerate legal training and dissemination of legal codes, redress corruption and monitor community-based justice, while reforming archaic laws and laws that restrict the rights of women'.[56] This process is organized through the Liberian National Decentralization and Local Development Program.[57] Decentralization involves the devolution of state power to subnational county governments, articulates a need for local participation in peacebuilding and development projects and establishes the strategic framework for organizing Liberia's various peacebuilding interventions in Liberia's interior counties.

The centerpiece of Liberia's decentralization strategy is the justice and security hub concept. In early 2011, The Liberian government broke ground on a pilot Hub in Gbarnga.[58] The hub strategy merges justice sector reform with security sector reform's heavy emphasis on policing, thereby securitizing justice. Each Hub functions as a forward-operating base for a range of security actors to include the Liberian National Police as well as agents from the Bureau of Immigration and Naturalization. They also serve as regionalized command and control centers for more rapid deployment and crisis response for domestic security threats as well as potentially destabilizing regional threats. The Hubs house an administrative building, an operational control center, a training school, staff and police barracks and a court house. The security and justice Hub model therefore is an attempt to project and establish the formal legal apparatus of the state into the Liberian interior. Yet, it also functions as a platform for community outreach and for incorporating local input.

In this sense, the Hubs are intended to serve as community justice resources where complaints against both statutory and customary systems can be reported. For this purpose the Hubs provide a Public Support Office (PSO), designed to carry out perception surveys to assess the security and justice challenges as well as local need. Based on this data, PSOs are designed to work with local CSOs to develop and implement legal education interventions that reflect local practices and respond to local needs.[59] Additionally, the PSO provides continued technical and financial support and training for these regional CSOs with the aim of establishing networks of CSOs as 'clear entry points and referral pathways for the community', thereby creating a stream of feedback from the communities.[60] In this way, CSO networks function like regional circulatory systems with the Hub pumping legal information and education out into communities though CSOs and receiving complaints, cases and other forms of feedback which can then be reincorporated into outgoing projects. As the five regional justice and security Hubs come online over the coming years, organizations like TCC have been tasked with developing such a network of CSOs. However, designing and maintaining such a complex network of organizations and projects is a difficult undertaking. The following chapter turns to explore how TCC managed this complex political situation and how they set about developing and implementing this experimental informal network of justice practitioners.

Conclusion

From colonialism through conflict to peacebuilding, Liberia's history reflects a contentious relationship between the state and Liberia's rural inhabitants. Clearly, the overarching dynamic of the relationship is one in which the Liberian capital has continually attempted to assert its sovereign authority over its territory and population. Understood this way, Liberian history is characterized by the persistent attempt by the state to rationalize, institutionalize, order, criminalize or harmonize the local, traditional, informal and customary justice practices characterizing everyday life in the Liberian Hinterland. Certainly, the use of the formal statutory justice system was instrumental in this endeavor. The decentralized security and justice Hub project represents the most recent manifestation of this process, extending the power of the state into the Liberian interior. The Hub concept can certainly be explained as a panoptic projection of the state security and legal apparatus into rural Liberian communities, extending its gaze, collecting data, developing more efficient interventions, cultivating a sense of liberal legal subjectivity and attempting to establish a formal monopoly on the legitimate practice of justice.[61]

Meanwhile, Liberian history is also a story of persistent resistance to this process as state encroachment into Liberian communities has been continually confounded. Secret societies and the general culture of suspicion toward Monrovia they reflect are expressions of such strategies; the persistence of the customary justice system indicates widespread resistance to the formal law.[62] Indeed, many international justice practitioners involved with the Hub project express deep concerns that the Hubs would be perceived as a police fortress and Liberians simply would not show up. In this sense, the Liberian historical–political situation is significantly influenced by tensions between Americo-Liberians and indigenous Liberians, elites and the subaltern, state and hinterland, urban and rural and formal and customary justice. As such, Liberia's dual justice system is a *hybrid outcome* generated by the interactions between the Liberian state and local Liberians. While this hybrid explanation of Liberian history captures the general dynamics and overarching tension at play in Liberia, there is more. By emphasizing how justice is practiced rather than the difference between formal and customary justice systems brings a post-liberal reading of Liberian hybridity to the fore.

A post-liberal history of Liberia reveals an ongoing debate about what justice means in Liberia, how it should be practiced and who is authorized to practice it. From the colonial period into Liberia's current peacebuilding project, customary justice has been understood as an impediment the country's long-term peace, security and economic prosperity. However, this claim is being challenged, and customary justice is becoming a vital aspect of Liberia's peacebuilding strategy. Part of this process involves harmonizing customary practices under the legal authority of the state; but this reading conceals another process that is transforming postcolonial Liberia into a post-liberal state where a plurality of justice practices and new and different justice practitioners are becoming political possibilities.

6
Translating Statutory Justice into Legal Empowerment

The 2006 ICG report changed the political situation for justice practitioners involved in designing Liberia's justice reform strategy. The report found that customary justice practices and conflict resolution mechanisms were effective and enjoyed widespread legitimacy while the statutory system did not. The report therefore concluded that customary justice practices must form an integral part of Liberia's justice strategy. Following its publication, the Liberian Minister of Justice, Frances Johnson Morris, reached out to TCC and asked them to participate in developing the Access to Justice Initiative (A2J). The A2J Initiative called for a spectrum of peacebuilding interventions designed to reach out to rural communities where customary practices predominate, to work with chiefs in order to enhance their conflict resolution capacities and to gradually bridge the gap between customary and statutory systems. This A2J Initiative was also a part of the broader Security Sector Reform strategy designed to integrate the regional justice and security hubs with surrounding communities through networks of CSOs. This strategy required TCC to cultivate working relationships with chiefs who administered justice in their communities

However, in 2006 the political and material momentum behind Liberia's peacebuilding strategy was headed in the opposite direction. Chiefs and the customary justice system were seen as antithetical to peace, security and justice in Liberia. The statutory justice practitioners based in Monrovia claimed that the Liberian Constitution granted them a monopoly over the legitimate practice of justice.[1] Working through the statutory legal institutions such as Arthur Grimes Law School and the Liberian Bar Association, the Liberian legal establishment attempted to impose their political situation on Liberia's emerging justice landscape. As Lubekeman et al. point out, 'the fate of the dual system in

Liberia tends to occur among Monrovia-based elites and their international partners. Consequently, these debates tend to privilege the concerns of these actors'.[2] The Liberian legal establishment attempted to maintain control over what the law means, how it can be legitimately practiced and who is authorized to practice it.

With wide-ranging support from large international donors, the prevailing view within the fragile national government in Monrovia was that Liberia's dual justice system was the cause of the conflict and should not serve as the basis for a peacebuilding strategy.[3] Therefore, TCC faced a political situation in Liberia which was hostile to their objective. Yet, just as the Monrovian legal establishment was leery of any attempts to strengthen and legitimize the customary justice system, chiefs and the rural communities were highly suspicious of national and international interventions designed to inculcate an awareness of human rights and the rule of law. Amid this climate of mutual suspicion, TCC faced a precarious political situation. They had to develop a range of justice-related interventions that (a) were not rigidly committed to replacing customary justice with statutory law; (b) reflected the traditions and values of customary justice; while (c) addressing rural Liberian community members whose justice needs were going unmet by either statutory or customary systems. However, in 2006, there was no model for such an intervention. To overcome these obstacles and meet these needs, TCC had to start from scratch. They attempted to build a network of post-liberal justice practitioners in order to destabilize the existing statutory monopoly and transform the political situation in Liberia into one in which customary justice became a legitimate aspect of Liberia's justice landscape.

Problematization: Challenging the statutory legal establishment

Faced with a political situation in Liberia which was largely opposed to expanding the political role of customary system, TCC proceeded to build a counter network of justice practitioners which would enable them to displace the existing statutory monopoly on justice and to create a post-liberal political situation in which customary justice became a legitimate possibility. This process of network building is described by Callon as one of interessment and enrollment.[4] These processes describe how TCC set about locking various practitioners into the roles assigned to them. Through this process, TCC was able to draw these practitioners into an overlapping, shared political situation in which their practices could be orchestrated in ways that would displace the statutory monopoly while creating political conditions in which customary practices would become a vital feature in Liberia's emerging justice landscape. To this end, cultivating a close relationship with Liberia's customary practitioners was essential. So TCC reached out to the chiefs.

The national traditional council

In Liberia, the chieftaincy is not a unified institution. Liberian chiefs speak different dialects and identify with different ethnic groups. However, to the extent that the chieftaincy is a national institution, it is through the National Traditional Council (NTC). During a meeting with a group of ranking NTC members chaired by Bouku Zulu, the Council vice chairman explained that before the war, the NTC functioned as a committee to promote, advocate and participate in discussions of issues that affect customary peoples in Liberia. But during the war, they were disbanded. After the conflict, he explained how TCC helped to reestablish the NTC as a political entity in Monrovia. He explained how the customary system enjoyed the widespread legitimacy of the population and how, as customary justice practitioners, chiefs were necessary to the success of Liberia's justice strategy. Taking care to emphasize the complimentary relationship of the chief's and the long-term sustainability of the Liberian peacebuilding enterprise, the vice chairman noted how the customary system absorbs the vast majority of the everyday justice burden in Liberian communities, solving disputes at the lowest level, before they reach the overworked formal courts.[5]

In close collaboration with TCC and the MoIA, the NTC signed a resolution on a particularly contentious issue between customary and formal justice – trials by ordeal. Trial by ordeal is the main enforcement mechanism in the customary system and provides a coercive deterrent to behavior that runs counter to customary laws and restorative social values of community life. There are two basic types of trial by order practiced in Liberian customary justice: sassywood and cowfur.[6] Sassywood involves physical disciplinary coercion that can include burning the accused with a hot cutlass or forcing them to ingest poison. The coercive rationale behind sassywood is that it will either force a confession or, according to Liberian mysticism, will only cause harm to a guilty party while sparing the innocent. Cowfur, meanwhile is socially rather than physically coercive. These practices include being forced to ingest dirt, or take an oath of innocence. The passive coercive logic behind this approach is to compel the truth from the accused based on a mystic threat of later physical harm.[7] The resolution agreed that sassywood 'should be abolished but that other forms of traditional dispute resolution [...] should be allowed as long as the practitioners are licensed by the Minister of Internal Affairs'.[8] Yet, the resolution also recognizes that if sassywood is abolished, then an alternative must be provided that will be 'inexpensive, transparent, reliable and credible in the eyes of the traditional people'[9]

Working with the NTC, TCC increased the political legitimacy of the chieftaincy and customary justice practices. They introduced customary justice practitioners into the statutory legal establishment, challenging the widely held perception that customary justice practitioners were unreliable partners in the peacebuilding process. TCC's direct involvement in building, extending and sustaining links between formal and customary justice actors, systems and practices culminated at the three-day National Conference on Enhancing Access to Justice in Gbarnga in April 2010. Supported by USAID funding and trained by TCC and UN conflict mediation experts, the NTC negotiated an end to the outbreak of violence in Lofa County in May 2010. They successfully mediated and resolved a dispute between local Mandingo and Lorma traditional elders.[10] According to Tom Crick, when TCC first began working with the NTC in 2007, 'they were located in a small, side office in the old Ministry of Internal Affairs building. Now the NTC is an independent body that is pretty much part of the protocol order'.[11]

The justice and peace commission

Just as TCC was attempting to introduce customary practices into sites where statutory practices circulate, they were also developing a new range of programing that would introduce statutory practices into sites where customary justice circulates. To this end, TCC began organizing a network of CSOs that would travel to rural communities to raise the community's awareness about their rights under the rule of law. However, building a network of CSOs and then managing their daily activities required a significant degree of institutional expertise and grassroots capacity. Rather than developing this institutional capacity from scratch, TCC enlisted a local NGO, the Catholic Justice and Peace Commission as a partner.

The Justice and Peace Commission (JPC) was established in 1991 by a group of Liberian bishops as a reaction to the widespread violence and human rights abuses perpetrated during the civil war. The JPC's work in Liberian communities during and after the conflict has earned the organization a significant amount of local legitimacy and grassroots support, and it is one of the largest Liberian NGOs today.[12] They operate a parish-based network of regional administrative compounds, churches, schools and local offices situated throughout Liberia. The JPC's established national presence enabled TCC to extend its network by cultivating working relationships with county-based local CSOs. These CSOs include human rights-based youth drama associations, local peacebuilding organizations and traditional women's groups. In this way, the JPC provided an existing and locally legitimate institutional backbone capable of supporting TCC's civic education program.

However, when the CSOs began working in their communities, they were quickly overwhelmed. They were increasingly solicited for legal advice and approached for legal assistance in resolving long-held local disputes – assistance that the CSOs were not qualified to provide. Faced with this initial feedback, TCC reasoned that there were a large number of unresolved disputes underlying the relative stability of local communities, disputes which could potentially destabilize the broader Liberian peacebuilding process.[13] While the ICG report highlighted the need to incorporate customary practices in Liberia peacebuilding strategy, the initial feedback from the CSOs indicated that the customary system was no panacea. In order to satisfy the demand for legal information and assistance exposed by the CSO program, TCC began to consider a more robust justice intervention. However, as mentioned, strengthening customary institutions and increasing their political role was seen as counterproductive to liberal peacebuilding. Therefore, no established program model existed.

Appropriation: Reimagining justice in Liberia

While the ICG report called for more engagement with customary practitioners and institutions, such engagement unfolded within the long-term strategic peacebuilding framework of national harmonization and the emerging One Liberia policy. According to that view, 'there can be no alternative adjudicative bodies' to the constitutional authority of the judiciary and therefore peacebuilding policy should 'limit the jurisdiction of the chief's court' bringing them 'under the supervision and hierarchy of the formal judiciary'.[14] In this way, harmonization was a strategy for translating the statutory legal *claim* to a monopoly on the legitimate practice of justice into a practical reality.

Amid the relatively apathetic environment among the Monrovian legal establishment and their international supporters, TCC reached out to a small and somewhat unorthodox group of international justice practitioners. Central among them were Deborah Isser, then working with the United States Institute of Peace (USIP), and Stephen Lubkemann of George Washington University. Working with TCC, this network of justice practitioners formed the Legal Working Group (LWG) in order displace to the existing liberal justice monopoly both within Liberia and to advance a post-liberal understanding of justice. This post-liberal network re-appropriated the liberal statutory meaning of justice, co-opted its practices and attempted to create a political situation for new justice practices and different justice practitioners. They ascribed their own meaning to justice in Liberia and attempted to transform the political situation from one that called for harmonization into one that embraces customary justice practices. Their approach was influenced by the notion of legal pluralism.

Legal pluralism

In the mid-2000s, the USIP was part of an emerging post-liberal network of international justice practitioners. Along with the USIP and TCC, this network included a number of academic practitioners operating from sites spread out over a number of organizations such as the International Development Law Organization, the Open Society Foundation's Justice Initiative, The Ford Foundation and the World Bank's Justice for the Poor (J4P) project. These practitioners sought to understand why the liberal, statutory system of justice was not taking hold in post-conflict and developing countries. However, as Caroline Sage and Michael Woolcock of the World Bank's J4P project point out, the failure of liberal approaches to justice reform in post-conflict and development contexts has a long history.

Starting in the 1960s, the Ford Foundation asserted that establishing the rule of law was essential to the success of economic development. Through the next decade, the Ford Foundation funded a number of legal aid interventions that 'rested on a belief that law could be used to change society, "that law itself was an engine for change" and that "lawyers and judges could serve as social engines" for change'.[15] Yet, Sage and Woolcock point out that these early legal aid interventions failed largely due to the false assumption 'that American-style "legal liberalism" could be transplanted wholesale to developing countries'.[16] Re-appropriating the 'poverty trap' slogan of economic development,[17] they point out how legal liberalism can often create and maintain unjust legal inequality traps. However, at the time, the prevailing liberal peacebuilding logic implicated the lack of local statutory capacity and the absence of more robust monitoring and evaluation as the problem. Facing such a political situation, this emerging post-liberal network of justice practitioners suggested that the problem was deeper. As Sage and Woolcock argue, the failure of previous legal aid interventions were not about political will or implementation capacity but 'a flawed ontological understanding of what norms, rules and law "are"'.[18] Therefore, Sage and Woolcock articulate an alternative vision for legal aid which prioritizes *function over form*.

In order to displace the liberal ontology of justice shaping international interventions, these justice practitioners proposed a post-liberal alternative rooted in the functional concept of legal pluralism. Legal pluralism therefore represents a direct challenge to 'the ideology of legal centralism' reflected in conventional development programs.[19] According to Brian Tamahana, a chief proponent of legal pluralism, the ideology of legal centrism is problematic because it rests on an essentialized definition of the law which articulates what the law is and what it is not. To define the law is also to essentialize justice. In order to circumvent such reductive essentialism, Tamahana argues, 'there is no "law is;" there are these kinds of law and those kinds of law.'[20] For Tamahana, 'the core credo of legal pluralist is that there are all sorts of normative orders [that are] not attached to the state which nevertheless are "law"'.[21] Accordingly, 'a non-essentialist concept of law thus requires that law be conceived in a way that is empty, or that at least does not presuppose any particular content or nature.'[22] He suggests instead that a nonessentialist understanding of the law must rest on how people *practice* it.

For Tamahana, the key insight offered by legal pluralism is that the 'law is whatever people identify and treat through their social practices as "law"'.[23] Contrary to statutory legal centrism, 'a state of legal pluralism then exists whenever more than one kind of "law" is recognized through the social practice of a group in a given social arena.'[24] In this way, a practice-based understanding offers a nonessentialist way to engage with the law, one which breaks the axiomatic connection between the law and the state and instead opens a space for exploring the customary justice practices which are often stronger and more relevant to everyday lives in postcolonial societies. According to a practice-based reading of the law, Tamahana argues that 'no presuppositions are made about the normative merit or demerit of a particular kind of law, or about its efficacy or functional or dysfunctional tendencies or capacity (if any).'[25] A practice-based understanding of the law is a re-appropriation of what justice amounts to. It increases the legitimate political space of non-statutory justice practices and customary justice practitioners. By extending this approach into post-conflict

Liberia, TCC created a political situation in which the centrality of statutory law became unstable and a post-liberal approach to practicing justice became politically possible. But what would an intervention based on the principles of legal pluralism look like?

Legal empowerment

Following its limited successes in the 1960s and 1970s, the Ford Foundation organized a thorough review of its Global Law Programs Learning Initiative (GLPLI). The aim of the review was to identify 'the challenges that grantees have faced around the world and provide a sense of how they have used particular legal strategies in very different settings.'[26] These efforts included developing innovative litigation strategies that leverage the rule of law in ways that create conditions of better accountability, social justice and change. Yet they also involved working with informal, alternative justice-related CSOs and training them to practice Alternative Dispute Resolution. In this way, the Foundation's review served to extend the meaning of justice beyond statutory law and to create space for new justice practitioners and different legal aid strategies. Based on their findings, the Foundation offered the following conclusion: 'one size does not fit all [...] Different organizations working under different circumstances proceed along different paths toward such common goals as promoting human rights and development.'[27]

Stephen Golub emerged as a central figure in reorganizing the Ford Foundation's GLPLI program and in promoting its post-liberal approach to legal aid and justice-related development. As an academic practitioner, Golub re-appropriated the Ford Foundation's findings, translating its various techniques, practices and strategies into a new legal aid approach called legal empowerment. Golub frames legal empowerment as a move beyond what he refers to as 'orthodox approaches' to the rule of law and development.[28] For him, orthodox legal aid is a top-down, state-centric, institutional approach involving the professionalization of justice, building legal, technical and administrative practices, all of which are oriented toward economic growth, poverty alleviation and good governance. Yet, Golub maintains that the problem is 'not these economic and political goals, *per se*, but rather [their] *questionable assumptions, unproven impact, and insufficient attention to the legal needs of the disadvantaged.*'[29]

Attempting to redress the lack of access to the formal system, Golub argues for a 'paradigm shift' in approaches to legal development that uses 'legal services and related development activities to increase disadvantaged populations' control over their lives'.[30] He therefore identifies this new post-liberal paradigm in legal aid as one of legal empowerment. For Golub, legal empowerment is simply 'the expansion of freedom of choice and action'.[31] In this reading, the purpose of legal empowerment is to use the law as a lever to counter the arbitrary exercise of either state or customary power. Therefore, a legal empowerment approach is 'community-driven and rights-based [...], grounded in grassroots needs and activities but [able to] impact on national laws and institutions'.[32] In order to enact these objectives, Golub outlines a series of practices which include 'counselling mediation, negotiation and other forms of non-judicial representation [...] enhancing people's legal knowledge and skill through training, media, public education advice and other mechanisms'.[33]

However, the paralegal is a crucial innovation of legal empowerment. Paralegals are not national or international legal aid practitioners, but legal 'laypersons, often drawn from the groups they serve, who receive specialized legal training and who provide various forms of legal education, advice and assistance to the disadvantaged [and] building the poor's capacities regarding legal, regulatory and policy reform'.[34] Hence, in addition to challenging the liberal monopoly on the meaning of justice in Liberia and how it can be practiced, a paralegal-based approach to legal empowerment also contests and expands the existing limits on who can practice justice. However, translating such an approach into the Liberian political situation was not a simple prospect.

Performance: Designing a legal empowerment intervention

In 2008, there was no established model for a legal empowerment intervention. It remained largely experimental – an ad hoc field-based innovation. There was only one paralegal program in operation: Timap for Justice in Liberia's northern neighbour, Sierra Leone. However, at the time there was no hard data to point to, no systematic review of lessons learned from the Timap project. Given its unique and experimental status and unverified political impact, designing a paralegal project for Liberia was politically sensitive. Indeed, when a paralegal approach was initially proposed in Liberia, the program was tentatively called the Community Legal Adviser program and the advisers were originally referred to as a 'paralegals'. Demonstrating the highly contested nature of 'the law' in Liberia, many in the formal legal establishment objected to referring to them as paralegals since they were not officially trained as paralegals and that their advice should not be confused with legal advice. Therefore, the program's name was changed to the Community Justice Adviser (CJA) program. Operating in this somewhat hostile environment, TCC and their USIP partners had to create a post-liberal political situation in Liberia in which these CJAs became not only politically viable but integral to Liberia's justice strategy.

Designing the CJA program

For TCC to implement their paralegal program, they had to create a post-liberal political situation in which paralegals became indispensable. But, in the absence of evidence suggesting that paralegals were effective in improving local perceptions and experiences of justice, TCC and the USIP set out to build a body of evidence that such an approach was both necessary and impactful. In 2007, TCC and the USIP were approached by two development economists from Oxford University's CSAE, Bilal Siddiqi and Justin Sandefur, who proposed designing the CJA program in such a way that its impacts could be evaluated using a Randomized Controlled Trial (RCT).

RCTs were originally developed to measure the impact of pharmaceutical interventions. If a researcher suspected that Drug A was an effective treatment for illness X, they would need a way to prove it; RCTs are a particularly effective way of doing so. For example, a large group of people infected with illness X are randomly divided into two groups. Drug A is administered to the first group (the treatment group) while Drug A is withheld from the second group (the control group). If Drug A were effective in treating the illness, then one would expect to see a dramatic difference between the treatment group and the control groups over time. This basic structure can also be applied to economic development interventions. In the case of the CJA program, legal empowerment is the 'treatment'. Following the basic structure of the RCT, Liberian communities can then be divided into treatment groups where the CJA regularly visits while the treatment group receives no CJA visits. After a period of time, treatment communities can be compared to control communities and any differences between them can be directly attributed to the CJA's legal empowerment intervention.

However, RCTs cannot be grafted onto an existing intervention. Instead, it requires an intervention to be configured according to the methodological demands and basic structure of the RCT. For these reasons, Siddiqi and Sandefur became directly involved in designing the CJA program. Commenting on the demanding nature of the RCT-based structure, Sandefur notes that it is 'definitely a case of the methodological tail wagging the dog'.[35]

the main consideration as to why we got so involved in the beginning of the program, and also the nature of the impact evaluation, means that you have to randomize from the get go... You have to do a baseline and then based on the baseline you assign treatment and control [groups]. You try to match apples to apples etc. So for all those reasons you get involved at the beginning of the design phase.[36]

In order to match 'apple' communities to other 'apple' communities, the CSAE proposed a programing innovation: the new CJAs would be *mobile*. The mobile dimension extended the scope of the CJA program. It called for 16 motorbike-bound community justice advisers. Each mobile CJA was assigned ten communities which they were required to visit on a regular basis. Their tasking would include raising the level of legal awareness and provide free legal assistance; however, they would be able to extend access to justice programing outside the larger communities and into more remote towns and villages previously unreachable (See Figure 6.1).

Organized within the framework of a RCT, the CJA program deployed mobile CJAs in 88 largely rural Liberian communities spread out over

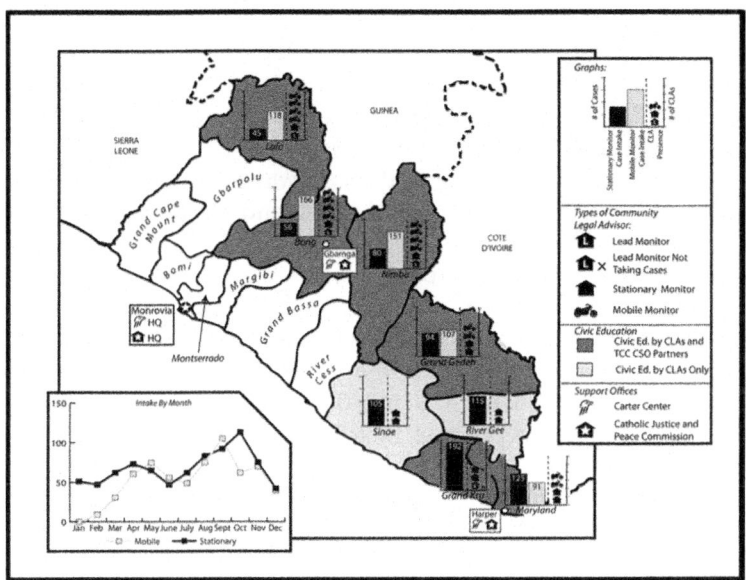

Figure 6.1 A map of the Community Justice Adviser program (The Carter Center; program document)

five counties: Bong, Nimba, Lofa, Grand Gedeh and Maryland. These 88 communities were designated as 'treatment' communities. In accordance with the survey design, the 88 treatment communities could be compared against 88 similarly composed 'control' communities where the CJAs would not be deployed. However, before deploying to their communities, a baseline survey had to be conducted in both treatment and control communities. The baseline survey entailed equipping a team of Liberian enumerators (data collectors) to interview one adult member of every household across the 88 treatment and 88 control communities (176 in total) which amounted to 2,100 households. These interviews consisted of administering a survey that probed respondent's income, nutrition, education, social position in the community, fluency in formal legal knowledge, history of disputes and their perceptions of justice in order to establish a baseline reading of the material well-being in each community. Once the baseline survey data was collected, a CJA would regularly visit their treatment communities. After a duration of two years, any differences between treatment and control groups could be attributed to the CJA intervention. The baseline survey was conducted under the auspices of a broader USIP project called *Looking for Justice*.

Looking for justice

In 2009, Bilal Siddiqi and Justin Sandefur of the CSAE along with Isser and Lubkemann of the USIP fielded a large-scale survey titled *Looking for Justice: Liberian Experiences and Perceptions of Local Justice Options* (L4J). L4J was a ten-month extended field survey which covered five Liberian counties: Nimba, Lofa, Bong, Grand Gedeh and Maryland. The report set out to 'develop evidence-based policy options for expanding the rule of law and consolidating peace over the next decade in Liberia in ways that account for the role of informal legal systems and grassroots understandings of justice'.[37] The research design consisted of qualitative and quantitative methods: while the USIP's team handled the qualitative aspects of the survey, the quantitative aspect was developed by Siddiqi and Sandefur as part of their baseline survey for the mobile CJA program.

L4J engaged directly with a range of actors involved in the customary justice system, including paramount chiefs, town chiefs, women's leaders and focus groups with community members. Through this approach, the researchers were able to trace *'the actual practice of dispute resolution, regardless of which institution – formal, customary or other – was involved'*.[38] By tracing the justice *practices* of Liberians as they attempt to resolve a dispute, the L4J report came to the conclusion that in the five counties surveyed, the perception of the formal justice system was overwhelmingly negative and that Liberians prefer to use the customary system. The report notes that these negative perceptions clustered around two general themes: 'first and second range concerns'.

The 'first-range concerns' were largely material in nature; they include affordability, timeliness, accessibility, transparency and effectiveness of formal vis-à-vis customary systems. Regarding the material, first-range concerns, L4J finds that

> The overwhelming majority of Liberians believe that the progress of a case in a formal court has virtually nothing to do with the substantive merits of the case. They believe that even the most meritorious, clear cut, or heinous cases will make absolutely no progress unless an often bewildering succession of 'fees' and costs are continuously being paid.[39]

Interfacing with this 'bewildering' formal justice process requires that a case is managed through a dizzying jumble of incomprehensible procedures that absorb an unacceptably high degree of not only money but time. The study concluded that the procedural nature of the formal system was 'invariably characterized by confusion and a deep sense of disempowerment'.[40] Yet, conceivably these material first-range concerns could be remedied by reducing court and representation fees, opening more legal clinics in more remote places and extending more legal education to clients. But, according to the USIP report: '[o]ne of the most striking findings [is] that most Liberians would still be unsatisfied with the justice meted out by the formal system, *even if it were able to deliver on the basics discussed above.*'[41] Hence, USIP finds that the more entrenched problems stem from 'second range concerns'.

These second-range concerns are normative in nature. The USIP survey assessed 'how most of [Liberia's] population defines "justice" itself in the first place'.[42] Contrary to the assumptions held by Monrovia elites and their international supporters, the report found that 'the core principles of justice that underlie Liberia's formal system (one based on the American legal system), differ considerably from those valued by most Liberians.'[43]

> There is a strong demand for justice results that comport with local conceptions of justice, as opposed to western norms that underlie the formal justice system. [...] Liberians also expressed their desire

for a locally relevant justice system – that is, one that embodies their values and social mores rather than seeking to supersede them; and one that addresses the full range of offenses, problems and crimes they believe they confront – including cases of 'witchcraft'.[44]

The survey concluded that Liberians want a justice system that reflects their values and beliefs – a 'fundamentally Liberian justice'.[45] Therefore, Liberian justice must reflect the restorative nature of customary justice in order to be perceived as legitimate. Contrary to the formal justice system which defines justice in individual terms (justice for the plaintiff over the defendant for example; a winner and a loser), Liberia's customary system defines justice in terms of the social cohesion of the community.

According to customary norms, punitive or redressive justice is 'considered deficient if it does not also produce reconciliation among the parties'.[46] Hence the management, maintenance or *restoration* of this social cohesion is the primary justice consideration in the customary system, not 'individual justice'. Rather than litigating the act or 'crime' as the formal system would, a restorative approach to justice must 'work to repair those relations, which are [seen as] the ultimate and more fundamental causal determinant, rather than merely treating the behavioral expressions that are viewed as its symptoms'.[47] Liberians understand the efficacy of the customary system as being closely related to the ability of the system to enforce its rules through these practices. Therefore, an essential aspect of the restorative justice practiced in Liberia is trial by ordeal.

The USIP report found that '[t]he vast majority of Liberians interviewed believed strongly that at least some forms of [trial by ordeal] should be allowed, and that the ban on its use was causing significant societal problems – most particularly the inability to control crime and a rise in witchcraft.'[48] While highly controversial in Monrovia, practicing sassywood (ingesting poison or burning with a hot cutlass in order to elicit a confession of guilt) is an integral aspect of restorative justice in Liberia. Along these lines, the L4J report determined that Liberians perceive the values embedded within the formal system to be eroding the capacity of customary systems to enforce the decisions and practices that sustain their restorative system of justice. Indeed the study found that 'to many Liberians the very term "human rights" has very negative connotations. For the most part, Liberians associate the term with children's rights and defendant's rights, and complain that these are undermining the social order.'[49] Consequently, it concluded that policies promoting the rule of law and formal justice were having *deleterious effects* on the very peace and security these policies purported to be securing.

However, L4J also revealed a significant range of negative perceptions of the customary system. Within the data, CSAE found that groups disadvantaged by the customary system such as 'women, poorer people, ethnic minorities, and the less locally connected people measured in distance from the chief would prefer to go to the formal system'.[50] The quantitative data collected in the baseline survey revealed what Siddiqi argued was 'a rationale to why people go to the customary system'; it indicated that if given the free choice between customary and formal systems, certain minority groups, would prefer to take their dispute to the formal system. Yet, because it is too expensive, the justice needs of these minority groups also go unmet in the customary system. Based on the negative perceptions of both formal and customary justice systems, the CJA program was designed to remove the economic and social barriers that factor into a Liberian's justice forum shopping decisions. Therefore, not only did the L4J suggest that the 'liberal', state-centric approach was undermining the customary justice practices maintaining the fragile peace in Liberia, but the report went on to point out where the customary system was also falling short.

The CJA program was designed to operate in the justice gaps between the formal and customary system. The CJA service is free of charge; it comes to the client rather than requiring the client to travel to a clinic. It is not a formal service; it appeals to restorative sensibilities and can therefore circumvent negative, alienating aspects of formal justice. The point of the CJA program was to provide a third justice option.[51] Whereas the ICG report indicated that the customary justice system was essential to Liberian peace and security, the L4J report went further; it found that active attempts to promote formal justice had an adverse effect on these essential customary practices, suggesting that 'the liberal peace' was detrimental to peace in Liberia. According to a senior UN operative who participated in the formation of Liberia's justice sector policy, L4J 'changed the discussion', and that 'the scale of the research and its findings in terms of volume, caused a moment of pause'.[52] Tom Crick, the associate director for TCC's Conflict Resolution Program in Atlanta, observed that 'cumulatively, these kinds of empirical studies were showing more and more clearly that the problems of rural justice were not going to be addressed simply by the formal justice system...which the international community was having a hard time in reforming from the top-down as it was'.[53]

Using data generated by this international-led survey, Liberia's 'justice problem' was redefined as a post-liberal problem rather than a liberal one: Liberia's justice problem could not be fixed by supplanting customary justice with formal justice, but by changing the formal justice system in a way which accommodates and reflects customary justice practices. This view was expressed by the post-liberal network of justice practitioners working through the Liberian Legal Working Group (LWG).

> The starting point for policies regarding justice reform should be focused on ways to functionally improve the quality of justice for all Liberians [...] Rather than only focusing on the legal framework, the approach should be a problem-solving one that focuses first and foremost on how best to meet the justice needs of the population [...] In other words, questions of structure and form are subordinated to those of function.[54]

With these findings, the LWG recommendations functioned to destabilize the historical hierarchy of formal over customary practices and called into question the claim that the formal system was the obvious approach to justice reform in peacebuilding. The group concluded that the customary system was essential to meet peacebuilding objectives in Liberia, rather than an obstacle to it.[55] They found that reform 'must focus on achieving far greater and more meaningful forms of local social participation than has hitherto been the case'.[56] Hence a range of new programing needed to be designed to reach out to and engage the 'full spectrum' of conflict resolution capacity in Liberia. This full spectrum approach created political space for a long-term, ongoing engagement with customary justice practitioners including further focus groups, meetings, research and surveys designed to 'focus efforts [on] working with traditional leaders and local communities to find alternative socially acceptable ways of addressing their concerns'.[57]

Conclusion

The process of designing the CJA program highlights the controversies within the international peacebuilding establishment; it exposes the contested limits of 'liberal' justice and reveals debates about how justice should be practiced and who should be able to practice it in post-liberal Liberia. TCC was enlisted by the Minister of Justice to develop a range of programing that could bridge the gap between the statutory and customary justice systems revealed by the ICG report. Based on these findings, TCC set out to create a post-liberal political situation in Liberia in which new justice practices and practitioners could be incorporated into the peacebuilding strategy. TCC cultivated a relationship with the JPC, a local NGO with an established national network that would allow them to extend statutory justice into rural communities. They also expanded the political role of the chiefs, incorporating them into statutory procedures and helping to establish them as legitimate justice practitioners in Liberia. However, the prevailing liberal peacebuilding wisdom at the time assumed that strengthening customary justice was counterproductive to the goal of establishing the rule of law and protecting human rights.[58]

TCC had to create the political space for customary practices and practitioners. They enrolled an emerging post-liberal network of international justice practitioners who were advancing legal pluralism and legal empowerment as alternatives to orthodox liberal justice interventions. The result of this collaboration was the CJA Program. Part of designing and launching the CJA program was fielding USIP's L4J report. The report's findings contravened the established liberal peacebuilding orthodoxy; they indicated that extending the rule of law and human rights into Liberian communities was having a destabilizing effect. The USIP report created a post-liberal political situation in which customary justice became an indispensable part of Liberia's peacebuilding strategy.

In addition to highlighting the contested status of justice among international peacebuilding practitioners, the process of designing the CJA program exposes the post-liberal economy of disruptive data. The ICG and USIP reports highlight how powerful international practices can be performed in ways that destabilize how international power is practiced. Contrary to justifying liberal peacebuilding inventions, these international organizations mobilized powerful quantitative methodologies for the purpose of challenging its assumptions and creating space for a post-liberal justice in Liberia. Using these methods, they were able to transform customary justice from a problem that peacebuilding must overcome into an indispensable peacebuilding solution.

While these quantitative methodologies were essential to destabilizing the liberal monopoly and creating the post-liberal political space for the CJA program, these same quantitative methods would be used to determine its impact. But since relative levels of 'empowerment' are difficult to quantify and compare, the CSAE survey team used economic indicators – child food security for example – as a proxy. The hypothesis being tested by the RCT was whether a legal empowerment intervention could improve the material well-being in communities. In other words, the relative success of the CJA program would be determined by the ability of the CJAs to demonstrate quantifiable economic impacts in their assigned treatment communities.

7
Translating Legal Empowerment into Liberian Communities

The USIP report concluded that the liberal peacebuilding strategy to gradually supplant customary justice with statutory law was having a negative impact on peace and security in Liberia. The findings challenged the Monrovian legal establishment's claim to a monopoly on the legitimate practice of justice and created a post-liberal political situation in which a legal empowerment intervention became an indispensable aspect of Liberia's peacebuilding strategy. The USIP report found that for justice to be perceived as legitimate, it must comport to the restorative justice norms and values practiced in Liberian communities. However, the report also indicated that the customary system was failing to meet the justice needs of women, ethnic minorities, subsistence farmers and other less-connected community members. The CJA program was designed to address these gaps by providing legal education and free legal assistance in rural communities. In order to be able to determine whether or not the program was successful in filling these justice gaps, the CJA program was organized within the methodological structure of an RCT.

According to the RCT-based structure, data collected during USIP's L4J report provided the baseline measurement which would later be compared against an end-line survey to determine the impact of the CJA program. The RCT-based design created a need for the CJAs to generate quantifiable impacts on material well-being indicators such as child nutrition and household income. The goal of improving child nutrition using an unconventional and experimental legal empowerment intervention was ambitious and called for a proactive and transformative approach. However, the priority placed on generating quantifiable impacts in Liberian communities was in tension with the restorative customary justice practices circulating through them. Therefore TCC had to develop a legal empowerment strategy which was both transformative while also maintaining vital local legitimacy. In order to manage the tension between generating impact and maintaining legitimacy in the eyes of their communities, the CJA's training required a nuanced approach to practicing legal empowerment.

Problematization: Organizing legal empowerment

With the end-line survey looming, the CJAs met for their semiannual training retreat in Gbarnga in February 2011. Gbarnga lies roughly four hours from Monrovia; it is a former Charles Taylor stronghold and the site of the new Liberian regional security hub pilot project (see Chapter 5). The town is the capital of Bong County, where the district commissioner and county superintendent preside and where both the JPC and TCC have regional offices. The training was hosted by the JPC on their large compound set on a hill just outside the town center. Over the duration of the training, as many as 120 participants and partners involved in TCC's access to justice programing attended. The schedule was intense – six days a week for two weeks, from eight to nine hours each day. The training was designed to equip the CJAs with the practical understanding of legal empowerment that would enable them to creatively manage the political tension between generating impacts and maintaining local legitimacy in their communities. However, as mentioned, legal empowerment was very new to peacebuilding and development practitioners. Prior to the CJA program, there was only one paralegal-based legal empowerment intervention in operation – Timap for Justice in Sierra Leone.[1]

Timap for justice

As Liberia's northern neighbor, Sierra Leone experienced similar postcolonial dynamics that manifested in what is, functionally, a dual legal system. Following Golub's early work on legal empowerment, Vivek Maru cofounded Timap in 2003 where he was codirector until 2007. Prior to Timap, legal empowerment practices were largely field-based innovations on existing legal aid programs that emphasized two practices: provided formal legal services and statutory legal education. Though he emphasizes legal education as 'a critical first step in giving people power', Maru finds that legal education alone is 'inadequate to change a person's or a community's capacity to overcome injustice'.[2] Maru argues that earlier generations of justice aid in development contexts 'failed because of an unwillingness to heed socio-legal specificity'.[3]

As he explains, 'the successful provision of justice services requires serious engagement with the social and legal particularities of a given context.'[4] In such a context Timap's goal was to improve access to justice for poor and rural Sierra Leoneans through primarily 'pragmatic' means, and therefore, Timap draws 'on both sets of institutions in any given case, depending largely on which institutional course will best achieve our client's interests and the interests of justice'.[5] In this sense, Timap represented a move away from understanding legal development in terms of formal state institutions and toward engaging with local needs.

Compared to the 'far better funded and more established' practice of building state institutions, reforming formal courts, fighting corruption in the judiciary and police, Maru argues that legal empowerment 'focuses on directly assisting ordinary people, especially the poor, who face justice problems'.[6] To address the unmet justice needs in rural Sierra Leonean communities, Maru established a legal empowerment NGO that was based exclusively on *paralegals*. Paralegals are 'laypeople with basic training in law and formal government who assist poor and otherwise disempowered communities to remedy breaches of fundamental rights and freedoms'.[7] Timap paralegals are trained to provide legal education and mediation in Sierra Leonean communities 'where the social infrastructure is thinnest and the need for services is greatest'.[8]

> The institution of the paralegal offers a promising methodology of legal empowerment that fits between legal education and legal representation, one that maintains a focus on achieving concrete solutions to people's justice problems but which employs, in addition to litigation, the more flexible, creative tools of social movements.[9]

In development and post-conflict settings Maru finds that the paralegal-based approach requires practitioners to 'straddle plural legal systems, engaging traditional, religious, and formal institutions, depending on the needs of a given case'.[10] This new way of enacting legal empowerment includes 'working with and strengthening community organizations, organizing collective action to address justice problems, and engaging in community education and community dialogue on justice issues'.[11] In this sense, Maru describes legal empowerment as 'the use of the law to bolster human agency'.[12]

> For all our engagement with the formal system, however, we are not legal missionaries who would banish customary darkness with formal

legal light. Customary institutions deserve respect both for their link to tradition and for the fact that they, far more than the formal institutions, are accessible and relevant to most Sierra Leoneans [...] Our work in this regard departs from the exclusive focus of most law reform efforts on the formal system, and resonates instead with what Madhavi Sunder calls 'New Enlightenment' efforts to advance freedom from within cultures which traditionally have been viewed as outside the modern public sphere.[13]

Nevertheless, formal litigation is a vital aspect of Timap's work in Sierra Leone. As Maru explains, 'because litigation or even the threat of litigation carries significant weight in Sierra Leone [...] our capacity to litigate adds strength to our paralegals' work as advocates and mediators'.[14] But TCC wanted to take a slightly difference approach.

From Timap to the community justice adviser program

Building on the Timap program, TCC began translating legal empowerment into the CJA program in November 2007.[15] Jeff Austin, TCC's South East regional director in Harper, managed this process which required close collaboration with Maru and the Timap paralegals. As Austin recalls, 'we really attempted to replicate a lot of things from Timap.'[16] However, there were some significant changes that were made along the way. First, Timap was directly administered by its codirectors. It did not use a local implementing partner or work through existing local NGOs. The CJA program, on the other hand, worked through the JPC. The reasoning behind using the JPC was that they were more established in Liberian communities than TCC. The JPC had accrued a great deal of local legitimacy through their ongoing work in Liberian communities and was therefore more sustainable over the long term.

Second, the CJA program did not adopt a formal litigation strategy. Contrary to Timap, which employs a deeper legal staff who directly supervises case management and can actually litigate cases, TCC has never directly litigated a case.[17] While the CJAs often use the statutory system to resolve disputes, the CJA program places greater emphasis on the indirect influence of legal empowerment over the direct coercive mechanism of formal litigation. Lastly, Timap was not designed within an RCT. The RCT-based structure of the CJA program placed political pressure on the CJAs to generate impacts. Structured in this way, the CJA program assumed that positive political impact could be generated by opening and resolving cases in a way which was more aligned with restorative justice norms and would therefore be more locally legitimate. On the one hand, these changes reflected the political situation in Liberia and the associated need to balance between local legitimacy and the need to generate impacts. On the other hand, the changes also added to the complexity of the CJA program relative to Timap. It increased the degrees of institutional separation between program designers and practitioners while creating additional structural demands.

Appropriation: Indirect legal empowerment

When the CJA program was designed, TCC decided not to establish an entirely new organization as Timap had but took advantage of Liberia's comparative advantage regarding the JPC's local and national organization. For the kind of decentralized, community-based work the CJAs were doing, the JPC was 'a natural fit'.[18] The daily operations of the CJA program are managed by the JPC, not TCC. The CJAs are employed by the JPC. The CJAs were all locals of the region where they would be working and were brought up from within the Catholic education and parish network managed by the JPC.[19] CJAs are hired based on their knowledge of local dialects and their familiarity with local geography and customs. Most of them had a background working in community outreach or CSOs and some previously worked on baseline surveys by the CSAE. CJAs work in JPC facilities where available. The JPC keeps the records, organizes their activities and manages the day-to-day operations. Meanwhile, TCC provides the JPC institutional support, legal expertise, a promotional and funding apparatus and monitoring and oversight. The CJA program was expanding to a new county, Grand Basa, and ten new CJAs (eight men of various ages and two young women) had to be trained to fill the positions. The first week of the CJA training retreat focused on training the ten new CJAs on how to practice legal empowerment.

As the training began, Pewee Flomoku, the program coordinator for TCC walked a fine line, defining the limits of the program and the need to balance between maintaining local legitimacy while also making an impact. As he introduced them to the program, Flomoku explained how the CJAs should identify themselves. He explained that that CJAs were not lawyers, they were not 'paralegals', they were not international TCC employees, but local CJAs who work for the JPC – a local NGO which would be in Liberia long after Carter left.[20] He walked them through the program basics. They would be assigned to ten communities where they were required to visit twice a month. He explained that CJAs were often assigned to communities which are often geographically distant, requiring hours of motorcycle travel in very difficult road and weather conditions. While in their communities, the CJAs' goal is to open new cases and manage these cases through to their closure, a process which entails an administrative component and careful case documentation.

Between statutory and customary justice

A significant portion of their training focused on statutory law. This aspect of the training was conducted by Counselor Lemeuel Reeves, TCC's full-time Liberian staff lawyer. Counselor Reeves functions as the legal adviser for the CJAs while they are in the field. Should the CJAs require legal clarification or encounter a situation beyond their legal expertise, they were encouraged to contact Counselor Reeves. The new CJAs were given an initial exam to assess their base knowledge of the legal system and then given periodic quizzes to track their progress. Their training in formal law targeted specific, historically problematic laws and statutes flagged up during the baseline survey. These topics included corrections and pretrial detention, rape, domestic and gender-based violence, land, property, mining and resource law, and inheritance law. Each of these legal areas was discussed in relation to the criminal justice system, clarifying its limits as outlined in the Constitution. In the course of the training, Counselor Reeves paid particular attention to the precarious, unsettled status of customary law within the formal system. However, with the exception of violent felonies such as rape, murder and serious violent assault, the training emphasized the importance of CJA impartiality vis-à-vis formal or customary justice systems. For example, if a CJA is personally opposed to divorce (being recruited from within the Liberian Catholic system, most of the new trainees were opposed to divorce), they are required to provide all options available to the client, including the option of divorce provided under the statutory and customary system and to assist them in proceeding.

However, compared to TCC, the JPC was more closely connected and often embedded in the communities where they operated. Therefore, the JPC was concerned about the potentially destabilizing effects that any legal empowerment intervention may have on the restorative customary practices in their community. They feared that being too active in pursuing and opening cases might negatively affect their local reputation and undermine their other community work. After all, the JPC and the CJAs were not internationals or Monrovia-based operators but local people who, while brought up in the Catholic Liberian education system, were also from communities where customary systems predominate. In fact these qualities – the familiarity with navigating both systems – are the reasons why they were selected in the first place.

Thomas Mawolo, the JPC regional coordinator from Cape Palmas, Maryland County, explained that the disruptions caused in communities when members take each other to court run counter to restorative values of customary justice and breeds animus between disputants. In discussing the balancing act the JPC performs between its commitment to formal law and the customary system, Mawolo maintains that there must be an acceptance of the dual system. His position vis-à-vis the customary system is to 'keep the good and change the bad'.[21] Using trial by ordeal or sassywood as an example, he made a distinction between bad sassywood such as 'the cutlass' (burning a suspect with a hot sword to compel a confession) and the more mystical customary practices of good sassywood.[22] However, this position walks a fine line, a line which is actively being contested in Liberia. Given the JPC's precarious position in their communities, Jeff Austin recalled that there was a need to 'balance our message to the staff about how active they should be' in seeking out or soliciting cases.[23] The result of this compromise was an *indirect* legal empowerment strategy in which the CJAs were not allowed to actively solicit cases. In this way, the JPC appropriated the CJA program, imposing their own political situation on its legal empowerment practices.

Practicing indirect legal empowerment

In order to manage the tension between local legitimacy and generating impactful changes in communities, The CJAs were trained to use an indirect legal empowerment strategy. Rather than actively solicit cases, this indirect strategy was designed to act upon the social milieu of the community to create the conditions in which community members would feel empowered to approach the CJA for help. A training PowerPoint slide that read 'The Empowerment Oriented Approach' was projected on the wall. It defined 'empowerment' as striving to 'increase the capacity' of individuals and institutions and stated: 'to empower someone is simply helping someone to help themselves. When you empower someone, you give them the tools and resources that they will need in order to be successful.'[24]

> All TCC partners should always develop the attitude that instead of doing something for them, you are doing something with them. You should pass on the knowledge to others so that the next time they have a similar problem, they will have the knowledge to help

themselves and they won't have to depend on someone else to come in and help them.[25]

The presentation posed a number of questions: 'How can you empower this woman?' 'How can you empower this community?' and was followed by a discussion in which trainees were presented with a number of scenarios they might encounter in their communities. Contrary to a more proactive approach to seeking out cases, the training carefully articulated that the role of the CJA is not to directly solicit cases but to employ an indirect, longer-term strategy for providing legal information at the community level and then assisting people in using that information to resolve disputes. Their training repeatedly reinforced the idea that CJAs must be approached by community members, and that their assistance must be requested. This indirect empowerment strategy is undertaken on the assumption that if provided with legal information that spousal abuse, for example, is a crime, then community members who experience spousal abuse would feel empowered to reach out to the CJA. Allowing the client to lead the process, the CJAs can maintain local legitimacy by appealing to the restorative nature of customary justice while also providing clients with the option of statutory court should they choose.

While indirect legal empowerment provides a strategy that is open to the restorative justice norms of their clients, it is also in tension with the RCT-based demand to generate quantifiable impacts. In fact, the purpose of the CJA program is to improve access to justice in Liberia, to bring about some change in the way justice is practiced in Liberia. It was for this reason that the CJA program was embedded within the framework of an RCT in the first place (see Chapter 6). The RCT is a way of measuring the changes that the CJAs are able to bring about in their communities. Therefore, the political situation facing the CJAs in their communities was a difficult one: they had to manage the light footprint of the indirect, client-led, legal empowerment approach while working around the implicitly disruptive effects of introducing new justice actors and a different way of practicing justice into Liberian communities for the purpose of generating transformative impacts. In order to manage this political situation, the CJAs were trained on how to use their various legal empowerment tools.

Performance: The tools of indirect legal empowerment

Indirect legal empowerment is designed to create a political situation in communities in which community members feel empowered to approach a CJA. This strategy begins with entering a community for the first time. In order to build the lasting partnerships in the communities that the program envisions, the trainees were instructed on the proper etiquette and protocol for making a good first impression. CJAs were taught to approach the chief first and to introduce themselves as the JPC seeking to conduct rule of law education in the community on an ongoing basis. CJAs were instructed to request from the chief a regular time to interact with the community members where a maximum audience can be gathered with a minimal disruption to the daily work of the community. The goal was to establish the terms of their conduct in the community so as to avoid problems. The group was instructed not to incite action against the chief and emphasized the importance of maintaining a cooperative rather than an antagonistic relationship with traditional community leaders. As Flomoku explained, 'the chiefs have been here hundreds of years', and he cautioned the CJAs not to enter their communities 'acting refined', using 'big English' and to refrain from conducting themselves arrogantly and imposing their ideas.[26] Using satire to demonstrate the point, Flomoku and the lead-CJA from Grand Gedeh, staged a role-play where they walked the trainees through the dos and don'ts of community entry, emphasizing professional conduct, respect for restorative community norms and for the chief's authority.

The tools of indirect legal empowerment

In order to translate an indirect legal empowerment strategy into legally empowered communities, the CJAs were provided with a set of 'tools'. This aspect of the training was conducted by experienced lead CJA monitors. These tools function as both the 'service' the CJAs provides and a resources which can be applied creatively. In this way, these legal empowerment tools comprise the practical understanding which enables the CJAs to perform their indirect legal empowerment strategy in a quantifiably impactful way. The most frequently used tool in the CJA's toolbox is community awareness-raising (tool #1). This is the CJA's opportunity to reach a wide audience. They were trained to keep as regular a schedule as possible, establishing a routine of community awareness-raising in order to address the range of disputes flagged-up by the L4J baseline survey. Domestic violence and spousal abuse is a common dispute. For example, community members may simply be unaware that spousal abuse is illegal under statutory law. Therefore, the objective is to raise awareness that domestic violence is illegal, creating a political situation in which community members, particularly the abused spouses, will feel encouraged to seek out the CJA for help in resolving their dispute.

As part of these regular community visits, the CJAs were taught to conduct ongoing investigations into the justice demands and needs of the specific community and to tailor awareness-raising accordingly. If, for example, a woman in the community shows a repeated pattern of bruising suggestive of an abusive spouse, the CJAs were trained *not* to approach the woman and tell her that she should open a case; their legal empowerment training emphasized that CJAs *cannot actively solicit cases* from community. Instead, they are trained to create a condition in which the bruised woman would feel encouraged to approach the CJA. To this end, they were trained to tread lightly by adjusting the theme of their awareness-raising session to emphasize the illegality of spousal abuse, the rights of the woman under the law and the broader negative social impact of spousal abuse on the community.

If the bruised woman approaches the CJA, then they can provide her with information (tool #2). Here, the CJA is trained to gather the details of the case, present the potential client with her rights under the law and then lay out the options available to the client. If the CJA learns that the case is legally complex (e.g., if the spousal violence stems from an inheritance she received), then they may need to enlist the help of the county's lead CJA monitors (tool #3) or contact TCC's on-call staff lawyer, Counselor Reeves (tool #4) in order to clarify the clients legal options. In the instance that the investigation reveals that the woman was raped, the case *must* be referred to the formal system. Indeed for all violent felonies such as rape and murder, CJAs were instructed to refer cases directly to the formal system. However, the training was careful to distinguish between providing free legal *information* and dispensing legal *advice*. In providing legal advice, the CJA takes the lead in directing the client. Providing free legal information, on the other hand, stems from the indirect legal empowerment strategy. Rather than the directing clients toward the formal system, CJAs present their clients with their available legal options under each justice system and then impartially allow the clients to choose according to their perceived justice needs.[27]

Having been provided with free legal information, a client has options for resolving a dispute, which generally proceeds down three distinct but often intersecting pathways. The first path is customary justice. Should a client choose this path, the CJA will assist their client to 'navigate the authority' of the customary system (tool#5). If using this tool, the CJA was encouraged to take advantage of the JPC's local reputation and credibility, along with TCC's network of customary justice practitioners to leverage the formal system in order to resolve a dispute in the client's favor. For example, if a chief rendered a decision on an inheritance which contravenes statutory law, the CJA is advised to inform the chief on behalf of the client who has the option to select formal court.

The formal court, therefore, is the second path generally available to the client. If the client wishes to take their dispute through the formal system, the CJA will assist in familiarizing the client with the procedures of the formal system, again bringing the resources of JPC and TCC to bear on the client's behalf. This dimension involves monitoring the formal system (tool #6) – ensuring that a client's rights are respected through their interaction with the criminal justice and correctional institutions by, for example, monitoring local police and correctional facilities. Along similar lines, CJAs are also trained to be community advocates (tool #7). Advocacy involves leveraging the formal law on behalf of an individual or group who may have leased some of their customary land for lumbering in exchange for a new school which was never built. In this instance, the CJA is trained to advocate on the community's behalf to ensure that they are properly compensated. However, the innovation of the CJA program in the Liberian context is that they provide a third option for resolving a dispute, an alternative justice pathway to customary and formal systems – CJAs provide a free mediation service (tool #8).

New justice practices; different justice practitioners

The experienced CJAs walked the new recruits through the mechanics of the mediation process from preparation – shuttling between parties, establishing 'the facts' and obtaining an agreement on CJA-led mediation from both parties – to managing the process through to resolution. The CJAs were trained in mediation techniques by TCC's legal staff through a combination of lecturing, role-playing and discussion. They were introduced to mediation terminology and conflict-resolution approaches and strategies.[28] The mediation aspect of the training involved teaching the trainees psychosocial techniques of communication: 'active listening', eye-level communication, tone of voice and showing empathy.[29] They were also trained on how to engage with traumatized victims of domestic violence, victims of gender-based violence, abused children and suicide intervention. According to their training manual, mediation 'does not aim to find objective truth, but rather to find an agreed solution that acknowledges and is based upon the perceptions and experience of all sides'.[30]

Mediation enables the CJA to practice legal empowerment in a way that reflects the restorative values of customary justice. Mediation training emphasized the need for the CJA to find the core issue or 'root causes' of the dispute. This restorative approach treats minor crimes or disputes as an expression or symptom of a deeper problem. Simply, litigating the symptom does not resolve the core problem.[31] In the case of the bruised woman, should she approach the CJA and request their assistance, the CJA would attempt find out if there was something else which may be agitating the husband – was there an exacerbating economic problem? Was he in debt? Was he not paid by his employer? Was there an underlying marital problem? Did he have another family that was monopolizing his resources? If so, the CJA would mediate the core or root cause of the dispute rather than its effect or the crime. While CJA-led mediation walks a careful line between statutory law and restorative justice, CJAs are prevented from performing trials by ordeal or other customary practices that contravene formal law. Should the client opt for mediation, then the task of the CJA is to bring all their resources, training and practical understanding to bear in attempting to resolve the dispute in a way which is not only satisfactory to the client but also sensitive to the restorative nature of community, all the while operating in accordance with the rule of law.

This requires a nuanced approach. Through the use of daily role-plays, the CJAs were continually challenged to use their tools in different and creative ways. Every afternoon, the trainees were provided with a tricky scenario – a political situation – and then encouraged to bring the entire array of 'tools' and training to bear on that situation. These role-play scenarios were monitored by the senior CJAs and Counselor Reeves. Following the scenario, the entire group discussed and provided the trainee with feedback, enlisting the other trainees to comment on what was done correctly and what could be done to improve. These role-plays were essential in the translation of a practical understanding of legal empowerment into CJA practice. Coupled with regular pop quizzes that tracked the translation and transfer of practical understanding, the new CJAs demonstrated a marked improvement in their baseline knowledge of the law. Through this ongoing, daily routine of lecture and discussion-based learning in the morning and role-playing in the afternoons, the legal empowerment *approach* was gradually translated into a *performance* of legal empowerment that enabled them to balance between the need to generate impact and maintaining local legitimacy.

Conclusion

The process of importing a legal empowerment model into Liberia highlights the precarious relationship between the design of a legal empowerment intervention and the practice. The USIP and ICG reports indicated that the rural Liberians were deeply suspicious of statutory justice system and the internationally led legal aid interventions that promote them. Rural Liberians hold a negative perception of human rights and the rule of law because the adversarial procedures enshrined in statutory law contravene the restorative practices of customary justice. The legal empowerment model imported from Sierra Leone was sensitive to restorative justice and emphasized client needs over programmatic benchmarks. The JPC was enrolled to implement the CJA program in a way that balanced between restorative justice and being able to leverage statutory law to help clients. But, the CJA program was designed as an RCT that measured 'impact' as increases in the level of economic well-being in treatment communities. In this sense, the program was designed to transform communities rather than to restore them.

The JPC was concerned that maximizing economic impact and prioritizing case generation would have a disruptive effect on the restorative justice that was practiced in their communities. They suggested that an active approach where the CJAs would seek out disputes and attempt to convince community members to open cases would exacerbate existing tension and latent disputes. The JPC favored an indirect legal empowerment practice that would prevent the CJA from actively soliciting cases in the community. The indirect legal empowerment approach that was reflected in their training was designed to create a political situation in communities where community members would feel empowered to approach the CJA for help. Using their legal empowerment tools, the CJAs were trained to use awareness-raising sessions as an indirect pathway to generate new cases and create an impact. The indirect strategy was based on the assumption that if community members were provided with legal information about common disputes and their rights under statutory law, then they would approach the CJAs. As a result, the awareness-raising session was treated as the highest priority.

The indirect approach to legal empowerment emphasized in the CJA training was at odds with the quantifiable economic impacts emphasized in the RCT-based design of the CJA program. On the one hand, the CJA program and indirect legal empowerment reflects the adaptability of international practices. It illustrates how international biopolitical interventions target the social milieu to cultivate neo-liberal subjectivity. But it also demonstrates the fragility of international power. The discontinuity between program design and performance shows how international interventions become co-opted, how projects can be re-appropriated and how practices can be reinscribed with new meaning and organized for new and different purposes.

8
Translating Legal Empowerment into a Randomized Controlled Trial

After two-and-a-half years of practicing an indirect legal empowerment strategy in their assigned communities, it was time to determine the impact the CJAs were making. According to the methodological structure of the RCT-based evaluation, the end-line survey mirrored the original baseline survey; it entailed resurveying all original 176 communities (88 treatment and 88 control) and each of the original 2,100 households spread out across five counties – Maryland, Grand Gedeh, Nimba, Lofa and Bong. Consequently, organizing and implementing an RCT of this size in rural Liberia was an expensive, labor-intensive enterprise with many moving parts and unforeseen variables. The CSAE survey, led by Bilal Siddiqi and Justin Sandefur, reasoned that the end-line survey would require roughly 25–30 enumerators (data collectors) who could complete the survey in just over a month. The survey instrument was the actual digital multiple-choice questionnaire which was uploaded to the handheld computers or Personal Digital Assistants (PDAs). The PDAs display an interactive digital interface which the enumerator reads aloud to the respondent. The survey instrument prompts the enumerator to ask the respondent a question and displays the optional answers for selection. The answers are then recorded on the PDA and saved for later analysis.

However, it is important to understand how an RCT-based methodology defines impact: in an RCT one is 'looking for a correlation which is [statistically] significantly different from zero'.[1] For the CJA program to register an impact which was 'significant', the RCT must determine with a 95 percent statistical degree of confidence that the CJA program had *more than zero impact*. In other words, the threshold required for demonstrating impact is low (more than nothing); however, such impacts must be determined with a very high degree of confidence (95 percent). Yet, legal empowerment was a relatively new intervention and had never been evaluated using an RCT. Compared to the conventional health or education-based programs that are typically subjected to RCT methodology, legal empowerment was experimental. In order to capture the uncertain impacts of legal empowerment with a high degree of confidence, the CSAE survey team used economic proxies – changes in concrete material indicators such as increased income, more food on the table or higher attendance at school. By comparing these material markers across both treatment and control communities, the survey would be able to detect any changes in the material well-being of the treatment communities that could then be causally attributed to the CJA intervention (see Chapter 6). However, given the untested nature of legal empowerment interventions and the complexity of the end-line survey, Siddiqi and Sandefur wanted to pilot the end-line survey in a few communities first. The aim was to test the water – to pre-assess whether the CJA program was registering a detectable material impact in their communities.

Problematization: Evaluating the impact of indirect legal empowerment

The RCT was designed to measure impacts at the community level. The end-line survey would compare treatment *communities* to control *communities* to determine the impact of the CJA program. Liberian communities are dynamic and lively; many situations of everyday life – from preparing food to dispensing justice – are performed in these communities. Members of these communities live, work, trade, farm, raise children and grow old there. Justice practices in these communities are predominantly customary in nature; the formal justice system and state institutions are largely absent in everyday life. And to the extent it is present, the statutory justice system is viewed with suspicion.[2] In order to stress-test the research strategy and assess the kinds of impacts the CJAs were having in their communities, a piloting exercise was organized. In the first two pilot communities, Tarsah and Gayatea, familiarity with the CJAs was virtually zero.

Harry Momodu, was the CJA assigned to these communities.[3] When discussing the reason for the low level of recognition in the first two piloting communities, Momodu suggested that it was partly due to how the survey team was inquiring about his work. He noted that in their communities, they were not known as the JPC or as CJAs; instead they were known as 'the human rights man' – a name that reflected the political meaning which the community had ascribed to him. Despite the relative lack of recognition, in Tarsah and Gayatea, Momodu suggested that there was a large appetite in the communities for knowledge of the statutory law and the rights it provides. But he also expressed frustration over the difficulty of translating the community's interest in the statutory law into actual cases. He indicated that his impact in the community was not from helping specific clients. Instead he cited the less tangible element of community education and awareness-raising as having the most significant impacts.[4]

The third piloting community, Baila, was larger and more centrally located than the previous two communities and was assigned to a different CJA. Nineteen cases had been opened in Baila, ten of which had been closed. Describing the impact of his work in the community, Prince Nimlay[5] emphasized two aspects. First, echoing Harry Momodu's comments, Nimlay indicated that wide-net strategies such as community education and providing general awareness of the law were having the most significant impacts. Second, he pointed to their relationship with customary institutions. He indicated that working with the chief raised the chief's standing in the community because he was seen to be more closely associated with the law.[6] Prince Nimlay found that the presence of the JPC and general awareness of the law in the community provided the chief some legitimate cover in resolving difficult disputes or providing them with an option to pass the case to the CJA, whom the community members found less biased.[7] These discussions revealed the ways in which the chief had appropriated and retranslated the CJA's legal empowerment practices, deferring problematic cases to the CJA in a way which simultaneously strengthened his restorative customary claim to authority and reinforced his legitimacy. Compared to Tarsah and Gayatea, the overall level of recognition of the CJA in Baila was higher. However, it did not indicate that the impact from awareness-raising and resolved individual cases were enough to be detected in a random sampling of the broader community.

Assessment: Zero-impact?

By the end of the second day of piloting, both quantitatively and qualitatively, it appeared that the general recognition and familiarity with the JPC and CJA's service was lower than expected at the community level. For Siddiqi and Sandefur the issue was not the lack of impact in the community per se, but rather that the program had not been properly implemented.[8] A survey team memo written to TCC cited low awareness and take-up of Community Justice Adviser (CJA) services and poor case follow-up as contributing factors to the lower than expected impact. Siddiqi and Sandefur were concerned that the data pointed toward a 'zero-impact' outcome:

> As we all know at this point, the basic methodology being used for the [CJA] evaluation [RCTs] will compare outcomes – and their improvement over time – between treatment and control communities. These outcomes range from subjective perceptions of justice ('How satisfied were you with the resolution...?') to objective welfare indicators that successful dispute resolution might affect, such as child support payments by absentee fathers and, in turn, child nutrition and school enrolment. If, as we currently fear, the end-line survey detects no significant difference in these outcome indicators between treatment and control communities, two obvious categories of explanation would emerge: (a) legal aid in this context simply doesn't work; there is a flaw in the project design; or (b) the project design was never really tested because it was not adequately implemented. Our basic concern is that launching an end-line survey now will find no effect from two years of [CJA] work, and that the explanation for this is likely in category (b). As such, $65k in additional survey research will teach us very little about what might work in the area of dispute resolution, or how future programs should be designed.[9]

Summarizing the political situation at the end of the first round of piloting, Siddiqi and Sandefur concluded that 'our experience in Bong [County] raised doubts about whether investing [more funds] on a survey at this point would yield interesting results, from either a research or program perspective'.[10] However, it was not that the CJAs were simply having no impact – they were.

Based on internal TCC monitoring, follow-up interviews conducted with clients, JPC case records and interviews with the CJAs themselves indicated that the intervention was indeed making an impact. After all, the CJAs had opened 1,868 new cases and had resolved 47 percent. Indeed, some of the data collected in the first round of piloting suggested that the program *was*, in fact, making an impact. The problem was rather that the program's impacts were *not at the level or scale that was anticipated when the survey was originally designed*.

The survey was designed to measure impacts at the community level. This structure would enable Siddiqi and Sandefur to randomly survey the community population during the end-line rather than having to track down and resurvey every member of the community who had opened a case with the CJA. This design was based on the assumption that the program would have been implemented at a level and scale such that its impact could be detected in a random sampling of the general community population. If the program was implemented at a sufficient level and scale and if enough individuals registered a case with the CJA, then a random community-level sample could detect the community-level impacts in addition to the finer-grained individual-level impacts.

While the random sample collected during the first round of piloting did not detect the anticipated community-scale of impact, it indicated that the CJAs were having smaller-scale impacts on the individual clients who decided to open a case with them. This suggested a disjuncture between the impacts the survey was designed to detect and the scale of impact the CJAs' indirect legal empowerment practices were actually registering.

The community-level design was based on TCC and CSAE's assumption that, over time, continual exposure to CJA interventions would result in significant and measureable differences that could be detected by a random sampling of treatment and control communities. Essentially, the survey was designed on the assumption that the program would generate larger-scale impacts than it actually did. Yet, because the survey was designed as a *community*-level evaluation, the finer-grained, the smaller-scale individual-level impacts were lost in a random sampling of the community. Consequently, the CSAE survey team began considering ways to capture the individual-level impacts the CJAs were actually making in their communities.

Appropriation: Generating political impact

The zero-impact indication reflected how the Siddiqi and Sandefur appropriated the CJA program and ascribed their own meaning to its legal empowerment practices. They saw the CJA program as an opportunity to challenge conventional legal aid interventions using an RCT. RCTs are commonly considered the 'gold standard' in attributing cause and assessing the effect of a given 'treatment' or intervention.[11] Since the early 2000s, the use of RCTs in peacebuilding and development contexts has proliferated. During that period a significant amount of money was flowing into Oxford from several sources, such as the UK's DFID and the Open Society Foundation (OSF) to conduct research using RCTs. In this climate, Siddiqi and Sandefur recalled that 'resources were available and people were being encouraged to throw around ideas, and that's what we were doing'.[12] However, first they needed to find an intervention that could be measured using an RCT-based methodology. Upon learning of TCC's CJA program, Siddiqi went to Monrovia to meet with them and pitch the idea of designing their new paralegal project within an RCT-based framework.

Their interest in the CJA program sprang from a 2008 paper by development economists Martina Björkman and Jakob Svensson titled *Power to the People: Evidence from a Randomized Field Experiment on Community-Based Monitoring in Uganda*.[13] What Siddiqi and Sandefur found intriguing about this particular study was how it used RCTs to evaluate an unconventional development intervention. The study found that simply bringing the community together to 'talk about the performance of their health clinic, had big effects that [were] measureable in terms of child mortality rates'.[14] For Siddiqi and Sandefur, these impacts were interesting because they suggested that a non-conventional development intervention could deliver significant impacts on key development indicators that expensive mainstream brick-and-mortar development interventions could not. For them, being able to deliver significant reductions to child mortality rates using unorthodox community-based programs could compel large development donors to take notice and say, 'wow, these wishy-washy things we've ignored in the past are having some huge concrete returns relative to some of our more standard interventions.'[15] In other words, they were interested in these types of community-based justice programs because of their potential to challenge established development dogma.[16] Recalling their thinking during their initial discussions with TCC, Sandefur recalled:

> If you really want people to take notice of your justice sector stuff you need to show that it has impacts on the kinds of core welfare indicators that people are already paying attention to. So in the case of Liberia it's going to be 'can we test whether resolving these [household disputes...] has an impact on the food security of children? [If so] then a whole different class of people are going to start paying attention to the results.[17]

However, 'empowered' is difficult to measure. To capture the impacts of a legal empowerment intervention, its anticipated effects were translated into a more easily quantifiable set of indicators. Siddiqi and Sandefur used economic indicators such as an increase in disposable income as a proxy. They reasoned that an improvement in the economic conditions in individuals of treatment communities would reflect the economic spillover effects of a legal empowerment intervention. For Siddiqi and Sandefur, 'to cross that line from the law and justice folks to the rest of the development community was to try to test the claim that getting these justice sector issues sorted out was going to have material returns, economic returns defined in a more standard way, so that was the holy grail to us.'[18] Using RCTs to challenge established liberal assumptions rather than simply confirming and legitimizing them points to the potentially disruptive political impact of RCTs.

The randomistas

The profusion of RCTs in peacebuilding and development contexts is largely driven by a group of development economics practitioners who have become colloquially known as the *randomistas*.[19] In their book *Poor Economics: A Radical Rethinking of the Way to Fight Global Poverty*, Banerjee and Duflo of the Abdul Latif Jamil Poverty Action Lab (J-PAL) at MIT introduce a selection of findings generated by RCTs into the debate on international aid.[20] Acknowledging the oversimplification, they argue that the international aid debate centers on the differentiation between 'aid is good', on the one hand, and 'aid is bad', on the other. They represent the former camp through Jeffery Sachs' notion of the 'poverty trap', in which aid is necessary if poor people are to be able to escape.[21] The latter camp, represented by William Easterly[22] and Dambisa Moyo,[23] argues that aid destroys development and harms local economies.[24] Proposing that aid itself is the poverty trap, Easterly and Moyo find that giving away something for nothing leads poor people not to value it.[25] It is into this debate that the 'randomistas' introduce their findings.

The 'randomistas' maintain that this polemical aid debate is more about the application of worldview and the politics of given (ideological) dispositions to aid policy than about the engagement with actors, context and evidence. Positioning themselves against the 'universal answers' represented as the aid-is-good, aid-is-bad debate, Banerjee and Duflo caution against throwing the baby out with the bath water, instead championing an approach which seeks out whatever policy works to alleviate poverty and raise living standards in the developing world.[26] In this sense, the 'radical potential' of RCTs in development and peacebuilding is that these studies have become part and parcel of development while at the same time challenging and overturning conventional 'common sense' development practices. The 'randomistas' claim to offer an approach to development policy which is 'evidence-based', which engages with the 'realities' of 'the field' in order to inform policy with evidence of 'what actually works'. They find that doing so means confronting the problems of development through the micro, particular, contextual and local lenses provided by randomized controlled methodologies. Banerjee and Duflo contend that this approach reflects a 'shift in perspective from INSTITUTIONS in capital letters to institutions in lower case – the "view from below" '.[27]

Seen in this light, the political economy driving proliferation of RCT-based practices places a premium on data that upsets the conventional wisdom and guiding assumptions of peacebuilding and development orthodoxy. In other words, the political currency of the 'randomistas' is disruptive data. In this political economy of disruptive data, revealing that a conventional and 'common sense' peacebuilding intervention has zero-impact can translate into significant political impact. Likewise, findings which demonstrate that unconventional interventions can have positive impacts may also be politically significant. Attempting to explain this political economy, Sandefur pointed to an RCT conducted by Banerjee and Duflo that evaluated micro-lending programs in India that 'made a huge splash' *because* it was a zero-impact outcome.[28]

> [An] enormous industry in development is predicated on the idea that the group lending, micro-finance model works and changes the world and lifts poverty. And there was lots of qualitative evidence and a deep belief this was really effective, so finding a non-result was worth spending a lot of money on research.[29]

While disruptive data is valuable in this political economy, the CJA program and legal empowerment are not as politically popular or as entrenched as micro-lending. The experimental nature of the program meant that the survey team had no reliable way to estimate what the program's potential impact could be. This proved to be an exacerbating factor that increased the gap between community-level survey design and individual-level impact that the intervention was actually registering. According to Siddiqi,

> The objective was access to justice broadly speaking, [for] communities rather than [for] particular kinds of individuals. So the program [was designed], rather naively, assuming that community-level impact was the objective; community-level impact was what

the program was designed around and that community-level impact was what we were going to test for. So all of our results assumed that enough people would have been impacted by the presence of these paralegals in order to create a community-level impact.[30]

Reflecting on the disjuncture between the community-level survey design and the individual-level impacts the CJAs were actually having, Sandefur noted that 'in retrospect, our evaluation design was probably more fragile than we realized at the time to really robust implementation and high take-up rates. And that fragility got exposed by basically the opposite happening.'[31] To this point, Tom Crick of TCC agreed, concluding that 'we ended up being overly guided by the randomization without enough common sense going into it.'[32] However, from TCC's perspective, the CJA program had opened 1,868 new cases as of March 2011 – an impact which was indeed significantly less than zero in qualitative terms. As Crick explained, 'my conclusion was that the instrument being used to determine the presence of the CJAs in the communities was much too sophisticated, to put it one way, or just wasn't the right tool because we had cases from all of the places but the survey found there was no knowledge of the CJAs.'[33] Therefore the CSAE survey team, in collaboration with TCC and the JPC, needed to find a way to capture the individual-level impact that the program was registering.

Performance: Designing the lightning round

The community-level design of the RCT was simply the wrong tool to use for detecting the individual impacts that CJA practices were actually generating. Based on TCC's internal monitoring and evaluation processes and their case file data, it was clear that the CJA program was having a substantial impact, despite the methodological threshold and design of the RCT. Both TCC and the CSAE survey team were eager to avoid a zero-impact evaluation because such an outcome would not reflect the actual impact the program was making at the individual level. Therefore, the original community-level survey had to be substantially modified in order to capture the individual-level impacts and to generate politically useful, policy-relevant data. To capture the impacts on *treated individuals* (individuals who opened a case with the CLA), the team would have to develop *an entirely new individual-level randomized controlled trial*. This new individual-level RCT was called the *Lightning Round*.

Designing the Lightning Round survey

The Lightning Round (LR) was a radical overhaul of the original community-level RCT and was designed to capture the individual-level impact of the CJA program. To this end, the LR had two objectives: to generate many *new* cases as quickly as possible, and then to expeditiously move these new cases through to resolution. However, the LR design would also have to adhere to the basic methodological framework of an RCT. Therefore, the LR entailed an entirely new individual-level baseline survey, an entirely new process of individual randomization, new individual treatment and control groups, a new treatment period and a new end-line survey specifically designed to compare treatment and control individuals against the community-level data. In order to get through the constraints of the evaluation design, Siddiqi and Sandefur found room to maneuver *within* this community-level survey structure in a way which was methodologically consistent with the original RCT design. Therefore the original community-level end-line survey was postponed for three months in order to implement the LR. During the intervening three-month period, the CJAs would focus on opening new LR cases, treating LR clients and resolving only LR cases.

In its total scope, the LR called for opening and closing 600 *new* cases (See Figure 8.1). Considering that in the 28 months of its existence, the mobile CJA program generated a total of 1,868 cases; opening 600 new cases was an ambitious target. In fact, 600 new cases represented nearly one-third of the program's total cases over two-and-a-half years. Due to the narrow three-month treatment window, the survey team proposed creating LR teams consisting of a CJA and a survey enumerator. Because of their training and existing practical understanding of legal empowerment, the CJAs were made responsible for opening new cases, managing the case intake process and following the case through to resolution. Meanwhile, the enumerators were responsible for managing the technical aspect of the survey. These 600 new LR cases were divided among 14 teams with each team responsible for opening 44 new cases. In accordance with the RCT methodology, each of these 44 cases had to be randomized and separated into approximately 22 treatment cases and 22 control cases. Given that each team was assigned six LR communities, they were required to open an average of eight new cases per community – four treatment cases and four control cases.

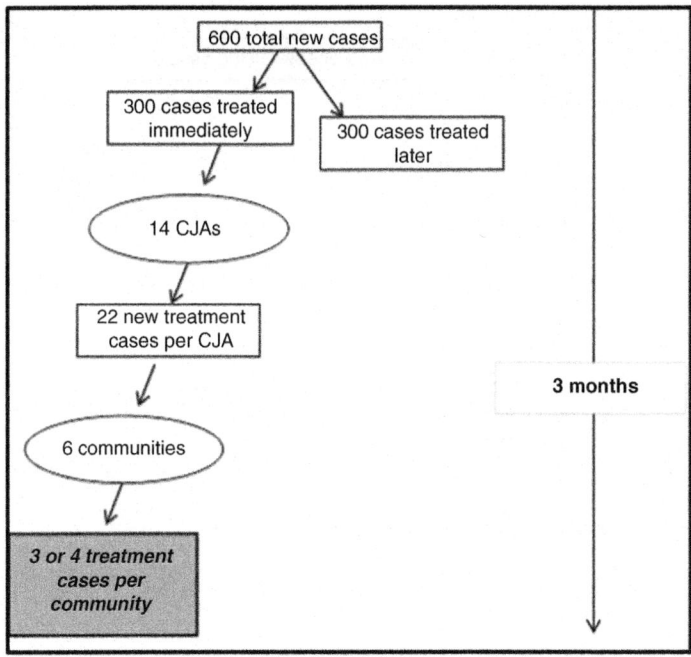

Figure 8.1 The Lighting Round survey design
Source: CSAE Survey Team: Lightning Round Proposal.

The LR entailed two phases: the first phase focused on opening new cases and randomly assigning them into treatment and control groups while the second phase focused on resolving the treatment cases. The key to the first phase was the awareness-raising session. During the session, the CJA and enumerators worked as a team to identify community members whose questions revealed a legitimate dispute. Once the team generated a pool of eight or more community members with legitimate disputes, the CJA then conducted brief screening interviews with the potential clients to determine the merits of each case. If a case had merit,[34] and if the potential client requested the CJAs assistance in resolving that dispute, then the enumerator was directed to administer a short case intake survey on their PDA (see Figure 8.2).

The 'case intake survey' simultaneously functioned as a baseline survey for the LR; it established a baseline reading for all individual LR clients before their cases were 'treated' by the CJAs. The baseline survey

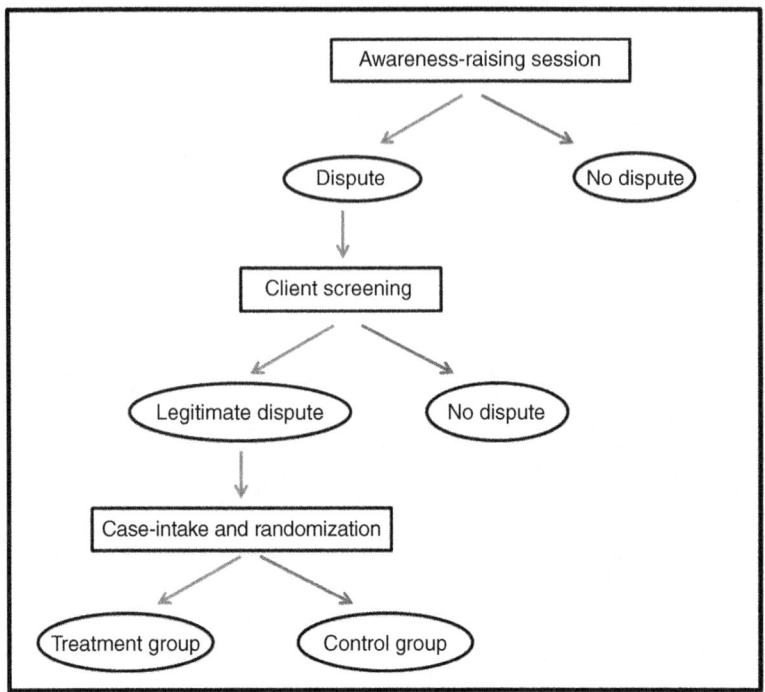

Figure 8.2 The Lighting Round process

assessed the material condition of each individual who opened a LR case with the CJA. The final step of phase one was randomization. Instead of randomizing at the *community* level, the LR cases were randomized at the *individual* level; the LR was designed to compare treatment individuals to control individuals. As the enumerator administered the baseline case-intake survey on the PDA, each case was *individually* randomized according to a preprogramed algorithm, assigning cases to treatment or control groups. This step determined which of the new LR cases would be 'treated' immediately and which would be assigned to the control group.

The second phase of the LR constituted the bulk of its three-month duration and focused entirely on resolving the new treatment cases. For phase two, the CJAs ceased taking new cases for the remainder of the LR and focused entirely on resolving their new treatment cases. The reasoning for allocating time in this way was to create sufficient space for the CJAs to manage their LR cases through to resolution.

During the second phase, the enumerators were no longer required (although they would return at the end of the three-month period to conduct the end-line). In phase two, CJAs were left alone to manage their new cases through to resolution. For three months the 'treatment' group would be treated and the 'control' group would not. After the three-month period, an end-line survey would be administered, both treatment and control *individuals* could be compared and the impact of the LR could be assessed at the individual level. Structured this way, the LR was designed as a self-contained, stand-alone RCT. The 'case intake survey' simultaneously functioned as a baseline survey for the LR. From these cases, the respondents were randomly assigned to entirely new treatment or control groups. The LR was then reincorporated into the broader community-level end-line survey.

By redesigning the survey in this way Siddiqi and Sandefur increased the range of practices under evaluation. Recalling the motivations behind the LR, Sandefur explained that it created a 'slightly more artificial environment [in which we could] focus in on actual cases that came to the CLAs'.[35] In this artificial environment, the LR created enough space for the CSAE to test their hypothesis: that under certain conditions, a legal empowerment intervention can generate concrete improvements in key material well-being indicators. In order to test their hypothesis, Siddiqi and Sandefur were able to work around the methodological constraints of the community-level survey by creating an entirely new individual-level RCT within the existing community-level structure. However, in order to generate the 600 new cases required by the LR design, the CJAs' approach to legal empowerment also had to be modified. The low uptake of CJA services reflected in the piloting exercise indicated that the indirect legal empowerment approach emphasized in the CJA training was insufficient. Therefore, the survey team began experimenting with a more direct approach to legal empowerment. In this sense, the LR then became a piloting exercise for an entirely new range of practices and techniques which, if they could demonstrate impact, could contribute to the formulation of future legal empowerment policy.

Conclusion

RCTs are the gold standard in determining which interventions generate impacts and which do not and are therefore increasingly important in determining which types of interventions received funding and which do not.[36] In this sense, RCTs represent a useful technology for perfecting intervention strategies and extending state power. However, they can also be practiced in ways that disrupt the liberal ideology reflected in conventional peacebuilding interventions and create new spaces for emancipatory local politics. The absence of detectable impacts in the CJAs' communities exposed a disjuncture between their indirect legal empowerment practices reinforced in their training and the RCT designed to measure their impact. The CSAE survey team anticipated that after two years of practising legal empowerment in their communities, the impacts of the CJA intervention would spillover into the general community, lifting the overall level of economic well-being. Based on these assumptions, the RCT was designed as a community-level impact evaluation – it would determine the impact of the CJA program by comparing treatment communities to the control communities. But the initial round of piloting indicated that the CJA program had generated no detectable impacts in their communities.

The hypothesis that Siddiqi and Sandefur were testing was whether an unconventional and inexpensive legal aid model like the CJA program could lead to decrease in key development indicators like infant mortality. Establishing such a connection could have significant political impact; it would raise questions about conventional liberal peacebuilding interventions and could potentially change how legal aid practitioners think about and design interventions in the future. Their hypothesis reflected the high value of disruptive data. In this emerging political economy, studies that establish positive impacts from unconventional interventions[37] and those that find zero-impact from conventional interventions are politically valuable.[38] But finding no impact from an unconventional intervention like the CJA program would have very little political value precisely because it was experimental and outside the mainstream. In order to salvage some politically impactful data, the CSAE survey team designed the LR, an entirely new RCT to measure the individual-level impacts the program was actually generating. However, the methodological constraints of the LR's RCT-based structure required a high volume of new cases (600) in a relatively short period of time (three months). This was an ambitious target and called for a more active legal empowerment approach.

The individual-level LR survey exposes the complex relationship between power and emancipation in the emerging post-liberal world. The discontinuity between the community-level survey design and the individual-level impacts of the CJAs' indirect performance reveals the fragility of powerful peacebuilding and development technologies and their susceptibility to appropriation. Yet it also highlights how powerful international practices like RCTs can be co-opted and performed in ways that pose challenges for peacebuilding orthodoxy and create political space for contenting visions of peace and emancipation. But challenging how international power is organized must not be confused with emancipation. The CSAE survey team also co-opted the CJA program and ascribed their own meaning to their practices including translating 'legal empowerment' into quantifiable economic impact.

9
Translating Legal Empowerment into Political Impact

The CJAs' indirect legal empowerment practices were not generating impacts on a scale such that they could be detected in a random sample of the treatment communities. The community-level structure of the RCT relied on robust and active implementation in order to generate large-scale impacts. However the CJA's indirect legal empowerment practices took the project in a different direction than the one anticipated when the survey was designed. The result was a mismatch between the community-level design of the RCT, on the one hand, and the indirect legal empowerment practices the CJAs were trained to perform, on the other. Following the first round of piloting, Siddiqi and Sandefur were concerned that a zero-impact assessment would hold little political value given the experimental and unconventional nature of the CJA program. From their perspective, a zero-impact assessment would only indicate that the CJA program had not been properly implemented; it would provide no politically valuable data about *why* the program had no impact and what the impact *could have been* had it been implemented more robustly.[1]

After the first round of piloting, the CSAE survey team's political situation shifted. The emerging strategy was to ensure that if there was a zero-impact outcome, it would generate as much academic and policy-relevant data as possible. The LR was an attempt to generate such politically useful data. It called for 600 new cases to be opened and closed within a narrow three-month period. However, given that the CJA program had opened approximately 1,800 cases over a two-and-a-half-year duration, the LR represented an ambitious undertaking. In order to generate and resolve 600 new cases within three months, the survey team had to first determine the reason for the low recognition and low uptake of the CJA and their services. To this end, the survey team conducted a second round of piloting. Going beyond simply increasing the sample size, the second round of piloting involved some additional components: understanding the reasons for the low uptake, identifying any impediments or obstacles which might be preventing community members from opening cases with the CJA and determining how the CJAs' legal empowerment practices could be adjusted in a way that would generate more cases and greater impacts.

Problematization: Indirect legal empowerment

The second round of piloting covered three counties, and eight communities that were serviced by four different CJAs. It entailed both quantitative and qualitative components and was designed to determine why the CJAs were not registering community-level impacts and how they could have greater impacts. The CSAE survey team therefore fielded a 'Quick Assessment Survey' (QAS) which was administered to 363 people (200 women and 163 men), 44 of whom were clients. It revealed that the general level of the JPC and CJA recognition in the community (79 percent) was actually higher than the first round indicated. The QAS probed the interviewee's contacts and interactions with the CJA: Had they heard of the CJA? Had they attended an awareness-raising session? Did they have a dispute, and if so, what was preventing them from seeking out the CJA's services? The QAS data found that of the 79 percent of the community members who had heard of the JPC, only 49 percent attended an awareness-raising session. The QAS also revealed that of those community members who did attend the awareness-raising sessions, only 17 percent actually approached the CJA with legitimate disputes. In other words, the majority of the attendees at the sessions simply were not opening cases.

However, the data also provided some indications of why this was the case. Of the attendees who did have a dispute but did not approach the CJA for assistance, 17 percent said they did not know how to approach the CJA, and 8 percent said they were unaware of what the CJA could do for them. The team reasoned that the attending community members were simply unaware of what to do with the information provided at the awareness-raising session. Lastly, the second round of piloting focused on those community members who did open cases with the CJA. The goal was to assess case follow-up and case closure among existing clients in order to identify any potential blockages. Of all the cases that had ever been opened only 55 percent had been resolved. Following the second round of piloting, the survey team's focus shifted toward understanding how the CJAs' legal empowerment practices could be adjusted to overcome these obstacles and generate the ambitious LR target of 600 new cases in a relatively slim three-month window of time.

Flelah

The survey team identified the CJA who had opened and closed the most cases: Zayzay Sawie.[2] He had opened 169 cases and closed 145 of them, almost double the average rate. The team arranged to observe him giving an awareness-raising session in his community Flelah to determine how he was able to open and close so many cases. Prior to the session, the team found that he frequently used a megaphone to notify and mobilize the community in advance of his awareness-raising sessions. The session was attended by two survey enumerators whose job was to track attendance levels (which peaked at 40 people) and transcribe the awareness-raising session (conducted in the regional Kpelle dialect). Their goal was to identify which attendees were asking questions, what those questions were and to determine whether these questions indicated that the attendee had a legitimate dispute and represented a potential new case. If a potential case was revealed during the discussion, then the enumerator would pass that information on to the CJA for a follow-up after the session.

The awareness-raising session was hosted in a large, dark community room just outside the town center. The topic was domestic violence. During the session, Sawie spoke about women's rights under formal law as well as the illegality and consequences of domestic violence. Enacting his legal empowerment training, he then spoke of the deleterious effects of domestic violence on the community and the household, which he defined very broadly to include economic and psychological violence. The session generated a significant number of questions from the audience. One woman self-identified as never having attended an awareness-raising session before. Her hair was tousled, and her skin and dress were covered in dirt. An infant was pressed to her chest. She was weeping. A female community elder sitting next to me leaned over and made a punching gesture saying, 'every day she is beaten and her husband sends all their money to his other family in Sinoe.' The woman had been beaten that morning. Sawie suggested that he could help, but, distraught, the woman left the session.[3]

Following the session, Sawie was resistant to the suggestion that he follow up directly with her. She obviously had a dispute and Sawie was there to solve it. So why not follow up directly? Sawie cited his empowerment training, noting that the community member must seek out the CJAs' assistance in resolving their dispute; they must choose to open a case. Nevertheless, Sawie's approach generated four new cases, the most cases he has ever opened in a single day. However, the substantial attendance and the high number of questions indicated that there were many other unresolved disputes in the community. As the post-awareness-raising screening exercise revealed, this was indeed the case: there were a significant number of legitimate and unresolved disputes in the community that were not being taken to the CJA. For the survey team, these unresolved disputes represented potential LR cases.

Socopa

The survey team also arranged to meet with Teta Jalloh,[4] a high-performing CLA from Nimba County in her community, Socopa. She was scheduled to give an awareness-raising session on the topic of the criminal justice system. However, unlike Sawie's community, Socopa was an hour from Jalloh's home near Ganta. Jalloh was also the only other CJA who regularly used a megaphone for community mobilization. While en route to the community that morning, her megaphone was damaged while strapped to the back of the motorbike. However, she did manage to meet with the chief and enlisted his help in dispatching the town crier. But, despite the community being roughly equal in size, attendance was lower than at Flelah, with roughly 25 attendees coming and going during the session. While the questions were continuous and covered a wide range of disputes revealing many potential clients in the community, nobody approached Jalloh to follow up their question. No new cases were generated that day; indeed, only one case had ever been opened in that community. Jalloh regarded this as a typical awareness-raising session insofar as there were numerous questions ranging across legal topics and concerns, questions that indicated legitimate disputes, yet no one followed up with Jalloh to open a new case.[5]

Assessment

Both the quantitative and qualitative data from the second round of piloting confirmed the problems that had been flagged in the first round. Despite uncovering higher levels of CJA recognition, uptake of the CJAs' services remained too low to register impacts at the community level. However, the second round also supplied an additional layer of data that proved useful for understanding *why* uptake of JPC services was lower than expected: indirect legal empowerment. The indirect legal empowerment approach that was emphasized in their training prohibited the CJAs from actively soliciting cases. According to their training, new cases must be initiated by an informed and legally empowered individual or community. CJAs must be approached by a potential client who must then decide to open a case with the CJA. However, this simply was not happening at the rate necessary to improve child food security across entire communities. Therefore, after two rounds of piloting, it was determined that the zero-impact outcome reflected a mismatch between the CJAs' legal empowerment practices and the community-level survey design. On the one hand, the survey was designed to detect improvements to the material well-being in a random sample of the community. On the other, the CJAs' actual practices prioritized an indirect, circumspect, community-sensitive approach. This indirect approach to practicing legal empowerment had been inscribed into the CJA program by the JPC who was weary of the destabilizing effects that a more proactive posture to case generation may cause.[6]

Acknowledging the survey design flaws and their overestimation of service take-up, Siddiqi noted that from the methodological perspective of an RCT-based impact evaluation, the CJAs' priority should have been to open cases: 'The paralegals were actually fulfilling [many] roles but if their impact was supposed to come from taking cases then they should have just focused on that [...] in order to have a community-level impact. But they weren't allowed to solicit cases; they didn't see themselves as really doing that'.[7] In other words, the survey team was detecting the priorities that were emphasized in the CJAs' legal empowerment training. The CJAs' indirect legal empowerment practices simply did not prioritize generating transformative community-wide impacts. Instead, the indirect legal empowerment approach prohibited the CJAs from actively soliciting cases in order to respect the restorative justice practices vital to maintaining local legitimacy.

The CJA program was unsettled by a process of translation in which the *practice* of 'legal empowerment' became increasingly dislocated from its intended design. Pointing to this contingent process of *translation*, Siddiqi maintains that the CJA program and the survey were originally designed on the premise that opening and resolving individual cases would spill over into the community, gradually lifting the level of economic well-being in the community.[8] However, as Siddiqi indicates, the CJAs did not treat case intake and resolution as the single priority. Instead, case intake was treated as one among many practices; the CJAs treated awareness-raising and legal education as equal objectives rather than as an indirect or passive means to the intended end: increasing case intake.[9] Summarizing the nature of the problem,

Siddiqi explains that the evaluation 'set out to measure a set of indicators that we eventually realized the program was never geared to change. Or rather, it may have wanted to change them but as the design of the program *evolved* we realized it wasn't actually attempting to change them'.[10] The 'evolution' of the CJAs' legal empowerment practices reflected a series of *performative discontinuities* in which meaning of legal empowerment became unstable. Based on this assessment, the team began considering where programmatic improvements, modifications and adjustments could be made to the CJAs' legal empowerment practices that could quickly and cheaply produce some measurable impacts and, therefore, some politically useful data.

Appropriation: Active legal empowerment

The second round of piloting illuminates the reasons for the zero-impact indications. Again, the tension between the RCT-based design and the CJAs' legal empowerment practices was implicated. However, the second round of piloting also suggested that there were a number of unresolved disputes in the community which were not being registered with the CJA. The QAS indicated that community members with legitimate disputes did not know how the CJA could help them. To address this problem, the survey team began to consider the CJAs' practices as *a chain of interactions* between community members, who may potentially have a dispute that they would like resolved, and the CJA, whose job it is to help them do so (see Figure 9.1).

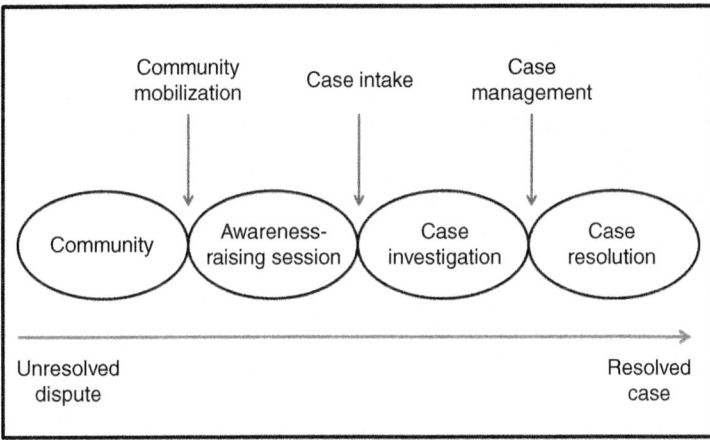

Figure 9.1 Weak links in the chain of client–CJA interaction (Created by Author)

The survey team identified four crucial points of interface separated by three weak links: (a) community mobilization: community members need to be aware of the JPC, their services and when and where they are holding awareness-raising sessions; (b) awareness-raising sessions: community members must be aware that they have a legitimate legal dispute and they must be aware that the CLA offers one avenue to resolve that dispute; (c) case intake: a client must choose to open a case with the CJA; and (d) case management and resolution: the ultimate objective. As the team arranged these four points of interface into a chain of interactions, the 'weak links' in the chain could be identified: community mobilization, case intake and case management. The survey team sought not only to identify these weak links, but to also overcome them by developing new practices to increase the CJAs' case load as dramatically as possible.

Community mobilization

The first programmatic impediment the team confronted was to ensure that as many community members as possible turned out for awareness-raising sessions. Clearly, in order to open a case with the CJA, a community member must first be aware of the services the CJAs provide and understand that they offer them a potential pathway for resolving their dispute. Awareness-raising sessions are the primary means for disseminating information about rights under the formal rule of law and function as important catalysts for generating new cases. If no one attends the awareness-raising session, there is a problem. Therefore, community mobilization – turning people out to the awareness-raising session – is a key moment of interface between the CJA and the wider community. The survey team determined that this aspect of the program was not receiving enough attention.

The LR strategy entailed a more active approach to mobilization. Interviews from the first round of piloting along with follow-up discussions indicated that for most CJAs the primary means of mobilization was the town crier, who was often deployed just prior to the commencement of the session. When the survey team found that Zayzay Sawie had an unusually high rate of case resolution, it turned out that he was only one of two CJAs using a megaphone to mobilize the community on a regular basis. The LR allotted sufficient time for the CJA and enumerator to conduct community mobilization both the night prior to the session and the morning of the session. This double-mobilization strategy entailed arriving the evening before the session, meeting the chief and introducing the project, spending the night in the community and then conducting a thorough mobilization early in the morning before the community departs for their farms. The CSAE equipped each LR team with a new megaphone and lights to use in mobilizing the community at night. The objective was to mobilize the community in such a way as to generate some excitement around the session the following day, thereby maximizing attendance at the awareness-raising session.

Case intake

Despite an abundance of unresolved disputes in the communities, piloting indicated that they were not being converted into cases. The CJAs were not following up with community members whose questions suggested that they had a legitimate dispute. Attendees were asking questions that revealed legitimate legal disputes and the CJA were providing them with legal information about their dispute and their rights under the law. But this interaction did not result in the community member opening a case with the CJA. The following excerpt from the LR proposal points to this 'weak link' in the chain.

> some of those who asked questions seemed satisfied simply by the fact that a CJA had answered their question, but did not seem inclined to take follow-up action. In one instance, a question was raised about inheritance, to which the [CJA] responded that the participant was entitled to recourse. The participant did not, however, follow up this case with the [CJA who] seemed to be under the impression that they should neither actively encourage participants in awareness-raising sessions to come to them with cases, nor follow up on disputes raised by participants during the awareness session. While registering a case with the [CJA] should be the client's prerogative, a more active encouragement or follow-up of cases raised could greatly raise impact and catch the relatively large number of cases that fall through the cracks due to lack of understanding or communication between participants and the [CJA].[11]

This finding suggested to the survey team that case intake was a fundamental weakness at a crucial moment of interface. Therefore, the survey team suggested a more active strategy for case intake during the LR, one that permitted the CJAs to follow up directly with potential clients after an awareness-raising session. As the CJAs conducted their session – facilitating a discussion, taking questions and providing answers – the enumerators would be responsible for tracking the questions from the audience, identifying which questions revealed legitimate disputes, and collecting details about those disputes. During the awareness-raising session, the CJA and enumerator work as a team to ensure that the enumerator recorded the community member's name and some detail about the dispute. Upon concluding the awareness-raising session, the CJA was instructed to reiterate who they are and what they do: 'we are from the JPC, we are here to assist you people resolve your disputes for free.' The CJA would then direct attendees toward the enumerator should they wish to register their dispute and open a case. In another departure from their indirect legal empowerment practices, the CJAs were instructed to use the data collected by the enumerator during the session to follow up directly with any attendees who did not open a new case, but whose question during the Q&A revealed a potential case. The CJA was directed to approach the attendee after the session, offer their assistance a final time and provide them an opportunity to register their dispute.

Case management

The third and final programmatic impediment was case management. Once a CJA did open a case, they often did not have the time to diligently manage it through to resolution. In follow-up interviews, the CJAs identified several problems in the program design that were preventing more expeditious case resolution. These issues had to do with the program's schedule. The CJAs were each assigned ten communities that they were required to visit twice a month. The program requires that a CJA spends 21 days per month out in their communities. Often, the distance between the communities was significant, sometimes requiring hours of travel by motorbike and additional walking. It emerged that the majority of the CJAs' time was spent in transit between their communities. Furthermore, while in their communities, the CJAs were required to maintain a regular schedule of awareness-raising sessions, alternating topics with each visit. The heavy emphasis on awareness took time away from client follow-ups and case management. On the days when they were not required to be in their communities, their time was spent managing their administrative demands for the month. As a result, open and unresolved cases were, at best, undercutting broader community-level recognition, and, at worst, undermining the CJA's credibility in the community. Therefore, it was determined that the CJAs' high workload was prohibitive.

Based on this assessment, the survey team determined that the CJAs' range of obligations, number of communities, field schedules, administrative tasks and the amount of time spent in transit between

> **Text Box A: The Lighting Round Schedule**
>
> The lightning round will consist of 14 teams of CJAs, CSOs, and enumerators who will each focus on 6 communities. Communities will be chosen in a way so as to minimize travel time and maximize time spent with clients. CJAs, supported by CSOs and enumerators, will visit these communities in 3-day increments (staying in each community for approximately 48 hours) according to the following schedule
>
> - Day 1: enter the community in the evening to conduct mobilization and follow-up existing cases.
> - Day 2: conduct morning mobilization, carry out awareness-raising session, take in new cases and take steps to resolve these, and follow-up existing cases.
> - Day 3: work on existing cases, including those taken in the previous day, exit the community in the afternoon.
>
> After the first week of activity, awareness raising may be eliminated from the schedule so that CJAs can focus only on case follow-up and resolution. During this time, CJAs can still take on new cases should they be approached by people with problems.
> This schedule is a guideline that should be generally adhered to in order to maximize activities of the lightning round. However, it can be altered in those instances where it is necessary to do so for the purposes of case intake, follow-up, resolution.

Figure 9.2 The Lightning Round schedule (CSAE Survey Team; Lightning Round Proposal)

communities were detracting them from the their ability to manage cases through to conclusion. Therefore, the LR strategy reduced the number of communities assigned to each CJAs from ten to six communities. The criteria for this selection were the community's demonstrated history of opening cases with the CJA and the community's proximity to the CJA's home. The narrow three-month LR window demanded a more intense daily pace so the CJA's work schedule was completely overhauled (see Figure 9.2). Each team would visit a new community every three days (or 48 hours). This pace would allow the teams to cover three communities per week (no work on Sundays). At the rate of three communities per week, the team could cover all six of their LR communities in the first two weeks. The rationale behind this intense initial scheduling was to create space for a two-phased approach to the LR. While phase one focused on case intake for the initial two weeks, phase two emphasized case management and resolution for the remaining two and a half months of the LR.

However, TCC raised some concerns. First, they wanted to ensure that the CJAs had time to wrap up any pending cases that were close to a resolution. They were also concerned about reducing the LR treatment communities from ten to six and therefore delayed launch for a week so that pending cases in the remaining four communities could be closed or passed to the stationary and lead CJAs. Finally, they wanted to ensure that there was a 'serious-case clause' built into the individual randomization which would allow serious cases such as rape, murder or other violent crime to go directly into the 'treatment' group. After those concerns were addressed, TCC gave CSAE the green light.

Performance: Generating politically impactful data

In the experimental environment created within the LR, the CSAE wanted to evaluate how a legal empowerment intervention *could* be organized and practiced in a way that would deliver the kinds of economic improvements that would be politically significant. The goal was to generate politically useful data – to determine whether a more proactive approach to practicing legal empowerment could generate greater impacts. To this end, the LR brought the CSAE survey team into a more active role; essentially, the CSAE assumed programmatic control of the CJA program. The rationale behind this approach was to minimize the degrees of institutional and organization separation between the program designers and the program practitioners. This approach required the CSAE survey team to assume an active role in designing and implementing a new field schedule, purchasing new equipment for the CJAs, rearranging the communities on the schedule and overseeing daily operations throughout the three-month duration of the LR. In order to generate politically useful data, the LR adopted a more active approach to legal empowerment relative to the approach reflected in the CJAs' training. This experimental approach reversed the relationship between the CJAs' legal empowerment practices and the RCT designed to measure them. Rather than designing the RCT to evaluate the impact of the CJAs' indirect legal empowerment practices, the CJAs' legal empowerment practices were redesigned in order to generate politically impactful data.

Lightning round findings

The LR generated a total of 443 new cases (249 treatment/194 control) out of a target of 667. It generated 66 percent of the new cases the LR was designed to randomize. Each team averaged 5.3 new cases per community with an average of 30–35 community members attending awareness-raising sessions. As discussed in Chapter 6, the original community-level baseline survey also revealed the types of disputes that were prevalent in Liberian communities: family disputes (child and martial) constituted approximately 16 percent of community disputes; economic disputes, such as land titling, debt, wages and theft, totaled approximately 58 percent; violent disputes, such as assaults, rapes and murders, constituted 15 percent; meanwhile a remaining 10 percent of disputes fell into other disparate categories. Compared to the original baseline findings, the LR revealed *five* politically impactful findings.

The first finding concerned the demand for service. The LR suggested that there was a high demand for CJA services among groups that are disadvantaged within customary system (women, ethnic minorities, subsistence farmers and migrants). For these clients, particularly females, the findings suggested that 'the impacts are distributed in favor of those whose rights are most limited under customary law'.[12] However, for these traditionally disadvantaged groups, there was 'no evidence of any difference in the average respondent's relationship with the community' as a result of seeking the CJA's assistance, meaning that they suffered no social consequences for seeking CJA assistance.[13] For the survey team, finding a high level of demand among these groups suggested that 'legal aid not only provides an attractive alternative to going directly to the formal sector, but also increases the number of reported disputes by providing an outlet for grievances that otherwise would have gone nowhere.'[14]

The second LR finding pertains to the subjective experience of working with the CJA. On this mark, treated individuals reported greater satisfaction with justice outcomes than control individuals. The data indicated that individuals who received CJA assistance 'were overall much happier' with the outcome of the case. Treated individuals considered the CJA service to be fairer and more just than those whose options were limited to either customary or statutory justice. The third politically significant finding revealed an increase in legal knowledge and familiarity with statutory law.[15] Treated individuals demonstrated a significant increase in their knowledge of the formal legal system as a result of their interactions with the CJA. This gain in legal knowledge was correlated with statistically significant decrease in bribes paid by treated individuals. In other words, after registering cases with the CJA, community members were willing to use their new legal knowledge to avoid paying extra-legal bribes often levied by customary and statutory justice practitioners. Fourth, the LR indicated statistically significant improvements in treated individuals' economic situations; it found 'significant downstream impacts on household wellbeing – in particular, on three measures: household food security, child food security, and proportion of households with single mothers receiving child support payments from absentee fathers'.[16] This finding confirmed the original hypothesis: that under certain conditions, an unorthodox legal empowerment intervention can deliver significant improvements in the material well-being where more conventional approaches have failed.

However, the fifth area of findings indicated that despite the politically significant impacts discussed above, there was no change in the underlying attitudes and associated behaviors. In other words, there was no indication that the CJA program was changing how treated individual and communities conduct their everyday affairs. For the survey team, it was 'somewhat striking that there is absolutely no hint of an impact on any of these measures, suggesting by implication that any downstream impacts on household wellbeing do not come from changes in attitudes, credit market behavior, or greater security of property'.[17] In this sense, the CJA program and the LR had not altered the underlying justice norms or perceptions in Liberian communities but was working at the edges. Taken together, the LR generated some politically useful data. According to Siddiqi and Sandefur's reading,

> Overall, we interpret these results as preliminary evidence that legal empowerment interventions aimed at improving access to justice and reviving dead letter laws can produce large socioeconomic benefits. Moreover, our results suggest that these gains can be achieved not by bringing the rural poor into the formal domain of magistrates' courts, government offices, and police stations, but by bringing the formal law into the organizational forms of the custom, through low-cost third-party mediation and advocacy.[18]

By implication, these findings suggest that politically significant impacts can be generated by embracing a post-liberal understanding of justice, one which is neither customary nor statutory but un-foreclosed and emergent. These findings correspond to a number of recent international justice surveys that have shown alternative, local and customary justice practices to be essential to peace and security in Liberia. For example, the International Development Law Organization published a study related to customary land rights in Liberia, Mozambique and Uganda.[19] This survey found that customary land titling processes are more effective than formal mechanisms and that their customary capacities should be utilized in the peacebuilding process. Chris Blattman's work in Liberia is entirely focused on managing RCT in the field. He finds that after modest Alternative Dispute Resolution training 'land disputes are resolved at higher rates, less violently, and with more satisfactory outcomes, especially longstanding land disputes'.[20] Taken together, these RCTs are chipping away at the liberal claim to a monopoly on peacebuilding and development practices.

Following the LR, a number of changes were made to the design of the CJA program as well as to its legal empowerment practices. Freed from the rigid treatment-control design constraints of the RCT, the CJAs acquired more independent discretion in selecting the communities where they operated. The CJAs were able to select communities based on travel time and cost, how well they worked in that community in the past, proximity to regional and county justice centers, access to justice actors and courts and familiarity with the community culture, custom and dialect. Rather than having their mobility, schedule and communities determined by the RCT, the mobile CJAs were integrated into the existing stationary office-based program, a change which enabled the CJAs to be more flexible in how they allocated their time and energy.

Additionally, the CJA's role was diversified to provide oversight and monitoring of the statutory justice system. Rather than being exclusively focused on interventions in rural communities, the CJA program began intervening in the statutory justice system. In this role, the CJAs increasingly monitor actors in the formal system, keeping a 'scorecard' on how accountable these formal justice actors are to their mandate and the law. The CJAs' legal empowerment services were also extended into new counties. USAID and Humanity United funded an expansion of the CJA program into Grand Bassa County, increasing the number of CJAs in the field from 34 to 44. Service was also extended into Montserrado County, where Monrovia is located. This expansion introduced the CJAs into underserved and densely populated urban areas, where the lines between customary or formal law are less pronounced. Many of these changes would have otherwise been undertaken long before had the program not been locked into the RCT-based design.[21] These changes to the CJA program highlight the continued transformation and retranslation of 'legal empowerment' and demonstrate how new justice practices and difference practitioners are taking active roles in shaping how justice is practiced in the emerging post-liberal peace in Liberia.

Conclusion

The LR highlights the problematic and complicated relationship between power and emancipation in the emerging post-liberal world. It shows how a peacebuilding project – organized to contest the liberal monopoly on peace and create legitimate political space for restorative customary justice practices – can simultaneously become an exercise in post-liberal international power. After finding zero-impact at the community level, the CSAE modified the survey structure and designed the LR to capture the individual-level impacts the CJAs were having. The LR called for 600 new cases within a three-month period – nearly one third of the 1,800 cases the program had generated over its two-and-a-half-year duration. To generate such a high volume of cases in such a short period of time the CSAE survey team advocated for a more proactive approach to case follow-up. The survey team pointed out that the CJA program 'evolved', as the JPC had appropriated its legal empowerment practices, limiting how active the CJA could be, and ascribing a more restorative approach than the transformative one envisioned when the project was designed. Therefore, the survey team scripted a more active legal empowerment practice for the LR, one that was designed to maximize impact and generate politically useful data. It called on the CJAs to follow up directly with community members who have a legitimate dispute rather than waiting to be approached. In this way, the CSAE survey team recaptured the CJA program; its legal empowerment practices were again co-opted by the methodological demands for the RCT. Rather than being an instrument designed to evaluate the impact of a legal empowerment project, the legal empowerment project was appropriated by the impact evaluation.

The LR reveals how peacebuilding can be appropriated by practitioners with different political agendas.[22] On the one hand, the LR data will be folded back into the repertoire of statebuilding technologies and can be used to design evermore effective neo-liberal economic interventions. Yet, on the other hand, the LR also poses problems for the liberal monopoly on justice in Liberia. It demonstrates that a legal empowerment intervention can improve economic well-being for those who seek help and weakens the liberal claim to a monopoly on justice, creating post-liberal political space for new justice practices and different justice practitioners. Furthermore, the LR had no transformative effects on the broader community and caused no change in the underlying justice perceptions or preferences for customary justice. Despite the proactive legal empowerment practices of the LR, its impact was made at the edges of customary justice in Liberia where community members could appropriate its practices and make their own justice decisions. The LR exposes how susceptible peacebuilding interventions are to being co-opted and also reveals the fragility of international statebuilding power and the limits of its technologies.

Conclusion

The process of designing, implementing and evaluating the CJA program exposes the complicated relationship between power and emancipation in the emerging post-liberal world. The concept of hybridity was introduced to the PCS literature in order to make sense of the overwhelming complexity of post-conflict peacebuilding interventions. In PCS, hybridity signifies a complex and unstable relationship of political alterity between local actors, institutions and practices, on the one hand, and the liberal international peacebuilding interventions designed to 'develop' them, on the other. The result is liberal–local hybridity: a process generated by the political tensions between the exercise of liberal international power and expressions of emancipatory local agency. While liberal–local hybridity captures the overarching dynamic at play in complex peacebuilding environments, it also conceals a problematic paradox: liberal–local hybridity is likely to reproduce the existing relationship between power and emancipation rather than expose the practices that transform it. This book set out to unsettle the axiomatic relationship between internationality and power and challenge the assumed connection between localness and emancipation that lies at the heart of the hybrid paradox in PCS.

The recent post-liberal turn in critical PCS has laid the foundation for moving beyond the liberal–local paradox. Chandler calls for a methodological orientation that emphasizes international policy-practices. Such an approach, he argues, enables researchers to understand statebuilding governmentality in its own terms rather than imposing reductive binaries and universal theories.[1] Richmond's post-liberal approach adopts a materialist orientation similar to Chandler's practice-turn. Rather than imposing a reductive liberal–local binary, Richmond suggests exploring peacebuilding as it emerges in everyday practices unfolding in sites.[2] While Chandler and Richmond's post-liberal approaches reflect a similar emergent materialism, they come to very different conclusions about the emerging post-liberal world.[3] For Chandler, post-liberalism represents the end of classical liberalism's emancipatory vision. Instead of protecting political autonomy and rights, post-liberalism is a form of international governmentality that treats local political autonomy as a problem to be overcome through statebuilding interventions. Post-liberal statebuilding is a bio-political strategy that acts upon the social milieu in order to indirectly cultivate social conditions that encourage economic subjectivity. Yet for Richmond, post-liberalism represents a process of emancipation *from* the statebuilding governmentality described by Chandler. According to Richmond, post-liberalism represents an emancipatory process of peace formation anchored in transversal and transnational local–local networks that seek to create political space for a pluralistic peace, one that includes local customs and practices and advances local peace epistemologies.[4]

Chandler and Richmond hold very different views about the emerging post-liberal world, yet both views were reflected in the process of implementing the CJA program in Liberia. International governmentality is implicated in the CJAs' legal empowerment practices. CJAs were trained to practice legal empowerment in a way that would allow them to discretely unsettle customary justice practices while simultaneously cultivating a sense of liberal legal and political subjectivity. The RCT reduced the political impacts of legal empowerment to economic well-being, providing international peacebuilding practitioners with the data to develop more effective intervention strategies. The emancipatory politics of peace formation also appears in the CJA program. Legal empowerment is part of an emerging network of international and local justice practitioners challenging the liberal monopoly on peace and justice in Liberia and creating political space of local peace epistemologies rooted in postcolonial everyday life. In this view, the use of an RCT was an essential part of creating the post-liberal political situation necessary to legitimize customary justice practices and practitioners. The complex process of designing, implementing and evaluating the CJA program highlights how power and emancipation are often bundled together as part of the same performance. As the post-liberal world continues to take shape, the limits of power remain unsettled, and the meaning of emancipation is at stake. A practice-based approach enables researches to expose the unfolding debate about what power and emancipation are becoming in the emerging post-liberal world.

A practice-based approach

The practice-based approach advanced over the previous pages adopted Chandler and Richmond's shared materialist emphasis and sought to contribute to the ongoing development of an emergent post-liberal ontology of peacebuilding practice. However, the practice-based approach adopted here goes further by challenging the international–local binary that circumscribes the relationship between power and emancipation in emerging hybrid processes. There are always two overlapping but unsettled aspects of hybridity: difference and transformation.[5] Liberal–local hybridity emphasizes the politics of difference and establishes a relationship of alterity between international and local entities. By emphasizing the politics of difference, the transformative aspects of hybridity are reduced to a secondary effect, an outcome generated by the tension between international power and emancipatory local agency.

A practice-based exploration of hybridity rests on an emergent ontology. Contrary to emphasizing the politics of difference in order to explain complex hybrid processes, a practice-based exploration of hybridity emphasizes the politics of transformation. By emphasizing the transformative aspects of hybridity, the politics of difference become ontologically unstable, a secondary phenomenon subject to the fluctuating performance of emergent peacebuilding practices.[6] Although the politics of difference remains a central aspect of emergent hybridity, the primary ontological tension at play is a temporal tension. A practice-based reading of hybridity explores the emergent pressures that cut across the liberal–local boundary and continually transform the politics of difference into the politics of becoming different. Emergent hybridity is defined here as the contested transformation of difference.

The ontologically precarious temporal relationship between the liberal peace and the emerging post-liberal world must be continually managed. This process is organized through peacebuilding practices. While peacebuilding interventions may reflect liberal ideology and Western cultural norms, these abstractions must be ultimately translated into and organized through various practices. Practices are the organized but unstable conduit for meaning; the continuity of culture, norms and ideas depend on the contingent performance of organized practices.[7] Practices are therefore material; they are the material manifestation and expression of 'peacebuilding' that unfolds in sites as an embodied performance. Like a theatrical performance, it is scripted and directed; the movement of its actors is organized and purposeful and is shaped by what a shared (and often contested) understanding of 'good acting' should be.

Peacebuilding is often organized through individual projects that are organized for specific purposes. Peacebuilding projects are designed to solve some perceived problem, to resolve an issue, to bring about some change and are therefore political projects.[8] They are constrained by budgets, schedules, codes of conduct, professional ethics and are dependent on the relative capacity of their participants to perform the tasks a project specifies. In order to manage the tension between the project's constraints and its objectives, peacebuilding projects synthesize these crosscutting demands by establishing a hierarchy of tasks and assigning them a relative priority. Projects single out what is to be done, identify goals and specify how to reach those goals. While peacebuilding projects are organized, they are not determinant. Just as a theatrical performance is purposefully scripted, it relies on the actor to embody the script, to enact its purposeful activities and to creatively translate the meaning or the essence of the play into a performance.

When subjected to an unstable emergent tension, the continuity between how a practice is organized and how it is performed is always uncertain. An organized peacebuilding project must be translated into a practice by practitioners. Translations take place on the ground as practitioners attempt to bring about the objectives specified in their project in sites where those objectives may be contested.[9] In this unstable political situation, peacebuilding practitioners must improvise and develop creative ways to manifest the goals that the project is designed to bring about. A translation can therefore be understood as a constrained innovation, an organized performance. Understood in such a way, a translation reflects the unstable emergent tension described above. They expose the uncertain continuity between the way a peacebuilding project is designed and how it is performed by peacebuilding practitioners. These translations are expressed as performative discontinuities – points at which practitioners change how a project is organized and transform how its practices are performed, imposing a new meaning upon them, and possibly establishing a new or different way of practicing.

In order to expose the performative discontinuities that emerged in the process of launching the CJA program, the process of translation was broken down into *four* overlapping and interrelated aspects.[10] First, a translation involves *problematization*. This refers to how practitioners establish what is at issue, what needs to be addressed and what needs to change. Problematizing may involve destabilizing the existing pattern of practices and creating a political situation in which new and different practices become possible. Second, a translation is an *appropriation*. When practitioners appropriate a given practice, they ascribe their own meaning to the project and impose their own political situation onto its practices. An appropriation takes a project in a different direction, for different political purposes and through difference practices. The third aspect of a translation is *performance*: a performance is the materially embodied expression of an appropriation. It introduces a new practice, a different way of organizing projects. This leads to the fourth aspect of a translation: *re-problematization*. This dimension speaks to the emergent tension in translations. New performances may lead to new problems. They may change the political situation and require new and different practices. When these translations are stretched out over the early life of a peacebuilding project like the CJA program, they reveal a series of performative discontinuities in which various participants captured and retranslated the project's legal empowerment practices. These performative discontinuities add up to an emergent process of post-liberal hybridity in which the terms and limits of peace are always at stake.

The community justice adviser program

There are two justice systems in Liberia. The peacebuilding strategy there outlines a vision of harmonization, a process in which customary justice practices would be incorporated under and subjected to the statutory laws of the state. Liberia's harmonization policy largely reflected the liberal claim to a monopoly on the legitimate practice of justice. The prevailing view within the statutory legal establishment in Monrovia and among their international supporters was that customary justice was antithetical to the goals of liberal peacebuilding.[11] Liberia's peacebuilding strategy embraced the assumption that statutory justice would be preferred by Liberians if they could access it. However, the liberal claim was challenged by an ICG report in 2006.[12] It revealed that most Liberians were deeply suspicious of statutory justice and that the customary system enjoyed far greater local legitimacy than previously thought. The report made the case that Liberia's justice strategy must incorporate customary actor and practices. The ICG report created a post-liberal political situation in Liberia where the liberal monopoly on justice became unstable and different justice approaches became possible solutions. In this context TCC was approached by the Minster of Justice to develop new justice programing which could help bridge the gaps between formal and customary justice systems. However, the

Liberian legal establishment and their international supporters were resistant to the idea of increasing the political role of customary justice practitioners and believed that legitimizing customary practices was counterproductive to the liberal peacebuilding objective of establishing the rule of law. The CJA program took shape in this politically contested post-liberal situation.

Translation point A: From statutory justice to legal empowerment

The ICG report revealed that the legal establishment's claim to a justice monopoly was far from legitimate. But national peacebuilding strategy favored harmonizing customary justice within the statutory law of the state. TCC had to *problematize* the statutory legal monopoly and create some post-liberal political space for new justice practices and practitioners. Part of this process involved enrolling both customary and international justice practitioners. TCC enrolled the National Traditional Council (NTC) and established them as part of the process of negotiating the future of justice in Liberia. The JPC is also a vital local partner for TCC. As a local Catholic NGO, the JPC maintains a network of churches, schools and parish offices that enable TCC to have a national reach as well as providing them with local legitimacy. Meanwhile TCC also reached out to a number of international justice practitioners such as the USIP. Two development economists from Oxford's CSAE were also enrolled. These practitioners were part of a budding post-liberal network of justice practitioners with a shared stake in reimaging what justice means in the peacebuilding and development community and how justice-related interventions should be organized. Working together, these local and international justice practitioners developed the CJA program.

The CJA program reflects how this post-liberal network *appropriated* justice in Liberia; they co-opted its liberal practices, ascribing them a post-liberal meaning, one which was more inclusive of customary justice and restorative norms and values. The CJA program incorporates the principles of legal pluralism. The legal pluralists are critical of the liberal monopoly on justice and argue that international peacebuilding and development organizations must embrace a broader ontology of justice. Legal pluralism is a political movement among international justice practitioners that highlights a post-liberal controversy about the status of justice in the emerging post-liberal world. Advocates of legal pluralism hold that international organizations must prioritize the function of justice over its institutional form;[13] they maintain that justice interventions must be rooted in local justice practices rather than a priori top-down liberal approaches.[14] The CJA program incorporates the principles of legal pluralism and organizes them into a flexible legal empowerment intervention which is neither statutory nor customary but draws on both systems opportunistically in order to meet the justice needs of a client.

However, the principles of legal empowerment had to be translated into a legal empowerment intervention. This translation was *performed* in consultation with the USIP and the CSAE survey team who fielded the L4J report in 2009.[15] The USIP report confirmed the previous findings but went on to outline the reasons why Liberians prefer customary justice: The statutory system was too expensive for most Liberians; it was too bureaucratic, too unaccountable, too procedural and impersonal. More importantly however, the USIP report indicated that the formal justice system simply did not reflect the restorative justice values of customary Liberian community life. Yet within the overwhelmingly negative view of statutory justice in Liberian communities, the USIP report also found that women, ethnic minorities and the poor were disadvantaged by the customary system and would prefer another justice option. The USIP report concluded that the attempt to extend the formal justice system of the Liberian state into rural communities was having an *adverse* effect on Liberia's peace and security.[16]

These findings cut against the assumptions guiding orthodox peacebuilding and development practices; they ran contrary to the prevailing justice-sector reform project being undertaken in Liberia and challenged the justice monopoly claimed by the Liberian legal establishment. This point of translation discloses how practices associated with 'the liberal peace' can be used in creative ways that challenge the entrenched top-down, formal justice practices associated with 'the liberal peace' and create room for new justice practitioners and different justice practices. In this way, the USIP report created a post-liberal political situation in which customary justice became an indispensable aspect of Liberia's emerging justice strategy. This translation reveals controversies within the international community about what justice amounts to in the post-liberal world, how it should be practiced and who should be authorized to practice it. These controversies cut across the international–local divide and extend to the communities where the limits of customary justice are also debated.

Translation point B: From a paralegal program to indirect legal empowerment

The USIP report created the post-liberal political condition for new justice practitioners like the CJAs. But it also functioned as the baseline survey in a broader two-year RCT that would evaluate the impact of the CJA program. The RCT was designed to measure economic impacts at the community level. It was designed on the assumption that the CJAs' legal empowerment practices would spill over into economic impact that could be more easily quantified. In this way, the need to generate impact was at the center of the CJA program. However, the negative perception of statutory law and human rights held by the rural population suggested to TCC that the need to generate impacts had to be weighed carefully against the need to maintain local legitimacy in their communities. This balancing act compelled TCC to look for the legal empowerment model that was both impactful and sensitive to restorative customary justice practices. Timap was the only paralegal-based empowerment model that existed. Although Timap upheld the client's needs over those of either justice system, it was not a perfect fit for Liberia. TCC had to *problematize* how Timap was organized and retranslate its legal empowerment practices, reorganizing them as the CJA program. Timap was a small, local NGO that was designed from scratch by its cofounders who then assumed direct administrative control over paralegals. Formal litigation was at the center of Timap's strategy. They did not use a local implementing partner nor was the program organized within the framework of an RCT. As Timap was translated into the CJA program, the need to establish and maintain local legitimacy over the long-term became a high priority. TCC was not equipped to directly administer such an intervention, so they enrolled the JPC as a local implementing partner. The JPC offered the CJA program a national network and the necessary local legitimacy in rural communities.

As the JPC was incorporated and became the organization responsible for implementing the project, they *appropriated* the CJA program; they captured its legal empowerment practices and assumed ownership of its political meaning. While the JPC works through the extensive Catholic network in rural Liberia, it is a local NGO, staffed by local Liberians who grew up in local communities and are familiar with the customary justice practices that circulate in there. As such, the JPC raised concerns about the potentially disruptive consequences of an aggressive legal empowerment approach that prioritized case generation and economic impact.[17] The director of the JPC office in Cape Palmas drew nuanced distinctions between the positive and negative aspects of customary justice while pointing out how the punitive, adversarial justice practices of statutory justice upset the restorative justice ethic practiced by the customary system, turning neighbor against neighbor.[18] Therefore, the

JPC advocated for a less disruptive and more subtle legal empowerment performance.

The CJAs were trained to *perform* an indirect form of legal empowerment. Their training prohibited them from directly soliciting cases from community members. Instead, they were trained to use the awareness-raising session and legal education as a way to gradually soften the community, to build trust and rapport and to create a post-liberal political situation in which community members would feel empowered to approach the CJA for assistance in resolving their disputes. This elevated the importance of awareness-raising as the crucial means through which the CJAs could have any impact. This indirect legal empowerment strategy was designed to passively shape the social conditions so that different justice practices would become political possibilities in Liberian communities.

The JPC's translation of legal empowerment exposes the disjuncture between the design and the performance of a peacebuilding project. The JPC's influence on the CJA program reveals how susceptible peacebuilding projects are to being co-opted and transformed into new practices and performed to bring about different objectives. This translation also discloses the fragile continuity of international 'power' and by extension shows how exercises of power and expressions of emancipatory agency are often part of the same emergent continuum. The JPC exerted 'power' through the CJA program while also imposing their own emancipatory meaning upon its legal empowerment practices, scripting an indirect performance. However, the indirect, passive legal empowerment practice advocated by the JPC was in tension with the RCT-based structure of the program that depended on a proactive direct use of legal empowerment to generate impacts.

Translation point C: From legal empowerment to economic impact

In order to determine the impact of the CJA program, the CSAE survey team had to conduct and end-line survey. According to the RCT-based survey structure, data from the end-line would be compared to the baseline data collected during the USIP survey and the impact of CJA program could be determined. Yet the CJA intervention was new and somewhat experimental, its legal empowerment practices had never been evaluated using an RCT and so there was no way to estimate its potential impact. Given the untested and experimental nature of the CJA program, the survey team wanted to first pilot the end-line survey in order to determine whether the CJAs were having the anticipated community-level impact.

The first round of piloting indicated zero impact in a random sample of the community. This required the CSAE survey team to *problematize* the community-level structure of the survey and salvage some politically useful data from the CJA program. The CSAE survey team designed the RCT on the assumption that the effects from the CJA program would spill over into the broader community. The community-level survey design defined 'impact' largely through economic proxies – improvements in certain key indicators of material and economic well-being such as household income, school enrollment and child food security. Generating economic impact at the community level depended on an active, direct and robust approach to practicing legal empowerment in order to produce spillover effects that could be detected in a random sample of the community. Nevertheless, the piloting exercise also indicated that the CJAs were having an impact at the *individual level* among those community members who did open a case with the CJAs. Hence, the CSAE survey team set out to capture these individual-level impacts.

The zero-impact evaluation reflected how the CSAE *appropriated* the CJA program. It exposes how the survey team ascribed their own meaning to the CJA program and imposed their own political situation on its legal empowerment practices. As Siddiqi and Sandefur of the CSAE were enrolled into the CJA program, they incorporated its legal empowerment practices into the framework of an RCT. They saw legal empowerment as a potentially transformative approach that could change how legal aid and justice interventions are organized in post-conflict and development settings. The hypothesis they were testing was whether an unconventional legal aid intervention like the CJA program improve mainstream development indicators. If they could establish such a connection, it would be a politically valuable finding. However, because it was new and unorthodox, a zero-impact finding for the CJA program would have little political value. In order to recapture some politically valuable data, the CSAE had to re-appropriate the CJA program and reconfigure the survey design to capture the individual-level impact that the JPC was actually producing.

The CSAE *performed* a translation that converted the community-level RCT into an individual-level RCT called the Lightning Round (LR). The LR included a new individual baseline survey, an individual-level randomization process, a new three-month treatment period and an individual-level end-line that could be reincorporated into the original community-level RCT. The methodological constraints of the RCT required a large sample size so the LR called for the CJAs to open 600 new cases and then resolve half of them within a narrow three-month period of time. This was an ambitious target that required a more direct legal empowerment practice.

This point of translation highlights the adaptability of peacebuilding. The zero-impact outcome and the compensatory LR reveal the reductive practices of packaging peacebuilding interventions into RCTs. It demonstrates how local Liberians and their everyday disputes can become instruments of knowledge production. This process exposes how the emancipatory political aspirations often channeled through peace and justice-related interventions can be captured by the authority of quantitative data and drawn toward the development priorities of large donor organizations. However, the relationship between the CJA program and the RCT also points to how this data can be used in ways that pose problems for the liberal monopoly on peace and justice. In this way, this translation point uncovers the emerging political economy of data. The RCT was designed to determine whether an unorthodox intervention like the CJA program could improve economic well-being more effectively and at a lower cost than conventional legal aid interventions. Establishing such a connection would be politically valuable precisely because it would contradict conventional peacebuilding and development orthodoxy. While instrumentalizing, the 'gold-standard' authority that has been bestowed to RCTs can also be disruptive to established liberal peacebuilding dogma and can create post-liberal political space for new peacebuilding practices and practitioners.

Translation point D: From indirect legal empowerment to active legal empowerment

The zero-impact findings revealed in the first round of piloting exposed a gap between the community-level survey design and the CJAs' indirect legal empowerment practices. The RCT-based framework depended on large community-level impacts but the CJAs were prohibited from proactively soliciting cases in order to maintain good relations in their communities. Yet, the JPC's indirect legal empowerment approach was having impact at the individual level. The LR survey was an attempt to capture these individual-level impacts and generate some politically valuable data. But the methodological constraints of the RCT required the CJAs to generate a large amount of new cases (600) within a narrow three-month timeframe. This meant that the CJAs had to abandon their indirect approach and become far more active in opening cases in their communities.

The CSAE survey team organized a second round of piloting in order to *problematize* the CJAs' indirect practices; the team wanted to determine why the program was not generating greater impacts and identify any weak links in their performance. The second round of piloting highlighted what were determined to be 'weak links' in the CJAs' performances. These so-called weak links included the lack of time and equipment necessary to properly mobilize the community in advance of an awareness-raising session. Community members also indicated that they were unaware of how the CJA could help them and how to approach them for help, suggesting that the CJAs were not communicating their services effectively. Most significantly, the second round of piloting indicated that the CJAs were not following up with community members who had a dispute and instead emphasized the awareness-raising sessions as their most impactful practice. Based on these observations, the survey team concluded that the indirect legal empowerment practice reinforced in the CJA training was part of the reason behind the zero-impact findings. This argument created a political situation in which a more active approach became necessary.

The structure of the LR called on the CJAs to generate 600 new cases and therefore required a more active legal empowerment performance. During the LR, The CSAE *appropriated* the CJA program, assumed direct control over the program's daily operations and designed a more active legal empowerment performance, one that would generate politically valuable data. The so-called weak links were strengthened and the CJAs' interactions in their communities were more tightly scheduled and scripted. The CJAs were provided with a megaphone and paired with an enumerator from the survey team to help actively mobilize the community and increase attendance at the awareness-raising sessions. The LR also cleared the way for CJAs to proactively and directly follow up with community members who disclosed a legitimate dispute during the awareness-raising session. Lastly, the LR set aside a sufficient amount of time for case management and resolution.

The active legal empowerment approach *performed* during the LR generated the impacts it was designed to produce. The LR found improvements in child food security and household income as well as increases in statutory legal knowledge. Although its duration was limited, the LR improvements did not change the underlying attitudes and behaviors in the community. Instead these individual-level impacts indicated how community members made their own calculations about legal empowerment, how they determined the CJAs' legal empowerment practices could be useful and appropriated the CJA's services accordingly.

These findings suggested that the CJA program was not transforming community life and displacing customary justice but was having an impact at the edges of the customary system as a third justice option.

This translation point exposes the complicated relationship between the exercise of power and expressions of emancipatory agency in the emergent post-liberal world. Echoing the quantitative instrumentalism uncovered in the previous translation, the active legal empowerment approach developed for the LR demonstrates how peacebuilding projects can be appropriated, how their practices become captured and their political objectives become transformed into something different. The LR represented a significant intervention into the daily operations of a peacebuilding program. Rather than using RCTs to assess the impact of the CJA program, the CJA program was being used to generate politically useful data that could be detected by the RCT. On the one hand, the LR exposes how peacebuilding interventions designed to problematize the liberal monopoly on justice can be re-appropriated in order to perfect neo-liberal, post-liberal statebuilding interventions.[19] On the other hand, it also uncovers a consequential debate within and across the various networks of international peacebuilding about what peace and justice mean in the emerging post-liberal world.[20]

Mapping the emerging post-liberal world

These points of translation add up to a process of emergent hybridity. The process of designing, implementing and evaluating the CJA program was not an outcome generated between liberal international power and emancipatory local agency but instead was an emergent phenomenon in which the limits of power and emancipation in Liberia were at stake. When subjected to this uncertain emergent tension of post-liberal becoming, the discontinuities between how the CJA program was designed and how it was performed can be revealed. These performative discontinuities disclose how new and different justice practices emerged in these unsettled temporal disjunctures. Through this process of emergent hybridity the difference between internationality and localness that circumscribe the complex relationship between demonstrations of power and expressions of emancipatory agency became unstable. The unstable process of emergent hybridity exposed an unsettled and ongoing debate that cuts across the differences between internationality and localness and is concerned about what peace and justice are becoming in the post-liberal world, how they should be practiced and who is authorized to practice them.

Conclusion 163

The emergent hybrid process that unfolded in the course of the CJA program also highlights a debate within critical PCS about the relationship between power and emancipation in the post-liberal world. Is the CJA program a demonstration of post-liberal international governmentality as Chandler would suggest? Or does it represent an emancipatory process of peace formation and the increasing pluralization of peace and justice as Richmond suggests?[21] The CJA program illustrates how power and emancipation are part of the same complicated and unstable emergent continuum of post-liberal becoming. Demonstrations of international power may create post-liberal political space for new practices and different practitioners thereby destabilizing how international power circulates and transforms what 'the international' amounts to. From this emergent view, expressions of emancipatory agency may also be assertions of power, appropriating peacebuilding practices, translating them into a new performance and organizing different ways of performing 'emancipation'. However, change must not be confused with emancipation. As the CJA program demonstrates, new and emancipatory practices can re-appropriated, their emancipatory claims captured and transformed into another emancipatory claim. In this way, emancipation can reemerge as a different regime of practices, stabilizing new injustices and asymmetries.

To avoid reproducing another manifestation of liberal–local hybridity where the relationship between power and emancipation has already been determined, the practice-based approach presented above enables a methodological turn in critical PCS and International Relations. The point of departure for a critical methodological orientation follows John Law's assertion that 'if we want to understand the mechanics of power and organization, it is important not to start out assuming whatever we wish to explain.'[22] Rather than drawing from theories of power in order to explain and understand how power circulates, a methodological investigation would trace power as it emerges in and through peacebuilding practice. A critical methodological orientation allows a move away from epistemologies of difference and toward a practice of mapping the ontological process of becoming different.

Such a methodological orientation provides International Relations and PCS with a pathway around the epistemological boundaries that reproduce the global–local binary. By prioritizing methodology over theory, established epistemologies can be explored as the objects of critique rather than the means of critique. A post-liberal methodological approach would require different research practices. Rather than developing concepts to explain how power circulates, a methodological practice would be concerned with developing *methodological strategies* for identifying and tracing the contingent post-liberal dynamics that transgresses the theoretical limitations projected onto them. This is not a historical, deconstructive or genealogical task. What is required is a methodological practice for assembling a living genealogy of the emerging present. A post-liberal methodological project of mapping peacebuilding practices requires new arrangements and combinations of methodological tools and techniques. As post-liberal methodology must be attentive to the many often subtle, but sometimes, dramatic changes that emerge through the proactive, creative, improvised and ad hoc labor of practitioners performing peacebuilding in new and different ways in and across multiplicities of sites. A post-liberal account of peacebuilding practices therefore adopts the task of charting the discontinuities that emerge as peacebuilding practitioners traverse through and between sites establishing new connections.

By mapping the performative discontinuities that emerged in the course of designing and implementing the CJA program, a post-liberal process of hybridity was revealed. In Liberia, this process emerged as a debate about what justice is, how it should be practiced and who should be authorized to practice it. This process has created a post-liberal political situation in Liberia where customary justice practices and practitioners have become an indispensable aspect of the peacebuilding strategy. The implications of this process carry over into international peacebuilding and development practices where an emerging network of post-liberal justice practitioners are actively disputing how peacebuilding and development interventions should be organized and are challenging the kind of peace they are organized to bring about.

Notes

Introduction

1. See, for example, Volker Boege et al., 'On Hybrid Political Orders and Emerging States: State Formation in the Context of "Fragility"' (Berghof Research Center for Constructive Conflict Management, 2008), http://www.berghof-handbook.net/documents/publications/dialogue8_boegeetal_lead.pdf; Roger Mac Ginty, *International Peacebuilding and Local Resistance: Hybrid Forms of Peace* (New York: Palgrave Macmillan, 2011); Oliver Richmond and Audra Mitchell, eds, *Hybrid Forms of Peace: From Everyday Agency to Post-Liberalism* (Houndmills, Basingstoke, Hampshire; New York: Palgrave Macmillan, 2012); Roger Mac Ginty and Gurchathen Sanghera, 'Hybridity in Peacebuilding and Development: An Introduction,' *Journal of Peacebuilding & Development* 7, no. 2 (August 2012): 3–8, doi:10.1080/15423166.2012.742800.
2. Mac Ginty, *International Peacebuilding and Local Resistance*, 77.
3. Jenny H. Peterson, 'A Conceptual Unpacking of Hybridity: Accounting for Notions of Power, Politics and Progress in Analyses of Aid-Driven Interfaces,' *Journal of Peacebuilding & Development* 7, no. 2 (August 2012): 9–22, doi:10.1080/15423166.2012.742802; John Heathershaw, 'The Practical Representation of Peacebuilding: An (Auto) Ethnography of Programme Evaluation in Tajikistan,' in *Hybrid Forms of Peace: From Everyday Agency to Post-Liberalism*, Rethinking Peace and Conflict Studies (New York: Palgrave Macmillan, 2012); Patrick Tom, 'In Search for Emancipatory Hybridity: The Case of Post-War Sierra Leone,' *Peacebuilding* 1, no. 2 (June 2013): 239–255, doi:10.1080/21647259.2013.783256; Oliver Richmond, 'The Dilemmas of a Hybrid Peace: Negative or Positive?,' *Cooperation and Conflict*, 12 June 2014, doi:10.1177/0010836714537053.
4. Mac Ginty, *International Peacebuilding and Local Resistance*, 77.
5. Roger Mac Ginty, 'Indicators+: A Proposal for Everyday Peace Indicators,' *Evaluation and Program Planning* 36, no. 1 (February 2013): 56–63, doi:10.1016/j.evalprogplan.2012.07.001.
6. Roger Mac Ginty and Oliver P. Richmond, 'The Local Turn in Peace Building: A Critical Agenda for Peace,' *Third World Quarterly* 34, no. 5 (June 2013): 763–783, doi:10.1080/01436597.2013.800750.
7. Bruno Latour, 'The Politics of Explanation: An Alternative,' in *Knowledge and Reflexivity: New Frontiers in the Sociology of Knowledge*, ed. Steve Woolgar (University of Minnesota: Sage Publications Ltd, 1988).
8. David Chandler, *International Statebuilding: The Rise of Post-Liberal Governance*, Critical Issues in Global Politics 2 (London; New York: Routledge, 2010).
9. Ibid., 13.
10. Richmond and Mitchell, *Hybrid Forms of Peace*, 12.

11. Oliver Richmond, 'Failed Statebuilding versus Peace Formation,' *Cooperation and Conflict* 48, no. 3 (26 July 2013): 389, doi:10.1177/0010836713482816.
12. Oliver Richmond, 'A Post-Liberal Peace: Eirenism and the Everyday,' *Review of International Studies* 35, no. 03 (6 July 2009): 572, doi:10.1017/S0260210509008651.
13. Ibid., 570.
14. David Chandler and Oliver Richmond, 'Contesting Post-Liberalism: Governmentality or Emancipation?' *Journal of International Relations and Development* (2014).
15. William E. Connolly, *A World of Becoming* (Durham, NC: Duke University Press, 2010).
16. Homi K. Bhabha, *The Location of Culture*, 2nd ed. (Abingdon, Oxon.: Routledge, 2004), 263.
17. Connolly, *A World of Becoming*; see also Diana H. Coole and Samantha Frost, *New Materialisms: Ontology, Agency, and Politics* (Durham, NC; London: Duke University Press, 2010).
18. Mark B. Salter, 'Introduction,' in *Research Methods in Critical Security Studies: An Introduction*, ed. Mark B. Salter and Can E. Mutlu (Abingdon, Oxon.: Routledge, 2013), 2.
19. Theodore R. Schatzki, *The Site of the Social: A Philosophical Account of the Constitution of Social Life and Change* (University Park: Pennsylvania State University Press, 2002), xi; Janice B. Mattern, 'A Practice Theory of Emotions for International Relations,' in *International Practices*, ed. Emanuel Adler and Vincent Pouliot (New York: Cambridge University Press, 2011), 70–71.
20. Schatzki, *The Site of the Social*, 71–72.
21. Madeleine Akrich, 'The De-Scription of Technical Objects,' in *Shaping Technology/Building Society: Studies in Technical Change*, ed. Weibe E. Bijker and John Law (London: MIT press, 1992), 205–224.
22. Michel Callon, 'Some Elements of a Sociology of Translation: Domestication of the Scallops and Fisherman of St. Brieuc Bay,' in *Power, Action, and Belief: A New Sociology of Knowledge*, ed. John Law (London: Routlage & Kegan Paul, 1986), https://bscw.uni-wuppertal.de/pub/nj_bscw.cgi/d8022008/Callon_SociologyTranslation.pdf; Bruno Latour, 'The Powers of Association,' in *Power, Action, and Belief: A New Sociology of Knowledge*, ed. John Law (Routledge, Kegan Paul, 1987), http://www.bruno-latour.fr/sites/default/files/19-POWERS-ASSOCIATIONS-GBpdf.pdf; John Law, 'Traduction/Trahison: Notes on ANT' (Department of Sociology, Lancaster University, 1997), http://www.lancaster.ac.uk/sociology/stslaw2.html
23. Raymond Caldwell, 'Reclaiming Agency, Recovering Change? An Exploration of the Practice Theory of Theodore Schatzki,' *Journal for the Theory of Social Behaviour* 42, no. 3 (September 2012): 283–303, doi:10.1111/j.1468-5914.2012.00490.x.
24. Richard Freeman, 'What Is "Translation"?' *Evidence & Policy: A Journal of Research, Debate and Practice* 5, no. 4 (1 November 2009): 433, doi:10.1332/174426409X478770.
25. Chandler, *International Statebuilding*; see also Michel Foucault, *Security, Territory, Population: Lectures at the Collège De France, 1977–78*, ed. François Ewald and Alessandro Fontana, trans. Michel Senellart (New York: Picador, 2007).

26. Oliver Richmond, *A Post-Liberal Peace*, Routledge Studies in Peace and Conflict Resolution (Milton Park, Abingdon, Oxon [England]; New York: Routledge, 2011); James C Scott, *The Art of Not Being Governed: An Anarchist History of Upland Southeast Asia* (New Haven: Yale University Press, 2009).
27. Bruno Latour, *Reassembling the Social: An Introduction to Actor-Network Theory* (New York: Oxford University Press, 2004).
28. Peterson, 'A Conceptual Unpacking of Hybridity.'
29. Richmond and Mitchell, *Hybrid Forms of Peace*, 21.
30. Stephen Golub, *Beyond Rule of Law Orthodoxy: The Legal Empowerment Alternative*, Working Paper, Rule of Law Series: Democracy and Law Project (Washington, DC: Carnegie Endowment of International Peace, October 2003), http://siteresources.worldbank.org/INTLAWJUSTINST/Resources/BeyondRuleOrthodoxy.pdf
31. Caroline Sage and Michael Woolcock, 'Breaking Legal Inequality Traps: New Approaches to Building Justice Systems for the Poor in Developing Countries,' in *Inclusive States: Social Policy and Structural Inequalities*, ed. Anis Dani and Arjan de Haan (Washington, D.C.: The World Bank, 2008), 369–394.
32. Brian Z. Tamanaha, 'A Non-Essentialist Version of Legal Empowerment,' *Journal of Law and Society* 27, no. 2 (June 2000): 296–321.
33. U.S. Department of Education, *Identifying and Implementing Educational Practices Supported by Rigorous Evidence: A User Friendly Guide* (Washington, D.C.: U.S. Department of Education and the Council of Excellence in Government, December 2003), http://www2.ed.gov/rschstat/research/pubs/rigorousevid/rigorousevid.pdf; Nancy Cartwright, 'Are RCTs the Gold Standard?' *BioSocieties* 2, no. 1 (March 2007): 11–20, doi:10.1017/S1745855207005029.
34. Bilal Siddiqi is an economist at the World Bank's Development Research Group. His research focuses on micro-institutions, formal and informal legal systems, peacebuilding and state accountability in post-conflict settings. He is currently involved in several field experiments in Sierra Leone and Liberia related to public health and community-based paralegal programs. Justin Sandefur is a research fellow at the Center for Global Development. His research focuses on the interface of law and development in sub-Saharan Africa. From 2008 to 2010, he served as an adviser to the Tanzanian government to set up the country's National Panel Survey to monitor poverty dynamics and agricultural production. He has also worked on a project with the Kenyan Ministry of Education to bring rigorous impact evaluation into the Ministry's policymaking process by scaling up proven small-scale reforms.
35. Foucault, *Security, Territory, Population*.
36. Pierre Bourdieu, *The Logic of Practice* (Stanford: Stanford University Press, 1990).
37. Emanuel Adler and Vincent Pouliot, 'International Practices: Introduction and Framework,' in *International Practices*, ed. Emanuel Adler and Vincent Pouliot (New York: Cambridge University Press, 2011).
38. Schatzki, *The Site of the Social*.
39. Latour, 'The Powers of Association'; Callon, 'Some Elements of a Sociology of Translation: Domestication of the Scallops and Fisherman of St. Brieuc Bay.'

1 A Genealogy of Hybridity in Peace and Conflict Studies

1. Michel Foucault, *Power/Knowledge: Selected Interviews and Other Writings, 1972–1977* (Brighton, Sussex: Harvester Press, 1980).
2. Neil Cooper, 'Review Article: On the Crisis of the Liberal Peace', *Conflict, Security & Development* 7, no. 4 (December 2007): 605–616, doi:10.1080/14678800701693025.
3. David Chandler, *International Statebuilding: The Rise of Post-Liberal Governance*, Critical Issues in Global Politics 2 (London: New York: Routledge, 2010); Oliver Richmond, *A Post-Liberal Peace*, Routledge Studies in Peace and Conflict Resolution (Milton Park, Abingdon, Oxon [England]; New York: Routledge, 2011); David Chandler and Oliver Richmond, 'Contesting Postliberalism: Governmentality or Emancipation?', *Journal of International Relations and Development*, 27 June 2014, doi:10.1057/jird.2014.5.
4. Chester A. Crocker, 'Southern African Peace-Making', *Survival* 32, no. 3 (1990): 223.
5. Boutros Ghali B., 'An Agenda for Peace Preventive Diplomacy, Peacemaking and Peace-Keeping A/47/277 – S/24111' (United Nations, 1992), http://www.unrol.org/files/A_47_277.pdf; Boutros Ghali B., 'An Agenda for Development: Report for the Secretary General (A/48/935)' (United Nations, 6 May 1994), http://www.un.org/Docs/SG/agdev.html
6. See for example Robert Keohane, *After Hegemony: Cooperation and Discord in the World Political Economy* (Princeton, NJ: Princeton University Press, 1984); Michael W. Doyle, 'Liberalism and World Politics', *The American Political Science Review* 80, no. 4 (1 December 1986): 1151–1169, doi:10.2307/1960861; Jack Levy S., 'Domestic Politics in War', in *The Origin and Prevention of Major Wars*, ed. Rotberg I. Robert and Rabb K. Theodore (New York: Cambridge University Press, 1989); Larry Diamond, 'Promoting Democracy', *Foreign Policy*, no. 87 (Summer 1992): 25–46; John R. Oneal and Bruce Russett, *Triangulating Peace: Democracy, Interdependence, and International Organizations*, 1st ed. (W. W. Norton & Company, 2001).
7. Cooper, 'Review Article'.
8. Edward Newman, 'Liberal Peacebuilding Debates', in *New Perspectives on Liberal Peacebuilding* (Tokyo; New York: United Nations University Press, 2009), 38.
9. Jarat Chopra, 'Introducing Peace-Maintenance', in *The Politics of Peace-Maintenance*, ed. Jarat Chopra (Boulder, CO: Lynne Rienner Publishers, 1998), 10.
10. Ibid., 8 emphasis added.
11. Stephen D. Krasner, 'Sharing Sovereignty: New Institutions for Collapsed and Failing States', *International Security* 29, no. 2 (October 2004): 119, doi:10.1162/0162288042879940.
12. Roland Paris, *At War's End Building Peace After Civil Conflict*, Reprinted (Cambridge [u.a.]: Cambridge University Press, 2005), 7.
13. Ibid., 179.
14. Clement E. Adibe, 'Accepting External Authority in Peace-Maintenance', in *The Politics of Peace-Maintenance*, ed. Jarat Chopra (Boulder, CO: Lynne Rienner Publishers, 1998), 113.
15. Mark Duffield, *Global Governance and the New Wars: The Merging of Development and Security*, 1.udg. ed. (London: Zed, 2001), 11.

16. Ibid., 194.
17. Simon Maxwell, *The Washington Consensus Is Dead! Long Live the Meta-Narrative!* (London: Overseas development institute (ODI), 2005), 3–9.
18. Michael Pugh, 'The Political Economy of Peacebuilding: A Critical Theory Perspective', *International Journal of Peace Studies* 10, no. 2 (Autumn/Winter 2005): 23–42; Michael C. Pugh, Neil Cooper and Mandy Turner, eds, *Whose Peace? Critical Perspectives on the Political Economy of Peacebuilding*, New Security Challenges Series (Basingstoke [England]; New York: Palgrave Macmillan, 2008).
19. Oliver Richmond, *The Transformation of Peace* (Basingstoke: Palgrave Macmillan, 2007), 204.
20. Shahrbanou Tadjbakhsh, ed., *Rethinking the Liberal Peace: External Models and Local Alternatives*, Cass Series on Peacekeeping (Abingdon, Oxon; New York: Routledge, 2011), 4.
21. Richmond, *The Transformation of Peace*, 215.
22. Gayatri Chakravorty Spivak, 'Can the Subaltern Speak?', in *Marxism and the Interpretation of Culture*, 1988, 271–315; Bhabha, *The Location of Culture*; James C. Scott, *Domination and the Arts of Resistance: Hidden Transcripts* (New Haven: Yale University Press, 1990); Scott, *The Art of Not Being Governed*.
23. Oliver Richmond, 'Resistance and the Post-Liberal Peace', *Millennium – Journal of International Studies* 38, no. 3 (10 May 2010): 669, doi:10.1177/0305829 810365017.
24. Roger Mac Ginty, 'Indigenous Peace-Making Versus the Liberal Peace', *Cooperation and Conflict* 43, no. 2 (1 June 2008): 140, doi:10.1177/001083670808 9080.
25. See for example Richard Fanthorpe, 'On the Limits of Liberal Peace: Chiefs and Democratic Decentralization in Post-War Sierra Leone', *African Affairs* 105, no. 418 (September 2005): 27–49, doi:10.1093/afraf/adi091.
26. Newman, 'Liberal Peacebuilding Debates', 46.
27. Ibid., 45.
28. Roland Paris, 'Saving Liberal Peacebuilding', *Review of International Studies* 36, no. 02 (23 April 2010): 338, doi:10.1017/S0260210510000057.
29. Ibid., 340.
30. Ibid., 359.
31. Roland Paris and Timothy D. Sisk, *The Dilemmas of Statebuilding: Confronting the Contradictions of Postwar Peace Operations*, Security and Governance Series (London; New York: Routledge, 2009), 14.
32. Ibid., 7.
33. Roberto Belloni, 'Civil Society in War-to-Democracy Transitions', in *From War to Democracy*, ed. Jarstad K. Anna. and Sisk Timothy (Cambridge University Press, 2008), 182.
34. Ibid., 208; see also Jens Narten, 'Dilemmas of Promoting "Local Ownership": The Case of Post-War Kosovo', in *The Dilemmas of Statebuilding: Confronting the Contradictions of Post-War Peace Operations*, ed. Roland Paris and Sisk Timothy (London; New York: Routledge, 2010).
35. Timothy Donais, 'Empowerment or Imposition? Dilemmas of Local Ownership in Post-Conflict Peacebuilding Processes', *Peace & Change* 34, no. 1 (January 2009): 14, doi:10.1111/j.1468-0130.2009.00531.x.
36. Mac Ginty and Richmond, 'The Local Turn in Peace Building', 772.

37. Kristoffer Lidén, 'Peace, Self-Governance and International Engagement: From Neo-Colonial to Post-Colonial Peacebuilding', in *Rethinking the Liberal Peace: External Model and Local Alternatives*, ed. Shahrbanou Tadjbakhsh (Abingdon, Oxon; New York: Routledge, 2011), 57–74; Oliver Richmond, 'Critical Agency, Resistance and a Post-Colonial Civil Society', *Cooperation and Conflict* 46, no. 4 (1 December 2011): 419–440, doi:10.1177/0010836711422416.
38. Bhabha, *The Location of Culture*, 274–275.
39. Anne Brown, Volker Boege, Kevin P. Clements, Anna Noland, 'Challenging Statebuilding as Peacebuilding: Working with Hybrid Political Orders to Build Peace', in *Palgrave Advances in Peacebuilding: Critical Developments and Approaches*, ed. Richmond (London: Palgrave Macmillan, 2010), 102.
40. Ibid.
41. Roger Mac Ginty, 'Hybrid Peace: The Interaction Between Top-Down and Bottom-Up Peace', *Security Dialogue* 41, no. 4 (23 August 2010): 392, doi:10.1177/0967010610374312.
42. Mac Ginty, *International Peacebuilding and Local Resistance*, 89.
43. Ibid., 73.
44. Ibid.
45. Ibid., 77.
46. Roberto Belloni and Anna Jarstad K., 'Introducing Hybrid Peace Governance: Impact and Prospects of Liberal Peacebuilding', *Global Governance* 18, no. 1 (March 2012): 1–6.
47. Ibid., 1.
48. Ibid.
49. Ibid., 4.
50. Roberto Belloni, 'Hybrid Peace Governance: Its Emergence and Significance', *Global Governance* 18, no. 1 (March 2012): 34.
51. Peterson, 'A Conceptual Unpacking Of Hybridity', 13.
52. Ibid.
53. Ibid., 15.
54. Dominik Zaum, 'Beyond the "Liberal Peace"', *Global Governance*, Special Issue: Hybrid Peace Governance, 18, no. 1 (March 2012): 122.
55. John Heathershaw, 'Towards Better Theories of Peacebuilding: Beyond the Liberal Peace Debate', *Peacebuilding* 1, no. 2 (June 2013): 282, doi:10.1080/21647259.2013.783260.
56. Ibid., 275.
57. Audra Mitchell, 'Quality/Control: International Peace Interventions and "the Everyday"', *Review of International Studies* 37, no. 04 (12 May 2011): 1641, doi:10.1017/S0260210511000180.
58. Patrick Tom, 'In Search for Emancipatory Hybridity: The Case of Post-War Sierra Leone.' *Peacebuilding* 1, no. 2 (June 2013): 250. doi:10.1080/21647259.2013.783256.
59. David Chandler, 'The Uncritical Critique of "Liberal Peace"', *Review of International Studies* 36, no. S1 (26 August 2010): 155, doi:10.1017/S0260210510000823.
60. Richmond, *A Post-Liberal Peace*, 2011, 14.
61. Chandler, *International Statebuilding*, 23.
62. Ibid., 3.

63. Ibid., 12.
64. Ibid., 3.
65. Ibid., 13.
66. Ioannis Tellidis, 'The End of the Liberal Peace? Post-Liberal Peace vs. Post-Liberal States', *International Studies Review* 14, no. 3 (September 2012): 429–435, doi:10.1111/j.1468-2486.2012.01137.x.
67. Richmond, *A Post-Liberal Peace*, 2011, 20.
68. Richmond and Mitchell, *Hybrid Forms of Peace*, 10.
69. Richmond, *A Post-Liberal Peace*, 2011, 127.
70. Ibid., 10.
71. Ibid., 14.
72. Richmond, 'Failed Statebuilding Versus Peace Formation'.
73. Ibid., 386.
74. Richmond, 'The Dilemmas of a Hybrid Peace'.

2 A Post-Liberal Ontology of Peacebuilding Practice

1. Bruno Latour, 'The Politics of Explanation: An Alternative', in *Knowledge and Reflexivity: New Frontiers in the Sociology of Knowledge*, ed. Steve Woolgar (University of Minnesota: Sage Publications Ltd, 1988). Latour's definition of explanation should not be confused with Hollis and Smith's distinction between explaining and understanding. For Latour, the politics of explanation is the attempt to 'hold' complex ontological heterogeneous social phenomena to their epistemological explanation, that is, 'culture', 'globalization' or 'the liberal peace'.
2. Ibid., 157–159.
3. Ibid., 161.
4. Ibid., 156.
5. Ibid., 158.
6. Bruno Latour, *Reassembling the Social: An Introduction to Actor-Network Theory* (New York: Oxford University Press, 2004), 63.
7. Martin Hiedegger, *Being and Time* (New York: Harper & Row, 1963).
8. Ludwig Wittgenstein, *Philosophical Investigations* (Oxford: Blackwell, 1953).
9. Theodore R. Schatzki, 'Introduction', in *The Practice Turn in Contemporary Theory*, ed. Theodore R. Schatzki, Karin Knorr-Cetina and Eike Von Savigny (New York: Routledge, 2001); Joseph Rouse, 'Practice Theory', *Division I Faculty Publications: Paper 43*, 2007, http://wesscholar.wesleyan.edu/div1facpubs/43
10. See Rouse, 'Practice Theory'; Andreas Reckwitz, 'The Status of the "Material" in Theories of Culture: From "Social Structure" to "Artefacts"', *Journal for the Theory of Social Behaviour* 32, no. 2 (June 2002): 195–217, doi:10.1111/1468-5914.00183.
11. Michel Foucault, *Discipline and Punish: The Birth of the Prison* (New York: Random House, 1978); Michel Foucault, 'The Subject of Power', in *Michel Foucault: Beyond Structuralism and Hermeneutics*, ed. Hubert Dreyfus and Paul Rabinow (Chicago: Chicago University Press, 1982).
12. Michel de Certeau, *The Practice of Everyday Life* (Berkeley: University of California Press, 1984).

13. Judith Butler, *Gender Trouble* (New York: Routledge, 1989).
14. Latour, *Reassembling the Social: An Introduction to Actor-Network Theory*.
15. Pierre Bourdieu, *The Logic of Practice* (Stanford: Stanford University Press, 1990).
16. Anthony Giddens, *The Constitution of Society* (Berkeley: University of California Press, 1984).
17. Theodore R. Schatzki, *The Site of the Social: A Philosophical Account of the Constitution of Social Life and Change* (University Park: Pennsylvania State University Press, 2002).
18. See Michel Callon, 'Some Elements of a Sociology of Translation: Domestication of the Scallops and Fisherman of St. Brieuc Bay', in *Power, Action, and Belief: A New Sociology of Knowledge*, ed. John Law (London: Routledge & Kegan Paul, 1986), https://bscw.uni-wuppertal.de/pub/nj_bscw.cgi/d8022008/Callon_SociologyTranslation.pdf; John Law, *Organizing Modernity* (Oxford, UK; Cambridge, MA: Blackwell, 1994); Andrew Pickering, *The Mangle of Practice: Time, Agency, and Science* (Chicago: University of Chicago Press, 1995); Joseph Rouse, *Engaging Science: How to Understand Its Practices Philosophically* (Ithaca: Cornell University Press, 1996).
19. Clifford Geertz, *The Interpretation of Culture: Selected Essays* (New York: Basic Books, 1988); Sherry Ortner, 'Theory in Anthropology since the Sixties', *Comparative Studies in Society and History* 26, no. 1 (January 1984): 126–166; Paul Rabinow, *Essays on the Anthropology of Reason* (Princeton: Princeton University Press, 1996).
20. Keith Woodward, John Paul Jones III, and Sallie A Marston, 'Of Eagles and Flies: Orientations Toward the Site', *Area* 42, no. 3 (January 2010): 271–280, doi:10.1111/j.1475-4762.2009.00922.x.
21. Diddier Bigo, 'Security and Immigration: Toward a Critique of the Governmentality of Unease', *Alternatives: Global, Local, Political* 27, no. 1 (2002): 63–92; Mikkel Rasmussen, *The West, Civil Society, and the Construction of Peace* (Basingstoke Hampshire; New York: Palgrave Macmillan, 2003); Iver B. Neumann, 'To Be a Diplomat', *International Studies Perspectives* 6, no. 1 (February 2005): 72–93, doi:10.1111/j.1528-3577.2005.00194.x; Jef Huysmans, *The Politics of Insecurity: Fear, Migration, and Asylum in the EU*, The New International Relations (Milton Park, Abingdon, Oxon; New York: Routledge, 2006); Vincent Pouliot, 'The Logic of Practicality: A Theory of Practice of Security Communities', *International Organization* 62, no. 02 (3 April 2008), doi:10.1017/S0020818308080090; Emanuel Adler, 'The Emergence of Cooperation: National Epistemic Communities and the International Evolution of the Idea of Nuclear Arms Control', *International Organization* 46, no. 01 (22 May 2009): 101, doi:10.1017/S0020818300001466; Christian Büger, 'The Clash of Practice: Political Controversy and the United Nations Peacebuilding Commission', *Evidence & Policy: A Journal of Research, Debate and Practice* 7, no. 2 (19 May 2011): 171–191, doi:10.1332/174426411X579216.
22. See Christian Büger and Frank Gadinger, 'Reassembling and Dissecting: International Relations Practice from a Science Studies Perspective', *International Studies Perspectives* 8, no. 1 (February 2007): 90–110, doi:10.1111/j.1528-3585.2007.00271.x.
23. Schatzki, *The Site of the Social*, 71.

24. Janice B. Mattern, 'A Practice Theory of Emotions for International Relations', in *International Practices*, ed. Emanuel Adler and Vincent Pouliot (New York: Cambridge University Press, 2011), 73–74.
25. Ibid., 70.
26. Schatzki, *The Site of the Social*, 71.
27. Raymond Caldwell, 'Reclaiming Agency, Recovering Change? An Exploration of the Practice Theory of Theodore Schatzki', *Journal for the Theory of Social Behaviour* 42, no. 3 (September 2012): 283–303, doi:10.1111/j.1468-5914.2012.00490.x; Andreas Reckwitz, 'The Status of the "Material" in Theories of Culture: From "Social Structure" to "Artefacts"', *Journal for the Theory of Social Behaviour* 32, no. 2 (June 2002): 195–217. doi:10.1111/1468-5914.00183.
28. See Diana H. Coole and Samantha Frost, *New Materialisms: Ontology, Agency, and Politics* (Durham, NC; London: Duke University Press, 2010).
29. Reckwitz, 'The Status of the "Material" in Theories of Culture', 212–213.
30. Schatzki, 'Introduction', 2.
31. Rouse, 'Practice Theory', 512; see Foucault, *Discipline and Punish: The Birth of the Prison*.
32. Caldwell, 'Reclaiming Agency, Recovering Change?', 285.
33. Schatzki, *The Site of the Social*, 240.
34. Mattern, 'A Practice Theory of Emotions for International Relations', 72 emphasis original.
35. Reckwitz, 'The Status of the "Material" in Theories of Culture', 212.
36. Diana Coole, 'Rethinking Agency: A Phenomenological Approach to Embodiment and Agentic Capacities', *Political Studies* 53, no. 1 (22 March 2005): 124–142, doi:10.1111/j.1467-9248.2005.00520.x.
37. Ibid., 125.
38. Ibid., 130.
39. Ibid., 125.
40. Ibid., 128.
41. Ibid., 131.
42. Latour, *Reassembling the Social: An Introduction to Actor-Network Theory*, 71.
43. Reckwitz, 'The Status of the "Material" in Theories of Culture', 210.
44. Latour, *Reassembling the Social: An Introduction to Actor-Network Theory*, 71, emphasis in original.
45. Rouse, 'Practice Theory', 506.
46. Reckwitz, 'The Status of the "Material" in Theories of Culture', 211.
47. Schatzki, 'Introduction', 2.
48. Schatzki, *The Site of the Social*, 18–19.
49. Ibid., xi.
50. see also Michel Foucault, *Security, Territory, Population: Lectures at the Collège De France, 1977–78*, ed. François Ewald and Alessandro Fontana, trans. Michel Senellart (New York: Picador, 2007).
51. See Schatzki, *The Site of the Social*, 61–66 for review.
52. Ibid., 59.
53. Ibid., 65.
54. Ibid.
55. Ibid., 140–141.
56. Ibid., 233.
57. Ibid., 242.

58. Ibid., 148.
59. Reckwitz, 'The Status of the "Material" in Theories of Culture'; Callon, 'Some Elements of a Sociology of Translation: Domestication of the Scallops and Fisherman of St. Brieuc Bay'; David Harvey, *The Condition of Postmodernity: An Enquiry into the Origins of Cultural Change* (Oxford: Blackwell, 1989); Latour, *Reassembling the Social: An Introduction to Actor-Network Theory*.
60. Bruno Latour, 'On Interobjectivity', *Mind, Culture, and Activity* 3, no. 4 (October 1996): 293, doi:10.1207/s15327884mca0304_2.
61. Woodward, Jones III and Marston, 'Of Eagles and Flies'; See Sallie A. Marston, John Paul Jones and Keith Woodward, 'Human Geography Without Scale', *Transactions of the Institute of British Geographers* 30, no. 4 (December 2005): 416–432, doi:10.1111/j.1475-5661.2005.00180.x; John Paul Jones, Keith Woodward and Sallie A. Marston, 'Situating Flatness', *Transactions of the Institute of British Geographers* 32, no. 2 (April 2007): 264–276, doi:10.1111/j.1475-5661.2007.00254.x; Arturo Escobar, 'The "Ontological Turn" in Social Theory. A Commentary on "Human Geography Without Scale", by Sallie Marston, John Paul Jones Ii and Keith Woodward', *Transactions of the Institute of British Geographers* 32, no. 1 (January 2007): 106–111, doi:10.1111/j.1475-5661.2007.00243.x; Andrew E G Jonas, 'Pro Scale: Further Reflections on the "Scale Debate" in Human Geography', *Transactions of the Institute of British Geographers* 31, no. 3 (September 2006): 399–406, doi:10.1111/j.1475-5661.2006.00210.x for debate.
62. Jones, Woodward and Marston, 'Situating Flatness', 265.
63. Marston, Jones and Woodward, 'Human Geography Without Scale', 421.
64. Woodward, Jones III and Marston, 'Of Eagles and Flies', 273.
65. Escobar, 'The "Ontological Turn" in Social Theory: A Commentary on "Human Geography Without Scale", by Sallie Marston, John Paul Jones Ii and Keith Woodward', 109.
66. Latour, *Reassembling the Social: An Introduction to Actor-Network Theory*, 64.
67. Ibid., 246.
68. Ibid., 174.
69. Ibid., 66 emphasis added.
70. John Law, *Traduction/Trahison: Notes on ANT* (Department of Sociology, Lancaster University, 1997), http://www.lancaster.ac.uk/sociology/stslaw2.html
71. John Law, 'After ANT: Complexity, Naming and Topology', in *Actor Network Theory and After*, ed. John Law and John Hassard (Wiley-Blackwell, 1999), 4.
72. Woodward, Jones III and Marston, 'Of Eagles and Flies', 273 citing; Benedictus de Spinoza, *Ethics*, Oxford Philosophical Texts (Oxford; New York: Oxford University Press, 2000).
73. Woodward, Jones III, and Marston, 'Of Eagles and Flies', 273 emphasis original.
74. Ibid., 273.

3 The Politics of Post-Liberal Peacebuilding Practice

1. Christian Büger, 'The Clash of Practice: Political Controversy and the United Nations Peacebuilding Commission', *Evidence & Policy: A*

Journal of Research, Debate and Practice 7, no. 2 (19 May 2011): 173, doi:10.1332/174426411X579216.
2. Emanuel Adler and Vincent Pouliot, 'International Practices: Introduction and Framework', in *International Practices*, ed. Emanuel Adler and Vincent Pouliot (New York: Cambridge University Press, 2011), 7.
3. Theodore R. Schatzki, *The Site of the Social: A Philosophical Account of the Constitution of Social Life and Change* (University Park: Pennsylvania State University Press, 2002).
4. David Chandler, *International Statebuilding: The Rise of Post-Liberal Governance*, Critical Issues in Global Politics 2 (London; New York: Routledge, 2010).
5. Oliver Richmond, 'Resistance and the Post-Liberal Peace', *Millennium – Journal of International Studies* 38, no. 3 (10 May 2010): 665–692, doi:10.1177/0305829810365017.
6. Raymond Caldwell, 'Agency and Change: Re-Evaluating Foucault's Legacy', *Organization* 14, no. 6 (1 November 2007): 769–791, doi:10.1177/1350508407082262.
7. Michel Foucault, *Security, Territory, Population: Lectures at the Collège De France, 1977–78*, ed. François Ewald and Alessandro Fontana, trans. Michel Senellart (New York: Picador, 2007), 216.
8. Ibid., xxii.
9. Michel Foucault, *The History of Sexuality: An Introduction.*, trans. Robert Hurley (New York: Vintage Books, 1990), 95.
10. Brent Pickett L., 'Foucault and the Politics of Resistance', *Polity* 28, no. 4 (Summer 1996): 458.
11. Ibid., 465.
12. Caldwell, 'Agency and Change', 3 citing from Anthony Giddens, *The Constitution of Society* (Berkeley: University of California Press, 1984).
13. Ibid.
14. Ibid; Pickett, 'Foucault and the Politics of Resistance'.
15. Pierre Bourdieu, *The Logic of Practice* (Stanford: Stanford University Press, 1990), 25.
16. Ibid., 87.
17. Ibid., 82.
18. Ibid., 78.
19. Vincent Pouliot, 'The Logic of Practicality: A Theory of Practice of Security Communities', *International Organization* 62, no. 2 (3 April 2008), doi:10.1017/S0020818308080090.
20. Raymond Caldwell, 'Reclaiming Agency, Recovering Change? An Exploration of the Practice Theory of Theodore Schatzki', *Journal for the Theory of Social Behaviour* 42, no. 3 (September 2012): 283–303, doi:10.1111/j.1468-5914.2012.00490.x; Janice B. Mattern, 'A Practice Theory of Emotions for International Relations', in *International Practices*, ed. Emanuel Adler and Vincent Pouliot (New York: Cambridge University Press, 2011).
21. Adler and Pouliot, 'International Practices: Introduction and Framework'.
22. Diddier Bigo, 'Security and Immigration: Toward a Critique of the Governmentality of Unease', *Alternatives: Global, Local, Political* 27, no. 1 (2002): 63–92; Emanuel Adler, 'The Emergence of Cooperation: National Epistemic Communities and the International Evolution of the Idea of

Nuclear Arms Control', *International Organization* 46, no. 01 (22 May 2009): 101, doi:10.1017/S0020818300001466; Pouliot, 'The Logic of Practicality'.
23. Bigo, 'Security and Immigration: Toward a Critique of the Governmentality of Unease', 243.
24. Etienne Wenger, *Communities of Practice: Learning, Meaning, and Identity* (Cambridge, UK; New York: Cambridge University Press, 1999); Etienne Wenger, *Cultivating Communities of Practice: A Guide to Managing Knowledge* (Boston, MA: Harvard Business School Press, 2002).
25. Adler and Pouliot, 'International Practices: Introduction and Framework', 17.
26. Adler and Pouliot, 'International Practices: Introduction and Framework'. citing James G. March, 'Footnotes to Organizational Change', *Administrative Science Quarterly* 26, no. 4 (December 1981): 563–577.
27. Adler and Pouliot, 'International Practices: Introduction and Framework', 16.
28. Ibid., 15.
29. Mattern, 'A Practice Theory of Emotions for International Relations', 71 emphasis original.
30. Ibid., 71.
31. Ibid., 72 fn; referencing Andreas Reckwitz, 'Toward a Theory of Social Practices: A Development in Culturalist Theorizing', *European Journal of Social Theory* 5, no. 2 (1 May 2002): 243–263, doi:10.1177/13684310222225432.
32. Mattern, 'A Practice Theory of Emotions for International Relations', 71.
33. Pouliot, 'The Logic of Practicality', 277.
34. Bruno Latour, 'The Politics of Explanation: An Alternative', in *Knowledge and Reflexivity: New Frontiers in the Sociology of Knowledge*, ed. Steve Woolgar (University of Minnesota: Sage Publications Ltd, 1988).
35. Mattern, 'A Practice Theory of Emotions for International Relations', 72.
36. Schatzki, *The Site of the Social*, 94.
37. Ibid., 73.
38. Ibid., 79.
39. Ibid., 74.
40. Theodore R. Schatzki, 'Introduction', in *The Practice Turn in Contemporary Theory*, ed. Theodore R. Schatzki, Karin Knorr-Cetina and Eike Von Savigny (New York: Routledge, 2001), 3.
41. Schatzki, *The Site of the Social*, 79.
42. Theodore R. Schatzki, *The Timespace of Human Activity: On Performance, Society, and History as Indeterminate Teleological Events*, Toposophia (Lanham, MD: Lexington Books, 2010), 504.
43. Caldwell, 'Reclaiming Agency, Recovering Change?', 297.
44. Schatzki, *The Site of the Social*, 72.
45. Joseph Rouse, 'Practice Theory', *Division I Faculty Publications: Paper* 43 (2007): 532, http://wesscholar.wesleyan.edu/div1facpubs/43
46. Ibid., 531.
47. Ibid., 532.
48. John Law, *Organizing Modernity* (Oxford, UK; Cambridge, MA: Blackwell, 1994), 101.
49. Richard Freeman, 'What Is "Translation"', *Evidence & Policy: A Journal of Research, Debate and Practice* 5, no. 4 (1 November 2009): 433, doi:10.1332/174426409X478770.
50. Ibid., 433.

51. See ibid.; George Steiner, *After Babel: Aspects of Language and Translation* (Oxford; New York: Oxford University Press, 1998), 246.
52. Freeman, 'What Is "Translation"?', 433.
53. Ibid., 440 emphasis added.
54. Michel Callon, 'Some Elements of a Sociology of Translation: Domestication of the Scallops and Fisherman of St. Brieuc Bay', in *Power, Action, and Belief: A New Sociology of Knowledge*, ed. John Law (London: Routlage & Kegan Paul, 1986), https://bscw.uni-wuppertal.de/pub/nj_bscw.cgi/d8022008/Callon_SociologyTranslation.pdf
55. Ibid., 16.
56. Ibid.
57. Ibid., 18.
58. Ibid., 1.
59. Bruno Latour, 'The Powers of Association', in *Power, Action, and Belief: A New Sociology of Knowledge*, ed. John Law (Routledge, Kegan Paul, 1987), 267, http://www.bruno-latour.fr/sites/default/files/19-POWERS-ASSOCIATIONS-GBpdf.pdf
60. Ibid.
61. Ibid., 268.
62. Ibid.
63. Ibid.

4 Mapping Peacebuilding Practice: A Post-Liberal Methodology

1. David Chandler, *International Statebuilding: The Rise of Post-Liberal Governance*, Critical Issues in Global Politics 2 (London; New York: Routledge, 2010),11–12.
2. Oliver Richmond, *A Post-Liberal Peace*, Routledge Studies in Peace and Conflict Resolution (Milton Park, Abingdon, Oxon [England]; New York: Routledge, 2011), 14–15.
3. Ibid., 139–141.
4. Victoria Loughlan, Christian Olsson and Peer Schouten, 'Mapping', in *Critical Security Methods: New Frameworks for Analysis*, ed. Claudia Aradau, Jef Huysmans, Andrew Neal and Nadine Voelkner (Abingdon, Oxon, England; New York: Routledge, 2015), 39.
5. Michel Callon, 'Some Elements of a Sociology of Translation: Domestication of the Scallops and Fisherman of St. Brieuc Bay,' in *Power, Action, and Belief: A New Sociology of Knowledge*, ed. John Law (London: Routledge & Kegan Paul, 1986), https://bscw.uni-wuppertal.de/pub/nj_bscw.cgi/d8022008/Callon_SociologyTranslation.pdf
6. Oliver Richmond and Audra Mitchell, eds, *Hybrid Forms of Peace: From Everyday Agency to Post-Liberalism* (Houndmills, Basingstoke, Hampshire; New York: Palgrave Macmillan, 2012), 20.
7. Ibid.
8. Richmond, *A Post-Liberal Peace*, 2011, 123.
9. Lynn Manzo and Nathan Brightbill, 'Towards a Participatory Ethics', in *Connecting People, Participation and Place: Participatory Action Research Approaches and Methods*, ed. Sara Kindon, Rachel Pain, and Mike Kesby (London:

178 Notes

Routledge, 2007), 37; Caitlin Cahill, Sultana Farhana and Pain Rachel, 'Participatory Ethics: Politics, Practices, Institutions', *ACME: An International E-Journal for Critical Geographies* 6, no. 3 (2007): 308.
10. Sonya C. Dwyer and Jennifer L. Buckle, 'The Space Between: On Being an Insider-Outsider in Qualitative Research', *International Journal of Qualitative Methods* 8, no. 1 (2009): 58.
11. Ibid.
12. Patricia A. Adler, *Membership Roles in Field Research*, Qualitative Research Methods, vol. 6 (Newbury Park, CA: Sage Publications, 1987), 85; from Dwyer and Buckle, 'The Space Between: On Being an Insider-Outsider in Qualitative Research', 58.
13. Ibid., 62.
14. Morgan Brigg and Roland Bleiker, 'Autoethnographic International Relations: Exploring the Self as a Source of Knowledge', *Review of International Studies* 36, no. 03 (8 July 2010): 792, doi:10.1017/S0260210510000689.
15. Dorothy E. Smith, ed., *Institutional Ethnography as Practice* (Lanham, MD: Rowman & Littlefield, 2006).
16. Richmond and Mitchell, *Hybrid Forms of Peace*, 27–29.
17. Melvin Pollner and Robert M. Emerson, 'Ethnomethodology and Ethnography', in *Handbook of Ethnography* (Thousand Oaks: Sage Publications Ltd, 2001), 119.
18. Ibid., 120.
19. Bruno Latour, *Reassembling the Social: An Introduction to Actor-Network Theory* (New York: Oxford University Press, 2004)170.
20. Ibid., 171.
21. Ibid., 63–64.
22. Ibid., 178.
23. Ibid., 220.
24. Callon, 'Some Elements of a Sociology of Translation: Domestication of the Scallops and Fisherman of St. Brieuc Bay'; John Law, "Traduction/Trahison: Notes on ANT." Department of Sociology, Lancaster University, 1997. http://www.lancaster.ac.uk/sociology/stslaw2.html
25. Latour, *Reassembling the Social: An Introduction to Actor-Network Theory*; see also Latour, 'The Powers of Association'.
26. Ibid., 171.
27. Ibid., 237.
28. Bruno Latour, 'On Recalling ANT', in *Actor Network Theory and After*, ed. John Law and John Hassard (Wiley-Blackwell, 1999), 20.
29. Ibid., 19.
30. Latour, *Reassembling the Social: An Introduction to Actor-Network Theory*, 23.
31. Latour, 'On Recalling ANT', 20.

5 Practicing Justice in Liberia: A Brief History

1. Jallah A. Barbu, 'An Analysis of the Formal Legal Framework Governing Customary Law in the Republic of Liberia (DRAFT)' (United States Institute of Peace: From Current Practices of Justice to Rule of Law: Policy Options for Liberia's First Post-Conflict Decade, n.d.), 7.

2. Ibid., 6; Stephen C. Lubkemann, Deborah Isser and Philip A. Z. Banks, 'Unintended Consequences: Constraint of Customary Justice in Post-Conflict Liberia', in *Customary Justice and the Rule of Law in War-Torn Societies*, ed. Deborah Isser, Peacebuilding and the Rule of Law (Washington, DC: United States Institute of Peace Press, 2011), 200.
 3. Harrison Akingbade, 'The Pacification of the Liberian Hinterland', *The Journal of Negro History* 79, no. 3 (Summer 1994): 277–278.
 4. Ibid., 278.
 5. Davis v. Republic, 1 LLR: 17 in Barbu, 'An Analysis of the Formal Legal Framework Governing Customary Law in the Republic of Liberia (DRAFT)', 7.
 6. Ibid. actual text of 1869 Act cited as 'currently unavailable'.
 7. Akingbade, 'The Pacification of the Liberian Hinterland', 279.
 8. Ibid., 278.
 9. Karmo v. Morris, 317; 1919 in Barbu, 'An Analysis of the Formal Legal Framework Governing Customary Law in the Republic of Liberia (DRAFT),' 11–12 This ruling was later upheld in 1914.
10. Ibid., 7–8.
11. Ibid., 8–9.
12. Akingbade, 'The Pacification of the Liberian Hinterland', 282.
13. Ibid., 286.
14. Ibid., 280.
15. Barbu, 'An Analysis of the Formal Legal Framework Governing Customary Law in the Republic of Liberia (DRAFT)', 11–12.
16. Ibid., 29–30.
17. Ibid., 21 emphasis added.
18. Akingbade, 'The Pacification of the Liberian Hinterland', 290.
19. Barbu, 'An Analysis of the Formal Legal Framework Governing Customary Law in the Republic of Liberia (DRAFT)', 11.
20. Karmo v. Morris, 317; 1919 in ibid., 12.
21. Ibid. emphasis added.
22. Stephen Ellis, *The Mask of Anarchy: The Destruction of Liberia and the Religious Dimension of an African Civil War* (New York: New York University Press, 2007), 47–48.
23. Barbu, 'An Analysis of the Formal Legal Framework Governing Customary Law in the Republic of Liberia (DRAFT)', 13.
24. Ibid., 28.
25. Ibid., 31.
26. Title 12 in Sections 25.2 (b), (i), and (l) respectively in ibid., 15.
27. Morten Bøås and Anne Hatløy, ' "Getting In, Getting Out": Militia Membership and Prospects for Re-Integration in Post-War Liberia', *The Journal of Modern African Studies* 46, no. 01 (31 January 2008), doi:10.1017/S0022278X07003060.
28. Paul Richards, *Fighting for the Rain Forest: War, Youth & Resources in Sierra Leone*, African Issues (Portsmouth, N.H: Heinemann, 1996); Amos Sawyer, *Beyond Plunder: Toward Democratic Governance in Liberia* (Boulder: L. Rienner Publishers, Inc, 2005); Ellis, *The Mask of Anarchy*; see also Joel S. Migdal, *Strong Societies and Weak States: State-Society Relations and State Capabilities in the Third World* (Princeton, NJ: Princeton University Press, 1988).

29. Richards, *Fighting for the Rain Forest*; see Mary Moran, *Liberia?: The Violence of Democracy* (Philadelphia: University of Pennsylvania Press, 2006).
30. Robert D. Kaplan, 'The Coming Anarchy', *The Atlantic* (February 1994), http://www.theatlantic.com/magazine/archive/1994/02/the-coming-anarchy/304670/?single_page=true
31. Ibid.
32. Ellis, *The Mask of Anarchy*, 146; 298–300.
33. Ibid., 298.
34. Ibid.; see also James C Scott, *Weapons of the Weak: Everyday Forms of Peasant Resistance* (New Haven; London: Yale University Press, 1985); Richmond, 'Resistance and the Post-Liberal Peace'.
35. William Reno, 'African Weak States and Commercial Alliances', *African Affairs* 96, no. 383 (April 1997): 165–185.
36. Ibid., 166.
37. William Reno, *Warlord Politics and African States* (Boulder: Lynne Rienner Publishers, 1998), 2.
38. Ibid., 5; see also Fanthorpe, 'On the Limits of Liberal Peace: Chiefs and Democratic Decentralization in Post-War Sierra Leone'.
39. Reno, *Warlord Politics and African States*, 1; see Michael Pugh, 'The Political Economy of Peacebuilding: A Critical Theory Perspective.' *International Journal of Peace Studies* 10, no. 2 (Autumn/Winter 2005): 23–42.
40. Richards, *Fighting for the Rain Forest*, xvii.
41. Ibid., xviii.
42. Sawyer, *Beyond Plunder*.
43. Ibid., 8–9.
44. Ibid., 9.
45. Ibid., 8–9.
46. Ibid., 57.
47. International Crisis Group, *Liberia: Resurrecting the Justice System*, Africa Report (International Crisis Group, 6 April 2006), 7, http://www.crisisgroup.org/~/media/Files/africa/west-africa/liberia/Liberia%20Resurrecting%20the%20Justice%20System.pdf
48. Ibid., i.
49. International Crisis Group 'Liberia: Resurrecting the Justice System', 6.
50. Ibid., 7.
51. Ibid., 10.
52. Ibid., 9–10.
53. Ibid., ii.
54. Republic of Liberia, 'Poverty Reduction Strategy (PRS)', April 2008, 175, http://www.emansion.gov.lr/doc/Final%20PRS.pdf
55. Republic of Liberia, and UNMIL, 'Priority Plan for Peacebuilding Fund (PBF): Liberia' (United Nations Peacebuilding Fund, March 2009), 3–6, mdtf.undp.org/document/download/6299.
56. Republic of Liberia, 'Poverty Reduction Strategy (PRS)', 68.
57. Republic of Liberia, *The Liberian National Decentralization and Local Development Program* (May 2007), http://www.infoliberia.org/doc_download/County%20development%20funds.pdf?a4705305cd27e04fb1f66830e7e0ef9d=MTMx

58. Republic of Liberia, 'Liberian Peacebuilding Programme DRAFT' (2 May 2011), http://www.unpbf.org/wp-content/uploads/Final-Approved-LPP-May-5-20111.pdf
59. Ibid., 18.
60. Ibid., 9.
61. David Chandler, *International Statebuilding: The Rise of Post-Liberal Governance*, Critical Issues in Global Politics 2 (London; New York: Routledge, 2010); Michel Foucault, *Security, Territory, Population: Lectures at the Collège De France, 1977–78*, ed. François Ewald and Alessandro Fontana, trans. Michel Senellart (New York: Picador, 2007).
62. James C. Scott, *The Art of Not Being Governed: An Anarchist History of Upland Southeast Asia* (New Haven: Yale University Press, 2009); Oliver Richmond, 'Resistance and the Post-Liberal Peace', *Millennium – Journal of International Studies* 38, no. 3 (10 May 2010): 665–692, doi: 10.1177/0305829810365017.

6 Translating Statutory Justice into Legal Empowerment

1. Deborah Isser, 'The Problem with Problematizing Legal Pluralism: Lessons From the Field', in *Legal Pluralism and Development: Scholars and Practitioners in Dialogue*, ed. Brian Z. Tamanaha, Caroline Sage, and Michael Woolcock (New York: Cambridge University Press, 2013), 237.
2. Stephen C. Lubkemann, Deborah Isser and Philip A. Z. Banks, 'Unintended Consequences: Constraint of Customary Justice in Post-Conflict Liberia', in *Customary Justice and the Rule of Law in War-Torn Societies*, ed. Deborah Isser, Peacebuilding and the Rule of Law (Washington, D.C.: United States Institute of Peace Press, 2011), 202.
3. Richard Fanthorpe, 'On the Limits of Liberal Peace: Chiefs and Democratic Decentralization in Post-War Sierra Leone', *African Affairs* 105, no. 418 (September 2005): 27–49, doi:10.1093/afraf/adi091; International Crisis Group, *Liberia: Resurrecting the Justice System*, Africa Report (International Crisis Group, 6 April 2006), http://www.crisisgroup.org/~/media/Files/africa/west-africa/liberia/Liberia%20Resurrecting%20the%20Justice%20System.pdf
4. Michel Callon, 'Some Elements of a Sociology of Translation: Domestication of the Scallops and Fisherman of St. Brieuc Bay', in *Power, Action, and Belief: A New Sociology of Knowledge*, ed. John Law (London: Routlage & Kegan Paul, 1986), https://bscw.uni-wuppertal.de/pub/nj_bscw.cgi/d8022008/Callon_SociologyTranslation.pdf
5. Bouku Zulu, Vice Chairman, National Traditional Council, Monrovia, Group Interview, 25 November 2009.
6. United States Institute for Peace, *Looking for Justice: Liberian Experiences and Perceptions of Local Justice Options* (Washington, D.C., May 2009), 10.
7. Ibid.
8. National Traditional Council, 'Resolution Regarding Critical Issues Facing Liberia and Its Traditional People as We Strive to Achieve Lasting Peace and Prosperity: Based on Three Consultative Conferences of Traditional Leaders Held in Bomi, Bong, & Grand Gedeh Counties' (National Traditinal Council, August 2009), http://www.cartercenter.org/resources/pdfs/peace/conflict_resolution/liberia/NTC-Resolution2008.pdf

9. Ibid.
10. The Carter Center, 'Liberia: Policy Dialogue and Reform' (Press Release, n.d.), http://www.cartercenter.org/peace/conflict_resolution/liberia-policy-dialogue-reform.html; National Traditional Council, 'The 26 February 2010 Resolution Held in the City of Voinjama Between the Lormas and Mandingos of Voinjama City, Lofa County, Republic of Liberia', 8 May 2010, http://www.cartercenter.org/resources/pdfs/peace/conflict_resolution/liberia/LormaMandingoElders-agreements.pdf
11. Tom Crick, Associate Director of Conflict Resolution Programing, Carter Center, Atlanta, Personal Interview, 27 November 2012.
12. Thomas Mawolo, South West Regional Coordinator, Justice and Peace Commission, Cape Palmas, Personal Interview, 18 February 2011 Personal Interview.
13. Crick, Associate Director of Conflict Resolution Programing, Carter Center, Atlanta.
14. Isser, 'The Problem with Problematizing Legal Pluralism: Lessons From the Field', 243.
15. Caroline Sage and Michael Woolcock, 'Breaking Legal Inequality Traps: New Approaches to Building Justice Systems for the Poor in Developing Countries'. in *Inclusive States: Social Policy and Structural Inequalities*, ed. Anis Dani and Arjan de Haan (Washington, D.C.: The World Bank, 2008), 371.
16. Ibid.
17. Jeffrey Sachs, *The End of Poverty: Economic Possibilities for Our Time* (New York: Penguin Books, 2005).
18. Caroline Sage and Woolcock, 'Breaking Legal Inequality Traps: New Approaches to Building Justice Systems for the Poor in Developing Countries', 387.
19. Brian Z. Tamanaha, 'A Non-Essentialist Version of Legal Empowerment', *Journal of Law and Society* 27, no. 2 (June 2000): 299.
20. Ibid., 313.
21. Ibid., 298.
22. Ibid., 313.
23. Ibid.
24. Ibid., 312.
25. Ibid., 318.
26. Ford Foundation, *Many Roads to Justice: The Law-Related Work of Ford Foundation Grantees Around the World*, ed. Mary McClymont and Stephen Golub (New York: Ford Foundation, 2000), 2.
27. Ibid., 15.
28. Stephen Golub, *Beyond Rule of Law Orthodoxy: The Legal Empowerment Alternative*, Working Paper, Rule of Law Series: Democracy and Law Project (Washington, D.C.: Carnegie Endowment of International Peace, October 2003), http://siteresources.worldbank.org/INTLAWJUSTINST/Resources/BeyondRuleOrthodoxy.pdf
29. Ibid., 5 emphasis added.
30. Ibid., 25.
31. Ibid.
32. Ibid., 3.
33. Ibid., 26.

34. Ibid.
35. Justin Sandefur, Principal Investigator, Centre for the Study of African Economies, Personal Interview, 29 May 2012.
36. Ibid.
37. United States Institute for Peace, *Looking for Justice: Liberian Experiences and Perceptions of Local Justice Options*, 16.
38. Ibid., 7 emphasis added.
39. Ibid., 44.
40. Ibid., 47.
41. Ibid., 3.
42. Ibid., 43.
43. Ibid., 51.
44. Ibid., 9.
45. Ibid., 51.
46. Ibid., 52.
47. Ibid., 4.
48. Ibid., 5.
49. Ibid., 55.
50. Bilal Siddiqi, Principal Investigator, Centre for the Study of African Economies, Personal Interview, 16 July 2012.
51. Crick, Associate Director of Conflict Resolution Programing, Carter Center, Atlanta.
52. Anonymous, Senior UNMIL Official, Personal Interview, 1 July 2011.
53. Crick, Associate Director of Conflict Resolution Programing, Carter Center, Atlanta.
54. The Carter Center, 'Findings of the Legal Working Group', 10 December 2009, 5, http://www.cartercenter.org/resources/pdfs/peace/conflict_resolution/liberia/LWG-findings-2010.pdf
55. Ibid., 1.
56. Ibid., 5.
57. Ibid., 7.
58. Isser, 'The Problem with Problematizing Legal Pluralism: Lessons From the Field'.

7 Translating Legal Empowerment into Liberian Communities

1. Tom Crick, Associate Director of Conflict Resolution Programing, the Carter Center, Atlanta, Personal Interview, 27 November 2012; Jeff Austin, Former Regional Program Coordinator, Carter Center, Harper, Personal Interview, 7 December 2012.
2. Vivek Maru, 'Between Law and Society: Paralegals and the Provision of Justice Services in Sierra Leone and Worldwide', *Yale Journal of International Law* 31 (2006): 428.
3. Ibid., 429.
4. Ibid.
5. Ibid., 460.
6. Ibid., 428.

7. Ibid., 429.
8. Ibid., 441.
9. Ibid., 428.
10. Vivek Maru, 'Access to Justice and Legal Empowerment: A Review of World Bank Practice', *Hague Journal on the Rule of Law* 2, no. 02 (17 December 2010): 269, doi:10.1017/S1876404510200076.
11. Ibid., 269.
12. Ibid., 261.
13. Maru, 'Between Law and Society: Paralegals and the Provision of Justice Services in Sierra Leone and Worldwide', 461–462.
14. Ibid., 452.
15. The Carter Center Document, 'The Carter Center/JPC Community Legal Advisors Program in South East and Central Liberia', n.d.
16. Austin, Former Regional Program Coordinator, Carter Center, Harper.
17. Ibid.
18. Crick, Associate Director of Conflict Resolution Programing, the Carter Center, Atlanta.
19. Thomas Mawolo, South West Regional Coordinator, Justice and Peace Commission, Cape Palmas, Personal Interview, 18 February 2011.
20. Pewee Flomoku, 'Introductions' (JPC Training Compound, Gbarnga, 16 February 2011) Participant Observation.
21. Mawolo, South West Regional Coordinator, Justice and Peace Commission, Cape Palmas.
22. Ibid. Personal Interview.
23. Austin, Former Regional Program Coordinator, the Carter Center, Harper.
24. The Carter Center, 'The Empowerment-Oriented Approach' (JPC Training Compound, Gbarnga, 23 February 2011).
25. Ibid.
26. Pewee Flomoku, 'Role Play: Entering a Community for the First Time' (JPC Training Compound, Gbarnga, 23 February 2011) Participant Observation.
27. The Carter Center, 'The Empowerment-Oriented Approach'.
28. The Carter Center, 'Manual for JPC Community Legal Advisers (DRAFT)' (The Carter Center, February 2011), 29–34.
29. Ibid., 42.
30. Ibid., 38.
31. Ibid., 32.

8 Translating Legal Empowerment into a Randomized Controlled Trial

1. Justin Sandefur, Principal Investigator, Centre for the Study of African Economies, Personal Interview, 29 May 2012.
2. International Crisis Group, *Liberia: Resurrecting the Justice System*, Africa Report (International Crisis Group, 6 April 2006), http://www.crisisgroup.org/~/media/Files/africa/west-africa/liberia/Liberia%20Resurrecting%20the%20Justice%20System.pdf; United States Institute for Peace, *Looking for Justice: Liberian Experiences and Perceptions of Local Justice Options* (Washington, DC, May 2009).
3. Name anonymized to protect client identities.

4. Harry Momodu, JPC Community Legal Advisor, Bong County, Group Disscussion, 27 May 2011.
 5. Name anonymized to protect client identities.
 6. Prince Nimlay, JPC Community Justice Advisor, Bong County, Group Disscussion, 27 May 2011.
 7. Ibid.
 8. Bilal Siddiqi, Principal Investigator, Centre for the Study of African Economies, Personal Interview, 16 July 2012.
 9. CSAE Evaluation Team, 'Lightning Round Proposal' (Internal Document, 2 June 2011), 2–3.
10. Ibid., 1.
11. U.S. Department of Education, *Identifying and Implementing Educational Practices Supported by Rigorous Evidence: A User Friendly Guide* (Washington, D.C.: U.S. Department of Education and the Council of Excellence in Government, December 2003), http://www2.ed.gov/rschstat/research/pubs/rigorousevid/rigorousevid.pdf; See also Nancy Cartwright, 'Are RCTs the Gold Standard?', *BioSocieties* 2, no. 1 (March 2007): 11–20, doi:10.1017/S1745855207005029; C.B. Barrett and M.R. Carter, 'The Power and Pitfalls of Experiments in Development Economics: Some Non-Random Reflections', *Applied Economic Perspectives and Policy* 32, no. 4 (8 December 2010): 515–548, doi:10.1093/aepp/ppq023.
12. Sandefur, Principal Investigator, Centre for the Study of African Economies.
13. Martina Björkman and Jakob Svensson, 'Power to the People: Evidence from a Randomized Field Experiment on Community-Based Monitoring in Uganda', *Quarterly Journal of Economics* 124, no. 2 (May 2009): 735–769, doi:10.1162/qjec.2009.124.2.735; from Sandefur, Principal Investigator, Centre for the Study of African Economies.
14. Sandefur, Principal Investigator, Centre for the Study of African Economies.
15. Ibid. The term 'wishy-washy' was used to convey the prevailing view of legal empowerment-type projects held by large international donors.
16. Ibid.
17. Ibid.
18. Ibid.
19. see Maureen Tkacia, 'The Pragmatic Rebels', *Bloomberg Businessweek*, 5 July 2010, http://www.businessweek.com/magazine/content/10_28/b4186056393103.htm
20. Abhijit Banerjee and Esther Duflo, *Poor Economics: A Radical Rethinking of the Way to Fight Global Poverty* (New York: PublicAffairs, 2011).
21. Jeffrey Sachs, *The End of Poverty: Economic Possibilities for Our Time* (New York: Penguin Books, 2005).
22. William Easterly, *The White Man's Burden* (London: Penguin Books, 2007).
23. Dambisa Moyo, *Dead Aid: Why Aid Is Not Working and How There Is a Better Way for Africa*, 1st American ed. (New York: Farrar, Straus and Giroux, 2009).
24. Easterly, *The White Man's Burden*, 241.
25. Banerjee and Duflo, *Poor Economics*, 3.
26. Ibid., 14.
27. Ibid., 243; Pande Rohini and Christopher Udry, 'Institutions and Development: A View from Below', *Yale University Economic Growth Center Discussion*

186 Notes

Paper, 2005, http://dev.wcfia.harvard.edu/sites/default/files/PandeUdry2005.pdf
28. Abhijit Banerjee, Esther Duflo, Rachel Glennerster, and Cynthia Kinnan, *The Miracle of Microfinance? Evidence from a Randomized Evaluation*, Working Paper, Bread Working Paper (Bureau for Research and Economic Analysis of Development, June 2010).
29. Sandefur, Principal Investigator, Centre for the Study of African Economies.
30. Siddiqi, Principal Investigator, Centre for the Study of African Economies.
31. Sandefur, Principal Investigator, Centre for the Study of African Economies.
32. Tom Crick, Associate Director of Conflict Resolution Programing, Carter Center, Atlanta, Personal Interview, 27 November 2012.
33. Ibid.
34. Sandefur, Principal Investigator, Centre for the Study of African Economies.
35. The term 'legitimate dispute' was used to distinguish between an actual dispute which the CJA could provide assistance in resolving as opposed to a hypothetical or abstract legal question.
36. Barrett and Carter, 'The Power and Pitfalls of Experiments in Development Economics'.
37. Björkman and Svensson, 'Power to the People'.
38. Banerjee et al., *The Miracle of Microfinance? Evidence from a Randomized Evaluation*.

9 Translating Legal Empowerment into Political Impact

1. Bilal Siddiqi, Principal Investigator, Centre for the Study of African Economies, Personal Interview, 16 July 2012, emphasis added.
2. Name anonymized to protect client identity.
3. Flelah, Participant Observation, 7 June 2011 Participant Observation.
4. Name anonymized to protect client identity.
5. Socopa, Participant Observation, 10 June 2011.
6. Thomas Mawolo, South West Regional Coordinator, Justice and Peace Commission, Cape Palmas, Personal Interview, 18 February 2011 Personal Interview; see Chapter 7.
7. Siddiqi, Principal Investigator, Centre for the Study of African Economies.
8. Ibid.
9. Ibid.
10. Ibid. Emphasis added.
11. CSAE Evaluation Team, 'Field Observations From Witnessing CJA Awareness Sessions', 12 June 2011.
12. Justin Sandefur and Bilal Siddiqi, 'Delivering Justice to the Poor: Theory and Experimental Evidence from Liberia', *DRAFT* (November 2013): 35, https://editorialexpress.com/cgi-bin/conference/download.cgi?db_name=CSAE2013&paper_id=1014
13. Ibid., 33.
14. Ibid., 32.
15. Ibid., 33.
16. Ibid.
17. Ibid., 34.

18. Ibid., 35.
19. Rachael Knight, Silas Kpanan'Ayoung Siakor, and Ali Kaba, *Protecting Community Lands and Resources: Evidence from Liberia, Mozambique, and Uganda* (Washington, DC: International Development Law Organization in Partnership with Namti, 2012), http://namati.wpengine.netdna-cdn.com/wp-content/uploads/2012/06/protecting_community_lands_resources_inter_FW.pdf
20. Christopher Blattman, Alexandra C. Hartman and Robert A. Blair, 'How to Promote Order and Property Rights under Weak Rule of Law? An Experiment in Changing Dispute Resolution Behavior through Community Education', *American Political Science Review* 108, no. 01 (February 2014): 20, doi:10.1017/S0003055413000543.
21. Tom Crick, Associate Director of Conflict Resolution Programing, the Carter Center, Atlanta, Personal Interview, 27 November 2012; Jeff Austin, Former Regional Program Coordinator, the Carter Center, Harper, Personal Interview, 7 December 2012.
22. Deborah Isser, 'The Problem with Problematizing Legal Pluralism: Lessons From the Field', in *Legal Pluralism and Development: Scholars and Practitioners in Dialogue*, ed. Brian Z. Tamanaha, Caroline Sage and Michael Woolcock (New York: Cambridge University Press, 2013), 237–247.

Conclusion

1. David Chandler, *International Statebuilding: The Rise of Post-Liberal Governance*, Critical Issues in Global Politics 2 (London; New York: Routledge, 2010), 13.
2. Oliver Richmond, *A Post-Liberal Peace*, Routledge Studies in Peace and Conflict Resolution (Milton Park, Abingdon, Oxon [England]; New York: Routledge, 2011); Oliver Richmond and Audra Mitchell, eds, *Hybrid Forms of Peace: From Everyday Agency to Post-Liberalism* (Houndmills, Basingstoke, Hampshire; New York: Palgrave Macmillan, 2012).
3. David Chandler and Oliver Richmond, 'Contesting Post-Liberalism: Governmentality or Emancipation?', *Journal of International Relations and Development* (2014).
4. Ibid.
5. Homi K. Bhabha, *The Location of Culture*, 2nd ed. (Abingdon, Oxon.: Routledge, 2004), 663.
6. William E. Connolly, *A World of Becoming* (Durham, NC: Duke University Press, 2010); Mark B. Salter, 'Introduction', in *Research Methods in Critical Security Studies: An Introduction*, ed. Mark B. Salter and Can E. Mutlu (Abingdon, Oxon.: Routledge, 2013).
7. Theodore R. Schatzki, K. Knorr-Cetina and Eike von Savigny, eds, *The Practice Turn in Contemporary Theory* (New York: Routledge, 2001); Joseph Rouse, 'Practice Theory', *Division I Faculty Publications: Paper* 43, 2007, http://wesscholar.wesleyan.edu/div1facpubs/43
8. Theodore R. Schatzki, *The Site of the Social: A Philosophical Account of the Constitution of Social Life and Change* (University Park: Pennsylvania State University Press, 2002), 71.

9. Richard Freeman, 'What Is "Translation"?', *Evidence & Policy: A Journal of Research, Debate and Practice* 5, no. 4 (1 November 2009): 429–447, doi:10.1332/174426409X478770.
10. Michel Callon, 'Some Elements of a Sociology of Translation: Domestication of the Scallops and Fisherman of St. Brieuc Bay', in *Power, Action, and Belief: A New Sociology of Knowledge*, ed. John Law (London: Routledge & Kegan Paul, 1986), https://bscw.uni-wuppertal.de/pub/nj_bscw.cgi/d8022008/Callon_SociologyTranslation.pdf
11. Stephen C. Lubkemann, Deborah Isser and Philip A.Z. Banks, 'Unintended Consequences: Constraint of Customary Justice in Post-Conflict Liberia', in *Customary Justice and the Rule of Law in War-Torn Societies*, ed. Deborah Isser, Peacebuilding and the Rule of Law (Washington, D.C.: United States Institute of Peace Press, 2011); Deborah Isser, 'The Problem with Problematizing Legal Pluralism: Lessons From the Field', in *Legal Pluralism and Development: Scholars and Practitioners in Dialogue*, ed. Brian Z. Tamanaha, Caroline Sage and Michael Woolcock (New York, NY: Cambridge University Press, 2013), 237–247.
12. International Crisis Group, *Liberia: Resurrecting the Justice System*, Africa Report (International Crisis Group, 6 April 2006), http://www.crisisgroup.org/~/media/Files/africa/west-africa/liberia/Liberia%20Resurrecting%20the%20Justice%20System.pdf
13. Caroline Sage and Michael Woolcock, 'Breaking Legal Inequality Traps: New Approaches to Building Justice Systems for the Poor in Developing Countries', in *Inclusive States: Social Policy and Structural Inequalities*, ed. Anis Dani and Arjan de Haan (Washington, D.C.: The World Bank, 2008), 369–394.
14. Brian Z. Tamanaha, 'A Non-Essentialist Version of Legal Empowerment', *Journal of Law and Society* 27, no. 2 (June 2000): 296–321.
15. United States Institute for Peace, *Looking for Justice: Liberian Experiences and Perceptions of Local Justice Options* (Washington, D.C., May 2009).
16. Ibid., 14.
17. Thomas Mawolo, South West Regional Coordinator, Justice and Peace Commission, Cape Palmas, Personal Interview, 18 February 2011; Jeff Austin, Former Regional Program Coordinator, Carter Center, Harper, Personal Interview, 7 December 2012.
18. Mawolo, South West Regional Coordinator, Justice and Peace Commission, Cape Palmas.
19. Chandler, *International Statebuilding*.
20. Richmond, *A Post-Liberal Peace*.
21. Chandler and Richmond, 'Contesting Post-Liberalism: Governmentality or Emancipation?'.
22. John Law, 'Notes on the Theory of the Actor-Network: Ordering, Strategy and Heterogeneity', *Systems Practice* 5 (1992): 1.

Bibliography

Adibe, Clement E. "Accepting External Authority in Peace-Maintenance". In *The Politics of Peace-Maintenance*, edited by Jarat Chopra. Boulder, CO: Lynne Rienner Publishers, 1998.

Adler, Emanuel. "The Emergence of Cooperation: National Epistemic Communities and the International Evolution of the Idea of Nuclear Arms Control". *International Organization* 46, no. 01 (22 May 2009): 101. doi:10.1017/S0020818300001466.

Adler, Emanuel and Vincent Pouliot. "International Practices: Introduction and Framework". In *International Practices*, edited by Emanuel Adler and Vincent Pouliot. New York: Cambridge University Press, 2011.

Adler, Patricia A. "Membership Roles in Field Research". *Qualitative Research Methods*, v. 6. Newbury Park, CA: Sage Publications, 1987.

Akingbade, Harrison. "The Pacification of the Liberian Hinterland". *The Journal of Negro History* 79, no. 3 (Summer 1994): 277–296.

Akrich, Madeleine. "The De-Scription of Technical Objects". In *Shaping Technology/Building Society: Studies in Technical Change*, edited by Weibe E. Bijker and John Law, 205–224. London: MIT press, 1992.

Anonymous. Senior UNMIL Official. Personal Interview, 1 July 2011.

Austin, Jeff. Former Regional Program Coordinator, the Carter Center, Harper. Personal Interview, 7 December 2012.

Banerjee, Abhijit and Esther Duflo. *Poor Economics: A Radical Rethinking of the Way to Fight Global Poverty*. New York: PublicAffairs, 2011.

Banerjee, Abhijit, Esther Duflo, Rachel Glennerster and Cynthia Kinnan. *The Miracle of Microfinance? Evidence from a Randomized Evaluation*. Working Paper. Bread Working Paper. Bureau for Research and Economic Analysis of Development, June 2010.

Barbu, Jallah A. "An Analysis of the Formal Legal Framework Governing Customary Law in the Republic of Liberia (DRAFT)". United States Institute of Peace: From Current Practices of Justice to Rule of Law: Policy Options for Liberia's First Post-Conflict Decade, n.d.

Barrett, C.B. and M.R. Carter. "The Power and Pitfalls of Experiments in Development Economics: Some Non-Random Reflections". *Applied Economic Perspectives and Policy* 32, no. 4 (8 December 2010): 515–548. doi:10.1093/aepp/ppq023.

Belloni, Roberto. "Civil Society in War-to-Democracy Transitions". In *From War to Democracy*, edited by Anna K. Jarstad and Timothy Sisk. Cambridge University Press, 2008.

Belloni, Roberto. "Hybrid Peace Governance: Its Emergence and Significance". *Global Governance* 18, no. 1 (March 2012): 21–37.

Belloni, Roberto and Jarstad K. Anna. "Introducing Hybrid Peace Governance: Impact and Prospects of Liberal Peacebuilding". *Global Governance* 18, no. 1 (March 2012): 1–6.

Bhabha, Homi K. *The Location of Culture*. 2nd ed. Abingdon, Oxon: Routledge, 2004.
Bigo, Diddier. "Security and Immigration: Toward a Critique of the Governmentality of Unease". *Alternatives: Global, Local, Political* 27, no. 1 (2002): 63–92.
Björkman, Martina and Jakob Svensson. "Power to the People: Evidence from a Randomized Field Experiment on Community-Based Monitoring in Uganda". *Quarterly Journal of Economics* 124, no. 2 (May 2009): 735–69. doi:10.1162/qjec.2009.124.2.735.
Blattman, Christopher, Alexandra C. Hartman and Robert A. Blair. "How to Promote Order and Property Rights under Weak Rule of Law? An Experiment in Changing Dispute Resolution Behavior Through Community Education". *American Political Science Review* 108, no. 01 (February 2014): 100–120. doi:10.1017/S0003055413000543.
Bøås, Morten and Anne Hatløy. " 'Getting In, Getting Out': Militia Membership and Prospects for Re-Integration in Post-War Liberia". *The Journal of Modern African Studies* 46, no. 01 (31 January 2008). doi:10.1017/S0022278X07003060.
Boege, Volker, Anne Brown, Kevin Clements and Nolan Anna. "On Hybrid Political Orders and Emerging States: State Formation in the Context of 'Fragility' ". Berghof Research Center for Constructive Conflict Management, 2008. http://www.berghof-handbook.net/documents/publications/dialogue8_boegeetal_lead.pdf
Bourdieu, Pierre. *The Logic of Practice*. Stanford: Stanford University Press, 1990.
Brigg, Morgan and Roland Bleiker. "Autoethnographic International Relations: Exploring the Self as a Source of Knowledge". *Review of International Studies* 36, no. 03 (8 July 2010): 779–798. doi:10.1017/S0260210510000689.
Brown, Anne, Volker Boege, Kevin Clements and Anna Nolan. "Challenging Statebuilding as Peacebuilding: Working with Hybrid Political Orders to Build Peace". In *Palgrave Advances in Peacebuilding: Critical Developments and Approaches*, edited by Richmond. London: Palgrave Macmillan, 2010.
Büger, Christian. "The Clash of Practice: Political Controversy and the United Nations Peacebuilding Commission". *Evidence & Policy: A Journal of Research, Debate and Practice* 7, no. 2 (19 May 2011): 171–191. doi:10.1332/174426411X579216.
Büger, Christian and Frank Gadinger. "Reassembling and Dissecting: International Relations Practice from a Science Studies Perspective". *International Studies Perspectives* 8, no. 1 (February 2007): 90–110. doi:10.1111/j.1528-3585.2007.00271.x.
Butler, Judith. *Gender Trouble*. New York: Routledge, 1989.
Cahill, Caitlin, Sultana Farhana and Pain Rachel. "Participatory Ethics: Politics, Practices, Institutions". *ACME: An International E-Journal for Critical Geographies* 6, no. 3 (2007): 304–318.
Caldwell, Raymond. "Agency and Change: Re-Evaluating Foucault's Legacy". *Organization* 14, no. 6 (1 November 2007): 769–791. doi:10.1177/1350508407082262.
Caldwell, Raymond. "Reclaiming Agency, Recovering Change? An Exploration of the Practice Theory of Theodore Schatzki". *Journal for the Theory of Social Behaviour* 42, no. 3 (September 2012): 283–303. doi:10.1111/j.1468-5914.2012.00490.x.

Callon, Michel. "Some Elements of a Sociology of Translation: Domestication of the Scallops and Fisherman of St. Brieuc Bay". In *Power, Action, and Belief: A New Sociology of Knowledge*, edited by John Law. London: Routledge & Kegan Paul, 1986. https://bscw.uni-wuppertal.de/pub/nj_bscw.cgi/d8022008/Callon_ SociologyTranslation.pdf

Caroline Sage and Michael Woolcock. "Breaking Legal Inequality Traps: New Approaches to Building Justice Systems for the Poor in Developing Countries". In *Inclusive States: Social Policy and Structural Inequalities*, edited by Anis Dani and Arjan de Haan, 369–394. Washington, DC: The World Bank, 2008.

Cartwright, Nancy. "Are RCTs the Gold Standard?" *BioSocieties* 2, no. 1 (March 2007): 11–20. doi:10.1017/S1745855207005029.

Certeau, Michel de. *The Practice of Everyday Life*. Berkeley: University of California Press, 1984.

Chandler, David. *International Statebuilding: The Rise of Post-Liberal Governance*. Critical Issues in Global Politics 2. London; New York: Routledge, 2010.

Chandler, David. "The Uncritical Critique of 'Liberal Peace'". *Review of International Studies* 36, no. S1 (26 August 2010): 137–155. doi:10.1017/S0260210510000823.

Chandler, David and Oliver Richmond. "Contesting Postliberalism: Governmentality or Emancipation?" *Journal of International Relations and Development* (27 June 2014). doi:10.1057/jird.2014.5.

Chopra, Jarat. "Introducing Peace-Maintenance". In *The Politics of Peace-Maintenance*, edited by Jarat Chopra. Boulder, CO: Lynne Rienner Publishers, 1998.

Connolly, William E. *A World of Becoming*. Durham, NC: Duke University Press, 2010.

Coole, Diana. "Rethinking Agency: A Phenomenological Approach to Embodiment and Agentic Capacities". *Political Studies* 53, no. 1 (22 March 2005): 124–142. doi:10.1111/j.1467-9248.2005.00520.x.

Coole, Diana H. and Samantha Frost. *New Materialisms: Ontology, Agency, and Politics*. Durham, NC; London: Duke University Press, 2010.

Cooper, Neil. "Review Article: On the Crisis of the Liberal Peace". *Conflict, Security & Development* 7, no. 4 (December 2007): 605–616. doi:10.1080/14678800701693025.

Crick, Tom. Associate Director of Conflict Resolution Programing, the Carter Center, Atlanta. Personal Interview, 27 November 2012.

Crocker, Chester A. "Southern African Peace-Making". *Survival* 32, no. 3 (1990): 221–232.

CSAE Evaluation Team. "Lightning Round Proposal." Internal Document, 2 June 2011.

CSAE Evaluation Team. "Field Observations from Witnessing CJA Awareness Sessions". 12 June 2011.

Diamond, Larry. "Promoting Democracy". *Foreign Policy*, no. 87 (Summer 1992): 25–46.

Donais, Timothy. "Empowerment or Imposition? Dilemmas of Local Ownership in Post-Conflict Peacebuilding Processes". *Peace & Change* 34, no. 1 (January 2009): 3–26. doi:10.1111/j.1468-0130.2009.00531.x.

Doyle, Michael W. "Liberalism and World Politics". *The American Political Science Review* 80, no. 4 (1 December 1986): 1151–1169. doi:10.2307/1960861.

Duffield, Mark. *Global Governance and the New Wars: The Merging of Development and Security.* 1.udg. ed. London: Zed, 2001.
Dwyer, Sonya C. and Jennifer L. Buckle. "The Space Between: On Being an Insider-Outsider in Qualitative Research". *International Journal of Qualitative Methods* 8, no. 1 (2009): 53–63.
Easterly, William. *The White Man's Burden.* London: Penguin Books, 2007.
Ellis, Stephen. *The Mask of Anarchy: The Destruction of Liberia and the Religious Dimension of an African Civil War.* New York: New York University Press, 2007.
Escobar, Arturo. "The 'Ontological Turn' in Social Theory. a Commentary on 'Human Geography Without Scale', by Sallie Marston, John Paul Jones II and Keith Woodward". *Transactions of the Institute of British Geographers* 32, no. 1 (January 2007): 106–111. doi:10.1111/j.1475-5661.2007.00243.x.
Fanthorpe, Richard. "On the Limits of Liberal Peace: Chiefs and Democratic Decentralization in Post-War Sierra Leone". *African Affairs* 105, no. 418 (September 2005): 27–49. doi:10.1093/afraf/adi091.
Flelah. Participant Observation, 7 June 2011.
Flomoku, Pewee. "Introductions". JPC Training Compound, Gbarnga, 16 February 2011.
Flomoku, Pewee. "Role Play: Entering a Community for the First Time". JPC Training Compound, Gbarnga, 23 February 2011.
Ford Foundation. *Many Roads to Justice: The Law-Related Work of Ford Foundation Grantees Around the World.* Edited by Mary McClymont and Stephen Golub. New York: Ford Foundation, 2000.
Foucault, Michel. *Discipline and Punish: The Birth of the Prison.* New York: Random House, 1978.
Foucault, Michel. *Power/Knowledge: Selected Interviews and Other Writings, 1972–1977.* Brighton, Sussex: Harvester Press, 1980.
Foucault, Michel. "The Subject of Power". In *Michel Foucault: Beyond Structuralism and Hermeneutics*, edited by Hubert Dreyfus and Paul Rabinow. Chicago: Chicago University Press, 1982.
Foucault, Michel. *The History of Sexuality: An Introduction.* Translated by Robert Hurley. New York: Vintage Books, 1990.
Foucault, Michel. *Security, Territory, Population: Lectures at the Collège De France, 1977–78.* Edited by François Ewald and Alessandro Fontana. Translated by Michel Senellart. New York: Picador, 2007.
Freeman, Richard. "What Is 'Translation'?". *Evidence & Policy: A Journal of Research, Debate and Practice* 5, no. 4 (1 November 2009): 429–447. doi:10.1332/174426409X478770.
Geertz, Clifford. *The Interpretation of Culture: Selected Essays.* New York: Basic Books, 1988.
Ghali, Boutros, B. "An Agenda for Development: Report for the Secretary General (A/48/935)". United Nations, 6 May 1994. http://www.un.org/Docs/SG/agdev.html
Ghali, Boutros, B. "An Agenda for Peace Preventive Diplomacy, Peacemaking and Peace-Keeping A/47/277 – S/24111". United Nations, 1992. http://www.unrol.org/files/A_47_277.pdf
Giddens, Anthony. *The Constitution of Society.* Berkeley: University of California Press, 1984.

Golub, Stephen. *Beyond Rule of Law Orthodoxy: The Legal Empowerment Alternative*. Working Paper. Rule of Law Series: Democracy and Law Project. Washington, DC: Carnegie Endowment of International Peace, October 2003. http://siteresources.worldbank.org/INTLAWJUSTINST/Resources/BeyondRuleOrthodoxy.pdf

Harvey, David. *The Condition of Postmodernity: An Enquiry into the Origins of Cultural Change*. Oxford: Blackwell, 1989.

Heathershaw, John. "The Practical Representation of Peacebuilding: An (Auto) Ethnography of Programme Evaluation in Tajikistan". In *Hybrid Forms of Peace: From Everyday Agency to Post-Liberalism*. Rethinking Peace and Conflict Studies. New York: Palgrave Macmillan, 2012.

Heathershaw, John. "Towards Better Theories of Peacebuilding: Beyond the Liberal Peace Debate". *Peacebuilding* 1, no. 2 (June 2013): 275–282. doi:10.1080/21647259.2013.783260.

Heidegger, Martin. *Being and Time*. New York: Harper & Row, 1963.

Huysmans, Jef. *The Politics of Insecurity: Fear, Migration, and Asylum in the EU*. The New International Relations. Milton Park, Abingdon, Oxon; New York: Routledge, 2006.

International Crisis Group. *Liberia: Resurrecting the Justice System*. Africa Report. International Crisis Group, 6 April 2006. http://www.crisisgroup.org/~/media/Files/africa/west-africa/liberia/Liberia%20Resurrecting%20the%20Justice%20System.pdf

Isser, Deborah. "The Problem with Problematizing Legal Pluralism: Lessons From the Field". In *Legal Pluralism and Development: Scholars and Practitioners in Dialogue*, edited by Brian Z. Tamanaha, Caroline Sage, and Michael Woolcock, 237–247. New York: Cambridge University Press, 2013.

Jonas, Andrew E. G. "Pro Scale: Further Reflections on the 'Scale Debate' in Human Geography". *Transactions of the Institute of British Geographers* 31, no. 3 (September 2006): 399–406. doi:10.1111/j.1475-5661.2006.00210.x.

Jones, John Paul, Keith Woodward and Sallie A Marston. "Situating Flatness". *Transactions of the Institute of British Geographers* 32, no. 2 (April 2007): 264–276. doi:10.1111/j.1475-5661.2007.00254.x.

Kaplan, Robert D. "The Coming Anarchy". *The Atlantic*, February 1994. http://www.theatlantic.com/magazine/archive/1994/02/the-coming-anarchy/304670/?single_page=true

Keohane, Robert. *After Hegemony: Cooperation and Discord in the World Political Economy*. Princeton, NJ: Princeton University Press, 1984.

Knight, Rachael, Judy Adoko, Teresa Auma, Alda Salomao, Silas Siakor and Issufo Tankar. *Protecting Community Lands and Resources: Evidence from Liberia, Mozambique, and Uganda*. Washington, DC: International Development Law Organization in Partnership with Namti, 2012. http://namati.wpengine.netdna-cdn.com/wp-content/uploads/2012/06/protecting_community_lands_resources_inter_FW.pdf

Krasner, Stephen D. "Sharing Sovereignty: New Institutions for Collapsed and Failing States". *International Security* 29, no. 2 (October 2004): 85–120. doi:10.1162/0162288042879940.

Latour, Bruno. "On Interobjectivity". *Mind, Culture, and Activity* 3, no. 4 (October 1996): 228–245. doi:10.1207/s15327884mca0304_2.

Latour, Bruno. "The Powers of Association". In *Power, Action, and Belief: A New Sociology of Knowledge*, edited by John Law. Routledge, Kegan Paul, 1987. http://www.bruno-latour.fr/sites/default/files/19-POWERS-ASSOCIATIONS-GBpdf.pdf

Latour, Bruno. "The Politics of Explanation: An Alternative". In *Knowledge and Reflexivity: New Frontiers in the Sociology of Knowledge*, edited by Steve Woolgar. University of Minnesota: Sage Publications Ltd, 1988.

Latour, Bruno. "On Recalling ANT". Edited by John Law and John Hassard. Wiley-Blackwell, 1999.

Latour, Bruno. *Reassembling the Social: An Introduction to Actor-Network Theory*. New York: Oxford University Press, 2004.

Law, John. "Notes on the Theory of the Actor-Network: Ordering, Strategy and Heterogeneity". *Systems Practice* 5 (1992): 379–393.

Law, John. *Organizing Modernity*. Oxford, UK; Cambridge, MA: Blackwell, 1994.

Law, John. "Traduction/Trahison: Notes on ANT". Department of Sociology, Lancaster University, 1997. http://www.lancaster.ac.uk/sociology/stslaw2.html

Law, John. "After ANT: Complexity, Naming and Topology". In *Actor Network Theory and After*, edited by John Law and John Hassard. Wiley-Blackwell, 1999.

Levy, Jack S. "Domestic Politics in War". In *The Origin and Prevention of Major Wars*, edited by Robert I. Rotberg and Theodore K. Rabb. New York: Cambridge University Press, 1989.

Lidén, Kristoffer. "Peace, Self-Governance and International Engagement: From Neo-Colonial to Post-Colonial Peacebuilding". In *Rethinking the Liberal Peace: External Model and Local Alternatives*, edited by Shahrbanou Tadjbakhsh, 57–74. Abingdon, Oxon; New York: Routledge, 2011.

Loughlan, Victoria, Christian Olsson and Peer Schouten. "Mapping". In *Critical Security Methods: New Frameworks for Analysis*, edited by Claudia Aradau, Jef Huysmans, Andrew Neal and Nadine Voelkner, 23–56. Abingdon, Oxon, England; New York: Routledge, 2015.

Lubkemann, Stephen C., Deborah Isser and Philip A. Z. Banks. "Unintended Consequences: Constraint of Customary Justice in Post-Conflict Liberia". In *Customary Justice and the Rule of Law in War-Torn Societies*, edited by Deborah Isser. Peacebuilding and the Rule of Law. Washington, DC: United States Institute of Peace Press, 2011.

Mac Ginty, Roger. "Indigenous Peace-Making versus the Liberal Peace". *Cooperation and Conflict* 43, no. 2 (1 June 2008): 139–163. doi:10.1177/0010836708089080.

Mac Ginty, Roger. "Hybrid Peace: The Interaction between Top-Down and Bottom-Up Peace". *Security Dialogue* 41, no. 4 (23 August 2010): 391–412. doi:10.1177/0967010610374312.

Mac Ginty, Roger. *International Peacebuilding and Local Resistance: Hybrid Forms of Peace*. New York: Palgrave Macmillan, 2011.

Mac Ginty, Roger. "Indicators+: A Proposal for Everyday Peace Indicators". *Evaluation and Program Planning* 36, no. 1 (February 2013): 56–63. doi:10.1016/j.evalprogplan.2012.07.001.

Mac Ginty, Roger and Gurchathen Sanghera. "Hybridity in Peacebuilding and Development: An Introduction". *Journal of Peacebuilding & Development* 7, no. 2 (August 2012): 3–8. doi:10.1080/15423166.2012.742800.

Mac Ginty, Roger and Oliver P. Richmond. "The Local Turn in Peace Building: A Critical Agenda for Peace". *Third World Quarterly* 34, no. 5 (June 2013): 763–783. doi:10.1080/01436597.2013.800750.

Manzo, Lynn and Nathan Brightbill. "Towards a Participatory Ethics". In *Connecting People, Participation and Place: Participatory Action Research Approaches and Methods*, edited by Sara Kindon, Rachel Pain, and Mike Kesby, 33–40. London: Routledge, 2007.

March, James G. "Footnotes to Organizational Change". *Administrative Science Quarterly* 26, no. 4 (December 1981): 563–577.

Marston, Sallie A., John Paul Jones and Keith Woodward. "Human Geography Without Scale". *Transactions of the Institute of British Geographers* 30, no. 4 (December 2005): 416–32. doi:10.1111/j.1475-5661.2005.00180.x.

Maru, Vivek. "Between Law and Society: Paralegals and the Provision of Justice Services in Sierra Leone and Worldwide". *Yale Journal of International Law* 31 (2006): 427–476.

Maru, Vivek. "Access to Justice and Legal Empowerment: A Review of World Bank Practice". *Hague Journal on the Rule of Law* 2, no. 02 (17 December 2010): 259–281. doi:10.1017/S1876404510200076.

Mattern, Janice B. "A Practice Theory of Emotions for International Relations". In *International Practices*, edited by Emanuel Adler and Vincent Pouliot. New York: Cambridge University Press, 2011.

Mawolo, Thomas. South West Regional Coordinator, Justice and Peace Commission, Cape Palmas. Personal Interview, 18 February 2011.

Maxwell, Simon. *The Washington Consensus Is Dead! Long Live the Meta-Narrative!*. London: Overseas Development Institute (ODI), 2005.

Migdal, Joel S. *Strong Societies and Weak States: State-Society Relations and State Capabilities in the Third World*. Princeton, NJ: Princeton University Press, 1988.

Mitchell, Audra. "Quality/Control: International Peace Interventions and 'the Everyday'". *Review of International Studies* 37, no. 4 (12 May 2011): 1623–1645. doi:10.1017/S0260210511000180.

Momodu, Harry. JPC Community Legal Advisor, Bong County. Group Discussion, 27 May 2011.

Moran, Mary. *Liberia: The Violence of Democracy*. Philadelphia: University of Pennsylvania Press, 2006.

Moyo, Dambisa. *Dead Aid: Why Aid Is Not Working and How There Is a Better Way for Africa*. 1st American ed. New York: Farrar, Straus and Giroux, 2009.

Narten, Jens. "Dilemmas of Promoting 'Local Ownership': The Case of Post-War Kosovo". In *The Dilemmas of Statebuilding: Confronting the Contradictions of Post-War Peace Operations*, edited by Roland Paris and Timothy Sisk. London; New York: Routledge, 2010.

National Traditional Council. "Resolution Regarding Critical Issues Facing Liberia and Its Traditional People as We Strive to Achieve Lasting Peace and Prosperity: Based on Three Consultative Conferences of Traditional Leaders Held in Bomi, Bong, & Grand Gedeh Counties". National Traditional Council, August 2009. http://www.cartercenter.org/resources/pdfs/peace/conflict_resolution/liberia/NTC-Resolution2008.pdf

National Traditional Council. "The 26 February 2010 Resolution Held in the City of Voinjama Between the Lormas and Mandingos of Voinjama City, Lofa County, Republic of Liberia", 8 May 2010. http://

www.cartercenter.org/resources/pdfs/peace/conflict_resolution/liberia/LormaMandingoElders-agreements.pdf

Neumann, Iver B. "To Be a Diplomat". *International Studies Perspectives* 6, no. 1 (February 2005): 72–93. doi:10.1111/j.1528-3577.2005.00194.x.

Newman, Edward. "Liberal Peacebuilding Debates". In *New Perspectives on Liberal Peacebuilding*. Tokyo; New York: United Nations University Press, 2009.

Nimlay, Prince. JPC Community Justice Advisor, Bong County. Group Discussion, 27 May 2011.

Oneal, John R. and Bruce Russett. *Triangulating Peace: Democracy, Interdependence, and International Organizations*. 1st ed. W. W. Norton & Company, 2001.

Ortner, Sherry. "Theory in Anthropology since the Sixties". *Comparative Studies in Society and History* 26, no. 1 (January 1984): 126–166.

Paris, Roland. *At War's End: Building Peace After Civil Conflict*. Reprinted. Cambridge [u.a.]: Cambridge University Press, 2005.

Paris, Roland. "Saving Liberal Peacebuilding". *Review of International Studies* 36, no. 02 (23 April 2010): 337. doi:10.1017/S0260210510000057.

Paris, Roland and Timothy D. Sisk. *The Dilemmas of Statebuilding: Confronting the Contradictions of Postwar Peace Operations*. Security and Governance Series. London; New York: Routledge, 2009.

Peterson, Jenny H. "A Conceptual Unpacking Of Hybridity: Accounting for Notions Of Power, Politics and Progress in Analyses of Aid-Driven Interfaces". *Journal of Peacebuilding & Development* 7, no. 2 (August 2012): 9–22. doi:10.1080/15423166.2012.742802.

Pickering, Andrew. *The Mangle of Practice: Time, Agency, and Science*. Chicago: University of Chicago Press, 1995.

Pickett, Brent, L. "Foucault and the Politics of Resistance". *Polity* 28, no. 4 (Summer 1996): 445–466.

Pollner, Melvin and Robert M. Emerson. "Ethnomethodology and Ethnography". In *Handbook of Ethnography*, 118–135. Thousand Oaks: Sage Publications Ltd, 2001.

Pouliot, Vincent. "The Logic of Practicality: A Theory of Practice of Security Communities". *International Organization* 62, no. 02 (3 April 2008). doi:10.1017/S0020818308080090.

Pugh, Michael. "The Political Economy of Peacebuilding: A Critical Theory Perspective". *International Journal of Peace Studies* 10, no. 2 (Autumn/Winter 2005): 23–42.

Pugh, Michael C., Neil Cooper, and Mandy Turner, eds. *Whose Peace? Critical Perspectives on the Political Economy of Peacebuilding*. New Security Challenges Series. Basingstoke [England]; New York: Palgrave Macmillan, 2008.

Rabinow, Paul. *Essays on the Anthropology of Reason*. Princeton: Princeton University Press, 1996.

Rasmussen, Mikkel. *The West, Civil Society, and the Construction of Peace*. Basingstoke, Hampshire; New York: Palgrave Macmillan, 2003.

Reckwitz, Andreas. "Toward a Theory of Social Practices: A Development in Culturalist Theorizing". *European Journal of Social Theory* 5, no. 2 (1 May 2002): 243–263. doi:10.1177/13684310222225432.

Reckwitz, Andreas. "The Status of the 'Material' in Theories of Culture: From 'Social Structure' to 'Artefacts' ". *Journal for the Theory of Social Behaviour* 32, no. 2 (June 2002): 195–217. doi:10.1111/1468-5914.00183.

Reno, William. "African Weak States and Commercial Alliances". *African Affairs* 96, no. 383 (April 1997): 165–185.
Reno, William. *Warlord Politics and African States*. Boulder, CO: Lynne Rienner Publishers, 1998.
Republic of Liberia. *The Liberian National Decentralization and Local Development Program*, May 2007. http://www.infoliberia.org/doc_download/County%20development%20funds.pdf?a4705305cd27e04fb1f66830e7e0ef9d=MTMx
Republic of Liberia. "Poverty Reduction Strategy (PRS)", April 2008. http://www.emansion.gov.lr/doc/Final%20PRS.pdf
Republic of Liberia. "Liberian Peacebuilding Programme DRAFT", 2 May 2011. http://www.unpbf.org/wp-content/uploads/Final-Approved-LPP-May-5-20111.pdf
Republic of Liberia and UNMIL. "Priority Plan for Peacebuilding Fund (PBF): Liberia". United Nations Peacebuilding Fund, March 2009. mdtf.undp.org/document/download/6299
Richards, Paul. *Fighting for the Rain Forest: War, Youth & Resources in Sierra Leone*. African Issues. Portsmouth, NH: Heinemann, 1996.
Richmond, Oliver. *The Transformation of Peace*. Basingstoke: Palgrave Macmillan, 2007.
Richmond, Oliver. "A Post-Liberal Peace: Eirenism and the Everyday". *Review of International Studies* 35, no. 03 (6 July 2009): 557. doi:10.1017/S026021050900 8651.
Richmond, Oliver. "Resistance and the Post-Liberal Peace". *Millennium – Journal of International Studies* 38, no. 3 (10 May 2010): 665–692. doi:10.1177/0305829810365017.
Richmond, Oliver. "Critical Agency, Resistance and a Post-Colonial Civil Society". *Cooperation and Conflict* 46, no. 4 (1 December 2011): 419–440. doi:10.1177/0010836711422416.
Richmond, Oliver. *A Post-Liberal Peace*. Routledge Studies in Peace and Conflict Resolution. Milton Park, Abingdon, Oxon [England]; New York: Routledge, 2011.
Richmond, Oliver. "Failed Statebuilding Versus Peace Formation". *Cooperation and Conflict* 48, no. 3 (26 July 2013): 378–400. doi:10.1177/0010836713482816.
Richmond, Oliver and Audra Mitchell, eds. *Hybrid Forms of Peace: From Everyday Agency to Post-Liberalism*. Houndmills, Basingstoke, Hampshire; New York: Palgrave Macmillan, 2012.
Richmond, Oliver. "The Dilemmas of a Hybrid Peace: Negative or Positive?" *Cooperation and Conflict* (12 June 2014). doi:10.1177/0010836714537053.
Rohini, Pande and Christopher Udry. "Institutions and Development: A View from Below". *Yale University Economic Growth Center Discussion Paper*, 2005. http://dev.wcfia.harvard.edu/sites/default/files/PandeUdry2005.pdf
Rouse, Joseph. *Engaging Science: How to Understand Its Practices Philosophically*. Ithaca: Cornell University Press, 1996.
Rouse, Joseph. "Practice Theory". *Division I Faculty Publications: Paper* 43, 2007. http://wesscholar.wesleyan.edu/div1facpubs/43
Sachs, Jeffrey. *The End of Poverty: Economic Possibilities for Our Time*. New York: Penguin Books, 2005.

Salter, Mark B. "Introduction". In *Research Methods in Critical Security Studies: An Introduction*, edited by Mark B. Salter and Can E. Mutlu. Abingdon, Oxon: Routledge, 2013.

Sandefur, Justin. Principal Investigator, Centre for the Study of African Economies. Personal Interview, 29 May 2012.

Sandefur, Justin and Bilal Siddiqi. "Delivering Justice to the Poor: Theory and Experimental Evidence from Liberia". *DRAFT*, November 2013. https://editorialexpress.com/cgi-bin/conference/download.cgi?db_name=CSAE2013&paper_id=1014

Sawyer, Amos. *Beyond Plunder: Toward Democratic Governance in Liberia*. Boulder, CO: L. Rienner Publishers, Inc, 2005.

Schatzki, Theodore R. "Introduction". In *The Practice Turn in Contemporary Theory*, edited by Theodore R. Schatzki, Karin Knorr-Cetina and Eike Von Savigny. New York: Routledge, 2001.

Schatzki, Theodore R. *The Site of the Social: A Philosophical Account of the Constitution of Social Life and Change*. University Park: Pennsylvania State University Press, 2002.

Schatzki, Theodore R. *The Timespace of Human Activity: On Performance, Society, and History as Indeterminate Teleological Events*. Toposophia. Lanham, MD: Lexington Books, 2010.

Schatzki, Theodore R., K. Knorr-Cetina and Eike von Savigny, eds. *The Practice Turn in Contemporary Theory*. New York: Routledge, 2001.

Scott, James C. *Weapons of the Weak: Everyday Forms of Peasant Resistance*. New Haven; London: Yale University Press, 1985.

Scott, James C. *Domination and the Arts of Resistance: Hidden Transcripts*. New Haven: Yale University Press, 1990.

Scott, James C. *The Art of Not Being Governed: An Anarchist History of Upland Southeast Asia*. New Haven: Yale University Press, 2009.

Siddiqi, Bilal. Principal Investigator, Centre for the Study of African Economies. Personal Interview, 16 July 2012.

Smith, Dorothy E., ed. *Institutional Ethnography as Practice*. Lanham, MD: Rowman & Littlefield, 2006.

Socopa. Participant Observation, 10 June 2011.

Spinoza, Benedictus de. *Ethics*. Oxford Philosophical Texts. Oxford; New York: Oxford University Press, 2000.

Spivak, Gayatri Chakravorty. "Can the Subaltern Speak?". In *Marxism and the Interpretation of Culture*, edited by Cary Nelson and Lawrence Grossberg, 271–315. Chicago, IL: University of Illinois Press, 1988.

Steiner, George. *After Babel: Aspects of Language and Translation*. Oxford; New York: Oxford University Press, 1998.

Tadjbakhsh, Shahrbanou, ed. *Rethinking the Liberal Peace: External Models and Local Alternatives*. Cass Series on Peacekeeping. Abingdon, Oxon; New York: Routledge, 2011.

Tamanaha, Brian Z. "A Non-Essentialist Version of Legal Empowerment". *Journal of Law and Society* 27, no. 2 (June 2000): 296–321.

Tellidis, Ioannis. "The End of the Liberal Peace? Post-Liberal Peace vs. Post-Liberal States". *International Studies Review* 14, no. 3 (September 2012): 429–435. doi:10.1111/j.1468-2486.2012.01137.x.

The Carter Center. "Findings of the Legal Working Group", 10 December 2009. http://www.cartercenter.org/resources/pdfs/peace/conflict_resolution/liberia/LWG-findings-2010.pdf

The Carter Center. "Liberia: Policy Dialogue and Reform". Press Release, n.d. http://www.cartercenter.org/peace/conflict_resolution/liberia-policy-dialogue-reform.html

The Carter Center. "The Empowerment-Oriented Approach". JPC Training Compound, Gbarnga, 23 February 2011.

The Carter Center. "Manual for JPC Community Legal Advisers (DRAFT)". The Carter Center, February 2011.

The Carter Center Document. "The Carter Center/JPC Community Legal Advisors Program in South East and Central Liberia", n.d.

Tkacia, Maureen. "The Pragmatic Rebels", *Bloomberg Businessweek*, 5 July 2010. http://www.businessweek.com/magazine/content/10_28/b4186056393103.htm

Tom, Patrick. "In Search for Emancipatory Hybridity: The Case of Post-War Sierra Leone". *Peacebuilding* 1, no. 2 (June 2013): 239–255. doi:10.1080/21647259.2013.783256.

United States Institute for Peace. *Looking for Justice: Liberian Experiences and Perceptions of Local Justice Options*. Washington, DC, May 2009.

U.S. Department of Education. *Identifying and Implementing Educational Practices Supported by Rigorous Evidence: A User Friendly Guide*. Washington, DC: U.S. Department of Education and the Council of Excellence in Government, December 2003. http://www2.ed.gov/rschstat/research/pubs/rigorousevid/rigorousevid.pdf

Wenger, Etienne. *Communities of Practice: Learning, Meaning, and Identity*. Cambridge, UK; New York: Cambridge University Press, 1999.

Wenger, Etienne. *Cultivating Communities of Practice: A Guide to Managing Knowledge*. Boston, MA: Harvard Business School Press, 2002.

Wittgenstein, Ludwig. *Philosophical Investigations*. Oxford: Blackwell, 1953.

Woodward, Keith, John Paul Jones III and Sallie A Marston. "Of Eagles and Flies: Orientations toward the Site". *Area* 42, no. 3 (January 2010): 271–280. doi:10.1111/j.1475-4762.2009.00922.x.

Zaum, Dominik. "Beyond the 'Liberal Peace'". *Global Governance*, Special Issue: Hybrid Peace Governance, 18, no. 1 (March 2012): 121–132.

Zulu, Bouku. Vice Chairman, National Traditional Council, Monrovia. Group Interview, 25 November 2009.

Index

Note: The letter 'n' following locators refers to notes.

Aborigines Law, 79
abstract machines, substantialization of, 53
ACS, see American Colonial Society (ACS)
active legal empowerment, 139–40
Actor Network Theory (ANT), 7
Adibe, Clement E., 21, 168 n.14
Adler, Emanuel, 13, 48, 49, 52, 167 n.37, 175 n.2, 175 n.21, 176 n.25–7
Adler, Patricia A., 178 n.12
Adoko, Judy, 187 n.19
Akingbade, Harrison, 77, 179 n.3, 179 n.7, 179 n.12, 179 n.18
Akrich, Madeleine, 166 n.21
Alternative Dispute Resolution, 94
American Colonial Society (ACS), 76
American-style "legal liberalism," 92
Anna, Jarstad K., 170 n.46
Anna, Noland, 170 n.39
ANT, see Actor Network Theory (ANT)
'apple' communities, 96
appropriation, 48, 57
 definition of, 58
 legal empowerment: into Liberian communities, 109–12; into political impact, 139–44; into randomized controlled trial, 123–7; statutory justice into, 91–5
a priori standard of reference, 65
Arthur Grimes Law School, 87
Auma, Teresa, 187 n.19
Austin, Jeff, 108, 111, 183 n.1, 184 n.16, 184 n.23, 187 n.21, 188 n.17

Banerjee, Abhijit, 125–6, 185 n.20, 185 n.25, 186 n.28, 186 n.38
Banks, Philip A. Z., 179 n.2, 181 n.2, 188 n.11

Barbu, Jallah A., 77–9, 178 n.1
Barrett, C. B., 185 n.11, 186 n.36
Belloni, Roberto, 23, 25–6, 169 n.33, 170 n.40, 170 n.50
Bhabha, Homi K., 5, 22, 24, 166 n.16, 169 n.22, 170 n.38, 187 n.5
Bigo, Diddier, 5, 172 n.21, 175 n.22, 176 n.23
Björkman, Martina, 124, 185 n.13, 186 n.37
Blair, Robert A., 187 n.20
Blattman, Christopher, 147, 187 n.20
Bleiker, Roland, 65, 178 n.14
Bøås, Morten, 179 n.27
Boege, Volker, 165 n.1, 170 n.39
Bosnia, democratization in, 21
bottom-up peacebuilding, 82–3
Bourdieu, Pierre, 13, 37, 48, 50–1, 53, 167 n.36, 172 n.15, 175 n.15
Brigg, Morgan, 65, 178 n.14
Brightbill, Nathan, 177 n.19
Brown, Anne, 25, 170 n.39
Buckle, Jennifer L., 64, 65, 178 n.10, 178 n.13
Büger, Christian, 49, 172 n.22, 174 n.1
Butler, Judith, 37, 172 n.13

Cahill, Caitlin, 178 n.9
Caldwell, Raymond, 50, 55, 166 n.23, 173 n.27, 173 n.32, 175 n.6, 175 n.12, 175 n.20, 176 n.42
Callon, Michel, 13, 48, 56–7, 59, 88, 166 n.22, 172 n.18, 174 n.59, 177 n.53, 178 n.24, 181 n.4, 188 n.10
Carter Center Document, 184 n.15
Carter, M. R., 109, 185 n.11
Cartwright, Nancy, 167 n.33, 185 n.11
Catholic Justice and Peace Commission (JPC), 10

200

Centre for the Study of African Economies (CSAE), 63, 97, 98, 101, 131, 132
   politically impactful data, 144–7
   survey, 14, 119, 120, 123
Certeau, Michel de, 37, 171 n.12
Chandler, David, 3–4, 21, 28–32, 61, 150–2, 163, 165 n.8, 166 n.14, 166 n.25, 168 n.2, 170 n.59, 171 n.1, 175 n.4, 181 n.61, 187 n.1, 188 n.19
   post-liberal approach, 3
Chopra, Jarat, 21, 168 n.9
   notion of 'peace maintenance,' 21
civil society organizations (CSOs), 84–5
   informal, alternative justice-related, 94
   network of, 90
   working relationships with county-based local, 91
CJA, *see* Community Justice Adviser (CJA)
classic hybridity trap, 64
Clements, Kevin, 170 n.39
colonial history of Liberia, 76–81
The Coming Anarchy (Kaplan), 80
communication, psychosocial techniques of, 115
communities of practice, 51–2
Community Justice Adviser (CJA)
   case intake, 141–2
   case management, 142–4
   justice gaps, 101
   legal empowerment practices, 12, 69, 70
   map of, 97
   performative continuity of, 69
   practice legal empowerment, 116
   toolbox, 113–15
Community Justice Adviser (CJA) program, 9–11, 63, 69, 109, 154–5
   complexity of, 109
   daily operations of, 109
   designing, 12, 96–8, 103
   impact of, 105
   implementation and evaluation of, 13

indirect legal empowerment, 112–13
   innovation of, 115
   justice option, 11
   launching, 103
   legal empowerment, 108
   purpose of, 112
   RCT-based design of, 117
   scope of, 97
   statutory *vs.* customary justice, 10, 110–11
Community Legal Adviser program, 95
community mobilization, 140–1
Connolly, William E., 166 n.15, 166 n.17, 187 n.6
control communities, 98
Coole, Diana H., 38–9, 166 n.17, 173 n.28, 173 n.36
Cooper, Neil, 168 n.2, 168 n.7, 169 n.18
cowfur, 89
Crick, Tom, 90, 101, 127, 182 n.11, 182 n.13, 183 n.51, 184 n.18, 186 n.32, 187 n.21
'critical' researcher, 64
Crocker, Chester A., 168 n.4
CSAE, *see* Centre for the Study of African Economies (CSAE)
CSAE Evaluation Team, 185 n.9, 186 n.11
CSOs, *see* civil society organizations (CSOs)
customary justice
   practitioners, 83, 89, 90
   restorative nature of, 100
   statutory justice *vs.*, 110–11
   system, 98
customary practices, 90

decentralization strategy in Liberia, 84
democracy, market-based, 20
democratization in Bosnia, 21
Diamond, Larry, 168 n.6
dilemmas analysis approach, 23
domestic civil society, emergence and development of, 23
domestic violence, 109, 115
Donais, Timothy, 169 n.35

Doyle, Michael W., 168 n.6
Duffield, Mark, 21, 168 n.15
Duflo, Esther, 125–6, 185 n.20, 185 n.25, 186 n.28
Dwyer, Sonya C., 64–5, 178 n.10, 178 n.12–13

Easterly, William, 125, 185 n.22, 185 n.24
economic development, poverty trap slogan of, 92
economic liberalization, 21–2
emergent hybridity, 3
  defined, 5
  post-liberal process of, 13
  temporal politics of, 5
  transformative politics of, 4–5
emerging hybrid processes, 20
Emerson, Robert M., 66, 178 n.17
Escobar, Arturo, 43, 174 n.61, 174 n.65
ethnography, 65–6
'explanation,' definition of, 3
explanatory hybridity, 3, 36

Fanthorpe, Richard, 169 n.25, 180 n.38, 181 n.3
Farhana, Sultana, 178 n.9
Flomoku, Pewee, 109, 113, 184 n.20, 184 n.26
Ford Foundation, 92, 94, 182 n.26
formal justice process, 99
Foucault, Michel, 13, 19, 29, 37, 48–50, 166 n.25, 167 n.35, 168 n.1, 171 n.11, 173 n.50, 175 n.7, 175 n.9, 181 n.61
  discursive determinism, 50
  notion of resistance, 50
  theories of power and resistance, 49
Freeman, Richard, 7, 55–6, 166 n.24, 176 n.48, 177 n.51, 188 n.9
Frost, Samantha, 166 n.17, 173 n.28
function over form, 93

Gadinger, Frank, 172 n.22
Geertz, Clifford, 172 n.19
gender-based violence, 115

genealogy of hybridity
  description, 19–20
  emerging post-liberal world, 28–31
  explaining, 24–8
  liberal peace to local, 20–4
Ghali, Boutros, B., 168 n.5
Giddens, Anthony, 37, 53, 172 n.16
Glennerster, Rachel, 186 n.28
global conspiracy, 23
Global Law Programs Learning Initiative (GLPLI), 94
GLPLI, *see* Global Law Programs Learning Initiative (GLPLI)
Golub, Stephen, 94–5, 106, 167 n.30, 182 n.28
governmentality, 49–50

habitus, 50–1
  description of, 52
  Mattern's critique of, 52
'harmonization' strategy, 84
Hartman, Alexandra C., 187 n.20
Harvey, David, 174 n.59
Hatløy, Anne, 179 n.27
Heathershaw, John, 27, 165 n.3, 170 n.55
Heidegger, Martin, 36
Hinterland Regulations of 1949, 79
Hub model, 84–5
human rights, 100
Huysmans, Jef, 172 n.21, 177 n.4
hybridity
  concept of, 1
  defined, 1
  explanatory, 3
  explanatory and emergent politics of, 52–3
  genealogy of, *see* genealogy of hybridity
  liberal–local: alterity *vs.*, 5; explanation of, 4
  paradox of, 2–3
  process of, 36

indirect legal empowerment, 109–12
  assessment, 137–9
  Flelah, 136–7
  impact of, 120–3

practicing, 111–12
Socopa, 137
tools of, 112–17
institutional ethnography, 65–6
institutionalization, 21
International Crisis Group (ICG)
  report, 82–3, 87, 91, 101, 103, 180 n.48, 180 n.50, 181 n.3, 184 n.2, 188 n.12
International Development Law Organization, 92–4
international peacebuilders, 21
international peacebuilding, 22
  projects, 1, 10
Isser, Deborah, 91, 98, 179 n.2, 181 n.1–2, 182 n.4, 183 n.58, 187 n.22, 188 n.11

Jonas, Andrew E.G., 174 n.61
Jones, John Paul, III, 43, 172 n.20, 174 n.61–5, 174 n.72–3
Justice and Peace Commission (JPC), 90–1, 106, 108–10, 113, 121, 127, 135, 137, 138, 140, 142, 148, 155, 157, 158
justice in Liberia, 75–6
  accepted duality of, 14
  colonial history, 76–80
  future of, 155
  liberal monopoly on, 148
  limits and meaning of, 70
  peacebuilding, 80–5
  post-liberal, 103
  reimagining, 91–2
  restorative, 100
justice practitioners, 115–16
  customary, 83, 89, 90, 93, 102, 114
  international, 86, 103
  network of, 85, 92
  political situation for, 87
  post-liberal justice, 88
  statutory, 87

Kaplan, Robert D., 80, 81, 180 n.30
Keohane, Robert, 168 n.6
Kinnan, Cynthia, 186 n.28
Knight, Rachael, 187 n.19
Knorr-Cetina, K., 171 n.9, 176 n.39, 187 n.7

Krasner, Stephen D., 168 n.11
problem-solving approach, 21

Latour, Bruno, 3, 9, 13–14, 34–5, 37, 39, 42, 44, 48, 60, 62, 67–8, 165 n.7, 166 n.22, 167 n.27, 167 n.39, 171 n.1, 171 n.6, 172 n.14, 173 n.42, 174 n.59–60, 177 n.58, 178 n.19, 178 n.28
  critique of the politics, 67
  mapping strategy, 9
  proposes a sociology of associations, 67
Law, John, 44, 55, 172 n.18, 174 n.70, 176 n.47, 178 n.24, 188 n.22
legal aid, 11, 92–5, 106, 117, 123, 132, 145, 159, 160
legal development, paradigm shift in approaches to, 94
legal empowerment, 10, 94–5
  active, 139–44
  CJA, 12
  Golub's work on, 106
  indirect, 109–12, 135–9
  intervention, 95–102
  into Liberian communities: appropriation, 109–12; performance, 113–16; problematization, 106–9
  Maru description of, 107–8
  organizing, 106–9
  peacebuilding practices, 11
  performance, 144–7
  into political impact: appropriation, 139–44; performance, 144–9; problematization, 135–9
  project in Liberia, 69–70
  into randomized controlled trial: appropriation, 123–7; performance, 127–31; problematization, 120–3
  and RCTs, 12–13
  statutory justice into, 88–102
  translating in political impact, 134–5
legal liberalism, American-style, 92
legal pluralism, 92–4

Legal Working Group (LWG), 77, 92, 102
  recommendations, 102
Levy, Jack S., 168 n.6
liberalization, 21
liberal–local alterity *vs.* hybridity, 5
liberal–local dichotomy, 4
liberal–local hybridity, 2
  explanatory lens of, 8
  explanatory theoretical limits of, 64
  paradox of, 2–3
liberal peace
  crisis, 20, 21
  defense of, 23
  Richmond's critique of, 22
Liberia
  colonial history, 76–81
  culture, 81
  decentralization strategy, 84
  dual justice system in, 87–8, 106
  formal justice process, 99
  and international donors fund, 83
  justice related interventions, 88
  legal empowerment intervention in, 57
  Liberian Government and United Nations Mission in, 84
  National Traditional Council (NTC), 89–90
  nature of law in, 95
  'over-centralization' of, 82
  paralegal project for, 95
  peacebuilding intervention in, 9
  peacebuilding strategy, 83–4
  power and emancipation in, 9
  reimagining justice in, 91–2
  statutory legal establishment, 88–9
  types of trials in, 89
Liberian Bar Association, 87
Liberian communities, legal empowerment into, 106–16
Liberian Constitution, 76, 87
Liberian Legal Working Group (LWG), 77
Liberian National Decentralization, 84
Liberian Supreme Court, 76
Lidén, Kristoffer, 170 n.37
Lightning Round (LR) survey, 128–31
Local Development Program, 84

local peace indicators, Mac Ginty's work on, 2
Looking for Justice: Liberian Experiences and Perceptions of Local Justice Options (L4J), 98–100
Loughlan, Victoria, 177 n.4
Lubkemann, Stephen C., 92, 98, 179 n.2, 181 n.2, 188 n.11
LWG, *see* Legal Working Group (LWG)

Mac Ginty, Roger, 1–2, 22, 25, 165 n.1–6, 169 n.24, 169 n.36, 170 n.40–1
Manzo, Lynn, 177 n.9
mapping peacebuilding practice, 61–2
  legal empowerment project in Liberia, 69–70
  methodological orientation, 65–9
  practicing critical methodology, 62–5
March, James G., 176 n.26
market-based democracy, 20
Marston, Sallie A., 43, 172 n.20, 174 n.61–5, 174 n.72–3
Maru, Vivek, 106–8, 183 n.2, 184 n.10, 184 n.13
Mattern, Janice B., 6, 37–8, 52–3, 166 n.19, 173 n.24, 173 n.34, 175 n.20, 176 n.29
Mawolo, Thomas, 111, 182 n.12, 184 n.19, 186 n.6, 188 n.17–18
Maxwell, Simon, 169 n.17
meta-theorizing, 23
methodological orientation, mapping peacebuilding practice, 65–9
methodology as practice, defined, 62
Migdal, Joel S., 179 n.28
Ministry of Internal Affairs (MoIA), 77
Mitchell, Audra, 4, 27, 63, 165 n.1, 167 n.29, 170 n.57, 171 n.68, 177 n.6, 178 n.16, 187 n.2
Momodu, Harry, 120–1, 185 n.4
Monrovian legal establishment, 91
Moran, Mary, 180 n.29
Moyo, Dambisa, 125, 185 n.23

Namibia, 1989 peacekeeping mission in, 20
Narten, Jens, 169 n.34

national harmonization, 91
National Patriotic Front of Liberia (NPFL), 80
National Traditional Council (NTC), 89–90, 181 n.5, 181 n.8, 182 n.10
network of justice practitioners, 88
Neumann, Iver B., 172 n.21
Newman, Edward, 20, 23, 168 n.8, 169 n.26
Nimlay, Prince, 121, 185 n.6
Nolan, Anna, 170 n.39

Olsson, Christian, 177 n.4
Oneal, John R., 168 n.6
ontological primacy, 54
ontology of practice, 53
organization of practice, 53
organized peacebuilding projects, 6
organized practices
  material manifestation of, 55
  relative continuity and stability of, 49
  unstable continuum of, 48
Ortner, Sherry, 172 n.19
'over-centralization' of Liberia, 82

paralegal, 95, 107
  programs, 83, 95, 156–7
  training, 10
Paris, Roland, 21, 23, 168 n.12, 169 n.28, 169 n.31
partrimonialism, 81
PCS, *see* Peace and Conflict Studies (PCS)
PDAs, *see* Personal Digital Assistants (PDAs)
peace
  dimensions of, 2–3
  formation, post-liberal process of, 4
  hybrid forms of, 2
  indicators, local, 2
  liberal international epistemology of, 2
  transformative politics of, 3
Peace and Conflict Studies (PCS), 1
  liberal–local hybridity, 2
  post-liberal change in, 3
  post-liberal turn in, 3–5

problem solving and critical approaches in, 20–1
peacebuilding
  alternative emancipatory approach to, 22
  contexts, complexity of hybridity in, 1
  political economy of, 22
  post-liberal politics of, 68
  in practice, 83–5
  practices, *see* practice, peacebuilding
  projects, 6
peacekeeping mission (1989) in Namibia, 20
performance, 48, 57
  definition of, 59
  legal empowerment, 144–9
  statutory justice into legal empowerment, 95–102
Personal Digital Assistants (PDAs), 119
Peterson, Jenny H., 27, 165 n.3, 167 n.28, 170 n.51
Pickering, Andrew, 172 n.18
Pickett, Brent, L., 50, 175 n.10, 175 n.14
pilot Hub in Gbarnga, 84
political impact
  generating, 123–7
  legal empowerment into, 135–49
politics of explanation, 34
politics of post-liberal peacebuilding
  practice, 47–8
  organizing, 48–60
politics of translation, 7–8
Pollner, Melvin, 66, 178 n.17
post-conflict Liberia, power and emancipation in, 9
post-liberal approach, 3–4
postliberalism, 4
  Richmond and Mitchell's reading of, 4
post-liberal ontology of peacebuilding practice, 33–4
  emergence, 34–6
  political situation, 43–5
  practice, 36–43
post-liberal politics, 6
  of peacebuilding, 68
  process of hybridity, 36

post-liberal politics – *continued*
   situation in Liberia, 154
   of translation, 7, 8, 60
   USIP report, 156
post-liberal practitioner, 48
Pouliot, Vincent, 13, 48, 49, 52, 167 n.37, 175 n.2, 175 n.21, 176 n.25–7
Poverty Reduction Strategy (PRS), 83–4
power *vs.* resistance, 49–50
practice-based approach, 152–4
practice, peacebuilding
   being *vs.* becoming, 36–8
   communities of, 51–2
   defined, 5–6, 49
   dimensions to, 6
   emerging, 1
   legal empowerment, 11
   mapping, 66–9
   materiality of, 38–9, 49
   methodological orientation, 8–9
   organization of, 53
   organized nature of, 54
   organizing, 48–9
   peacebuilding in, 83–5
   politics of, 47
   post-liberal politics of, 47
   practical understanding, 53–5
   RCTs, 12–13
   relationality of, 39–40
   relational nature of, 39–40
   re-organization and re-stabilization of, 6–7
   Schatzki's notion of, 7
   Schatzki's reading of, 55
   site-based ontology of, 40–3
problematization, 48, 57
   definition, 57–8
   legal empowerment, 120–3; into Liberian communities, 106–9; into political impact, 135–9; into randomized controlled trial, 120–3
PRS, *see* Poverty Reduction Strategy (PRS)
PSO, *see* Public Support Office (PSO)
Public Support Office (PSO), 85
Pugh, Michael C., 22, 169 n.18
   critique of political economy, 22

QAS, *see* Quick Assessment Survey (QAS)
Quick Assessment Survey (QAS), 135, 139

Rabinow, Paul, 172 n.19
Rachel, Pain, 178 n.9, 186 n.28
randomistas, 125–7
randomized controlled trial (RCTs), 12–13, 96
   basic structure of, 96
   community-level, 127, 128
   disruptive political impact of, 125
   framework of, 97
   individual-level, 15, 128, 131
   legal aid interventions using, 123
   legal empowerment and, 10, 12–13, 120–31
   Lightning Round survey, 128–31
   methodological framework of, 128
   methodological structure of, 12, 105
   original community-level, 128
   profusion of, 125
   'radical potential' of, 126
Rasmussen, Mikkel, 172 n.21
RCTs, *see* randomized controlled trial (RCTs)
Reckwitz, Andreas, 38, 40, 171 n.10, 173 n.27, 174 n.59, 176 n.31
reimagining justice in Liberia, 91–2
Reno, William, 81, 180 n.35, 180 n.37
re-problematization, 48, 57
   definition of, 59
Republic of Liberia, 180 n.55–9
resistance, power *vs.*, 49–50
restorative justice norms, 112
Richards, Paul, 81, 179 n.28, 180 n.29, 180 n.40
Richmond, Oliver P., 2, 4, 22, 28–32, 61, 63, 150–2, 163, 165 n.1, 165 n.3, 165 n.6, 166 n.11–12, 166 n.14, 167 n.26, 168 n.3, 169 n.19, 169 n.23, 170 n.37, 175 n.5, 177 n.2, 177 n.6, 187 n.2–3
   critical scholarship in, 22
   critique of liberal peace crisis, 22
Rohini, Pande, 185 n.27

Rouse, Joseph, 38, 39, 55, 171 n.9–10, 172 n.18, 176 n.44, 187 n.7
Russett, Bruce, 168 n.6

Sachs, Jeffrey, 125, 182 n.17, 185 n.21
Sage, Caroline, 92–3, 167 n.31, 182 n.15, 182 n.18, 188 n.13
Salter, Mark B., 166 n.18, 187 n.6
Sandefur, Justin, 12, 63, 96, 98, 119–28, 131–2, 134, 146, 159, 167 n.34, 183 n.35, 184 n.1, 185 n.12, 186 n.12
Sanghera, Gurchathen, 165 n.1
sassywood, 89
Savigny, Eike von, 171 n.9, 176 n.39, 187 n.7
Sawyer, Amos, 82, 179 n.28
Schatzki, Theodore R., 6–7, 13, 37–8, 40–2, 48–9, 53–5, 166 n.19, 167 n.38, 171 n.9, 172 n.17, 175 n.3, 176 n.39, 176 n.41, 187 n.7–8
Schouten, Peer, 177 n.4
Scott, James C., 22, 167 n.26, 169 n.22, 180 n.34, 181 n.62
Siakor, Silas, 187 n.19
Siddiqi, Bilal, 12, 63, 96, 98, 119–28, 131–2, 134, 146, 159, 167 n.34, 183 n.35, 184 n.1, 185 n.12, 186 n.12
Sierra Leone, dual legal system, 106
Sisk, Timothy D., 23, 169 n.31
Smith, Dorothy E., 65, 178 n.15
Smiths's institutional ethnography, 65–6
social practices
 circulating, 49
 components of, 39
 nexuses and sequences of, 40
 organized continuum of, 48–9
 site-based ontology of, 37
Spinoza, Benedictus de, 174 n.72
Spivak, Gayatri Chakravorty, 22, 169 n.22
spousal abuse, 109
statutory justice
 to customary justice, 83
 into legal empowerment, 88–102;
 appropriation, 91–5;
 performance, 95–102;
 problematization, 88–91
 practitioners, 87
 procedural practices of, 75
 vs. customary justice, 110–11
statutory legal centrism, 93
statutory practices, 10, 90
Steiner, George, 177 n.50
Svensson, Jakob, 124, 185 n.13, 186 n.37

Tadjbakhsh, Shahrbanou, 22, 169 n.20
Tamanaha, Brian Z., 167 n.32, 182 n.19, 188 n.14
Tankar, Issufo, 187 n.19
TCC, see The Carter Center (TCC)
Tellidis, Ioannis, 171 n.66
The Carter Center (TCC), 10
 access to justice programing, 106
 Conflict Resolution Program in Atlanta, 101
 customary practices, 90
 indirect legal empowerment, 111–12
 and MoIA, 89
 network of justice practitioners, 88
 paralegal program, 96
 statutory practices, 90
 training, 90, 109
Timap
 CJA program, 108–9
 for justice, 106–9
 paralegals, 107
 projects, 95
Tkacia, Maureen, 185 n.19
Tom, Patrick, 27, 165 n.3, 170 n.58
top-down peacebuilding, 80–2
translation
 art of, 57
 components, 7–8
 Michel Callon's sociology of, 56–7
 politics of, 7–8
 process of, 55–7
'treatment' communities, 98
Turner, Mandy, 169 n.18

Udry, Christopher, 185 n.27
United States Institute of Peace (USIP), 92, 99, 181 n.6, 183 n.37, 188 n.15
UNMIL, 180 n.56, 183 n.52
USIP, *see* United States Institute of Peace (USIP)

violence, 81
   domestic, 109, 115
   gender-based, 115

Wenger, Etienne, 52, 176 n.24
Wittgenstein, Ludwig, 36, 171 n.8
Woodward, Keith, 43–5, 172 n.20, 174 n.61–4, 174 n.72–3
Woolcock, Michael, 92–3, 167 n.31, 182 n.15, 182 n.18, 188 n.13
World Bank, 81
world-building capacities, *a priori* definition, 68

Zaum, Dominik, 27, 170 n.54
zero-impact assessment, 121–3
Zulu, Bouku, 89, 181 n.5

CPSIA information can be obtained at www.ICGtesting.com
Printed in the USA
LVOW04*1723170715

446659LV00013B/159/P